Windows® Phone 7
SECRETS

Windows® Phone 7
SECRETS

DO WHAT YOU NEVER THOUGHT POSSIBLE WITH WINDOWS PHONE 7

Paul Thurrott

WILEY

Wiley Publishing, Inc.

EXECUTIVE EDITOR: Carol Long
SENIOR PROJECT EDITOR: Kevin Kent
TECHNICAL EDITOR: Todd Meister
PRODUCTION EDITOR: Kathleen Wisor
COPY EDITOR: Mildred Sanchez
EDITORIAL DIRECTOR: Robyn B. Siesky
EDITORIAL MANAGER: Mary Beth Wakefield
FREELANCER EDITORIAL MANAGER: Rosemarie Graham
MARKETING MANAGER: Ashley Zurcher
PRODUCTION MANAGER: Tim Tate
VICE PRESIDENT AND EXECUTIVE GROUP PUBLISHER: Richard Swadley
VICE PRESIDENT AND EXECUTIVE PUBLISHER: Barry Pruett
ASSOCIATE PUBLISHER: Jim Minatel
PROJECT COORDINATOR, COVER: Lynsey Stanford
COMPOSITOR: Craig Woods, Happenstance Type-O-Rama
PROOFREADER: Jen Larsen, Word One New York
INDEXER: Robert Swanson
COVER IMAGE: © Chad Baker / Lifesize / Getty Images
COVER DESIGNER: Ryan Sneed

Windows® Phone 7 Secrets

Published by
Wiley Publishing, Inc.
10475 Crosspoint Boulevard
Indianapolis, IN 46256
www.wiley.com

Copyright © 2011 by Wiley Publishing, Inc., Indianapolis, Indiana

Published simultaneously in Canada

ISBN: 978-0-470-88659-5
ISBN: 978-1-118-00558-3 (ebk)
ISBN: 978-1-118-00661-0 (ebk)
ISBN: 978-1-118-00662-7 (ebk)

Manufactured in the United States of America

10 9 8 7 6 5 4 3 2 1

For general information on our other products and services please contact our Customer Care Department within the United States at (877) 762-2974, outside the United States at (317) 572-3993 or fax (317) 572-4002.

Wiley also publishes its books in a variety of electronic formats. Some content that appears in print may not be available in electronic books.

LIBRARY OF CONGRESS CONTROL NUMBER: 2010935564

To Stephanie, Mark, and Kelly, I love you all.

—Paul Thurrott

About the Author

Paul Thurrott, the author of over 20 books, is a technology analyst for Penton Media, the news editor at *Windows IT Pro,* and the majordomo of the Super-Site for Windows (winsupersite.com). He also writes a daily news column, "WinInfo Daily UPDATE," a weekly editorial for Windows IT Pro UPDATE, and a monthly column called "Need to Know" for the *Windows IT Pro* print magazine. Additionally, he blogs at the SuperSite Blog (community.winsupersite.com/blogs/paul) and the Windows Phone Secrets blog (windowsphonesecrets.com), and records a popular weekly podcast with broadcasting legend Leo Laporte called "Windows Weekly" (twit.tv/ww).

About the Technical Editor

Todd Meister has been developing using Microsoft technologies for over 15 years. He's been a Technical Editor on over 75 titles ranging from SQL Server to the .NET Framework. Besides technical editing titles, he is the Senior IT Architect at Ball State University in Muncie, Indiana. He lives in central Indiana with his wife, Kimberly, and their four brilliant children.

Acknowledgments

Thanks to Stephanie for once again understanding the time crunch and high stress levels that are necessitated by this process and responding like the class act you are. This book could never have happened without you, and you are arguably more responsible for its on-time delivery than I am.

Thanks to Mark and Kelly for putting up with my months-long absence, even though I was just in the next room, screaming at my computer and wondering, aloud, why nothing ever works. When did you both get so tall?

This book couldn't have happened without the support of Greg Sullivan and the Windows Phone team at Microsoft, and Lucas Westcoat and Jonathan Richardson at Waggener Edstrom, who provided me with very early access to prototype phone hardware, beta Windows Phone software, and many answered questions, all of which allowed me to begin documenting this exciting new platform. It was a wild, crazy, and all too quick ride. Thank you, thank you, thank you. I can't wait for v2.

Thanks to the amazing team at Wiley. I've been lucky to work with the same core group of people over several books now, and it makes a big difference. Thanks to Carol Long for working with me early on to figure out the right book to do next, Kevin Kent for his steady hand on both the direction and schedule for the book, technical editor Todd Meister, copy editor Mildred Sanchez, and production editor Kathleen Wisor. You are all amazing.

Thanks, too, to Rafael, my *Windows 7 Secrets* co-author, for the occasional, friendly reminders to rejoin the world, usually in the form of an "are you still alive?"-type IM. Yes, I am still alive. And I look forward to rejoining you on the next book.

Finally, thanks to my readers and listeners from around the world. I've always thought about my work as a conversation about technology, and that was never truer than during the development of this book, when I wrote about both Windows Phone and, for the first time, the process of writing a book from beginning to end. Let's keep the conversation going: It's this back and forth that makes the whole thing worthwhile.

Contents at a Glance

Contents

Introduction

In early 2009, I infamously wrote an article called "Saying Goodbye to the iPhone" (winsupersite.com/alt/iphone_goodbye.asp) in which I expressed my desire to drop Apple's iPhone in order to adopt a device based on Microsoft's then-current smart phone platform, Windows Mobile. The article was written more for my own benefit than anything else, and I was transparently using it as a prod to drop what was then the superior product—the iPhone—to use something dramatically inferior.

The reasons for this were many, but what it came down to was misguided pragmatism. I'm the *Windows* guy, after all, and had been writing about Microsoft technologies for over 15 years by that point, most notably via the SuperSite for Windows. Using and writing about the iPhone didn't make much sense from a product coverage perspective. In isolation, Windows Mobile made plenty of sense.

There was just one problem. And boy, was it a doozy. Windows Mobile, to put it bluntly, was *terrible*. The version that was current at the time, Windows Mobile 6.1, was a stinker, with an underlying user interface that had roots dating back over a decade to the days of PDAs and tiny metal styluses. (Not surprisingly, Windows Mobile 6.1 phones still shipped with the little metal toothpicks. It was the only way to accurately press some of the tiny onscreen controls.)

In early 2009, there was an iota of hope that Microsoft would turn Windows Mobile around, and I clung to that hope like it was a virtual life preserver. That year, I went through several Windows Mobile devices, and while I won't embarrass any of the companies or products by naming names here, suffice it to say they were all horrifically bad compared to the iPhone.

Microsoft's plan, we were told, was to provide Windows Mobile with a multitouch-compatible user interface that would bring it up to speed with the iPhone. This interface would debut in Windows Mobile 6.5 in late 2009 and be accompanied by new services like Windows Marketplace for Mobile (an Apple App Store clone) and My Phone, a surprisingly decent way to synchronize and back up important smart phone data to the Web.

Windows Mobile 6.5 was big on promise but weak on execution. And while the details of why this release was so disappointing are almost too complicated to bother with, I'll at least offer up a few relevant points here.

First, the initial batch of Windows Mobile 6.5 devices that shipped in late 2009 did not include an iPhone-like capacitive touch screen. Instead, they all shipped with inferior resistive touch screens. The difference is profound, and important. Where capacitive touch screens are silky smooth and easy to use, resistive touch screens require more pressure—causing you to press down on the screen harder than you feel is comfortable—and they are prone to mis-taps.

Second, while Microsoft did indeed provide an iPhone-like multitouch interface for Windows Mobile 6.5, this interface was only made available on the system's lock screen, Start screen, and in a handful of apps, such as the updated version of Internet Explorer that shipped with that product. The rest of the UI was based on that horrible, old, stylus-based UI from 10 years earlier. And you didn't have to navigate too far into the UI to reach these crusty, older bits, none of which were touch-friendly in the slightest.

Finally, Microsoft continued to bifurcate the market for its mobile platform by supplying two different versions of Windows Mobile, Standard and Professional, which ran on different kinds of hardware. Standard was designed for smaller, non-touchscreen–based devices, while Professional was aimed at more capable devices. Annoyingly, this strategy created a situation where apps written for one version often wouldn't work on the other.

I could go on, but you get the idea. By the close of 2009, I had purchased and evaluated several Windows Mobile 6.x phones, and they were all horrible. Moving from the iPhone to one of these lackluster devices wasn't going to be like taking a step back. It would be like taking a step back in time. They weren't even close.

What I didn't know at the time was that, internally, Microsoft had already given up on Windows Mobile. Yes, there was a half-hearted side effort to shore up Windows Mobile 6.5 with a few minor updates throughout early 2010. But for the most part, Microsoft was simply letting Windows Mobile run its course. Separately, and secretly, it was plotting a new mobile platform, one that would replace Windows Mobile and allow the company a rare mulligan, a do-over, a chance to finally right the wrongs and set its mobile wares down the right path. This new platform, which became known simply as Windows Phone, was like a sudden, bright shot of light in a dark room. And while it would take a year and a half, it allowed me to finally make good on my promise to abandon the iPhone. I'm not looking back.

Windows Phone is to the mobile industry what the iPhone was years ago, but is no longer: A new way of doing things, a *better* way of doing things. Windows Phone supports applications, or apps, like other smart phone platforms. But it also provides its users with a simpler way of doing things, a more visual presentation, and a more personalized and customizable experience. While Apple is busy cementing its position, Microsoft has been forced to retrench, and this necessity has resulted in a far more thoughtful platform, one that doesn't copy what others are doing.

The older I get, the harder it is for me to become excited by new technology. I remember key products along the way that renewed my excitement and interest—things like Windows 95, Windows Media Center, Windows Home Server, and Windows 7. Windows Phone is such a product, and I hope my excitement is transmitted throughout the book. No technology is perfect—and Windows Phone is no exception, as I've tried to document here—but Microsoft's new mobile platform has the right feature set and underlying capabilities to redefine the way we consume computing and online services on the go. I'm excited to be part of it, if only in a small way. I suspect you will be as well. Welcome aboard.

—Paul Thurrott

thurrott@gmail.com

Who This Book Is For

This book is for *people*, average users, not technical experts. I assume you have at least a passing familiarity with mobile phones like the iPhone or those based on Google Android, but it's not a requirement. I assume you use a Windows-based PC, and not a Mac. (Though I will at least point out that, despite the incongruity of using a device called Windows Phone in tandem with a Mac, it is at least possible for those who are interested in reverse switching. Yes, they're out there.)

The book doesn't need to be read from cover to cover. That said, I do recommend reading at least the first three chapters in sequence, since this is the foundation for understanding how the phone works and why things are the way they are. From that point on, feel free to cherry-pick as needed, and as you discover and wonder about specific new features.

What This Book Covers

Windows Phone is a brand-new mobile platform, and experience with a Windows Mobile device is no more relevant than iPhone or Android experience. For this reason, the book covers some background material related to the "whys" as well as the "hows" of Windows Phone before delving into specific applications and features. This background material is, I feel, very important to gaining an understanding and firm grounding in Windows Phone.

This book covers only those applications, hubs, and services that come with every Windows Phone. It is possible—no, almost a certainty—that Microsoft, device makers, and wireless carriers will bolster this base functionality with additional features, including custom applications and hubs, and more. It's also as likely that the basic Windows Phone feature set will expand over time, and Microsoft is working to shore up the missing features that will be present at launch. It's impossible to see the future, of course, but I will be covering any changes to Windows Phone over time at this book's web site, Windows Phone Secrets (windowsphonesecrets.com), as well as at my main web site, the SuperSite for Windows (winsupersite.com). More so than any product I've ever covered, Windows Phone is going to change, and change a lot. It should be an interesting ride.

How This Book Is Structured

This book is divided into logical sections that should help you easily find what you need to know. As noted before, I recommend starting with, and reading through, the first three chapters in sequence, if possible. This will give you a firm grounding in Windows Phone.

From there, the book progresses through sections dedicated to integrated experiences, entertainment, Internet and online services, productivity, phone and messaging, and settings and configuration. There's no reason to read these sections and chapters in order. Instead, treat *Windows Phone Secrets* as reference guide, referring to it as needed as you explore your own phone. Alternatively, you could use the book as an early exploration tool to find out about new features before you dive in yourself.

The point here is simple: For the most part, this book doesn't need to be read cover to cover. Instead, you can read it in the order that makes the most sense for you.

What You Need to Use This Book

To use a Windows Phone, and thus *Windows Phone Secrets*, effectively, you will need a Windows-based PC, preferably running the latest version of Windows, which is Windows 7 at the time of this writing. You will need a Windows Live ID, as I discuss in Chapter 1. And you will need the latest version of the Zune PC software, since that software is the sole link between the phone and your PC.

Web Site Supporting the Book

This book is only the beginning: More secrets can be found online, and of course since Windows Phone will be evolving over time, there's much more to come. For updates, errata, new information, and an ongoing blog with interactive discussions, please visit my Windows Phone Secrets blog (windowsphonesecrets.com). I will also be covering Windows Phone and related topics on my main web site, the SuperSite for Windows (winsupersite.com).

Features and Icons Used in This Book

The following features and icons are used in this book to help draw your attention to some of the most important or useful information in the book, some of the most valuable tips, insights, and advice that can help you unlock the secrets of Windows Phone 7.

Watch for margin notes like this one that highlight some key piece of information or that discuss some poorly documented or hard to find technique or approach.

SIDEBARS

Sidebars like this one feature additional information about topics related to the nearby text.

TIP The Tip icon indicates a helpful trick or technique.

NOTE The Note icon points out or expands on items of importance or interest.

CROSSREF The Cross-Reference icon points to chapters where additional information can be found.

WARNING The Warning icon warns you about possible negative side effects or precautions you should take before making a change.

CHAPTER 1

Pre-Flight Checklist: What to Do Before You Get Your Windows Phone

IN THIS CHAPTER

▶ Creating and managing a Windows Live ID to have the best Windows Phone experience

▶ Connecting your ID to the social networks and online services you use

▶ Joining Zune Social

▶ Connecting with Xbox Live

▶ Picking the right phone

Before you even set foot in a store and start thinking about which Windows Phone you want to buy, you need to do a bit of legwork. Don't worry, it's not painful. But if you put the right pieces in place before you buy a device, you'll have a much better experience with Windows Phone.

The first step is to create and cultivate a Windows Live ID. Strictly speaking, you don't need a Windows Live ID to use Windows Phone. But you're going to want one regardless, because the Windows Phone experience is dramatically better when you do have such an account. Windows Live provides an amazing variety of services, including integration with the social network and online services you really do care about, and integration with Microsoft's numerous online services, including Hotmail, Zune, and Xbox Live.

Next, you need to understand which hardware features come with every Windows Phone, and which do not. By understanding what's available, you can make more intelligent choices about the type of phone you'll eventually buy. So bone up on the basics and then hit the stores better educated, and ready to get exactly the phone you want.

WINDOWS LIVE ID: ONE ONLINE ID TO RULE THEM ALL

Way back when the Internet was dominated by gray web pages with blinking text, Microsoft created a *single sign-on service* called Windows Live ID. The point behind the service was that you could create a single account, with a username and password, and use that one account to securely access multiple web sites. That way, you wouldn't need to create and maintain multiple accounts, one for each web site.

> **NOTE** Windows Live ID, like a certain underworld denizen, has gone by many names. When it was originally announced in the late 1990s, it was called Microsoft Wallet, because the software giant hoped it would prove popular with the budding e-commerce sites of the day. But it went through a series of other names over the years, including Microsoft Passport, .NET Passport, and even the awkward Microsoft Passport Network, before it settled on Windows Live ID.

Like many good ideas, Windows Live ID was a better theory than reality. Third-party web sites—that is, those sites not created and owned by Microsoft—ignored Windows Live ID for the most part, and while there are a few exceptions, this system is today used almost exclusively by Microsoft's own web sites and services, such as Hotmail, MSN, Windows Live, Xbox Live, and Zune.

While a single web-wide sign-on would be nice, being able to access Microsoft's many services via a single account is still pretty convenient, even more so if you're heavily invested in what I call the Microsoft ecosystem. And if you're going to be buying a Windows Phone, this single sign-on, or Windows Live ID, is the key to having the best experience. And while I hate to ruin the ending, this simple fact is arguably the most important secret in the whole book.

Having a Windows Live ID is essential to having a great experience with a Windows Phone.

Here's why. After many fits and starts, Microsoft has recast its Windows Live service as a central hub of sorts, a way to "keep your lives in sync." So instead of competing with the Facebooks and Twitters of the world, Microsoft is instead providing a way to link to third-party services, allowing you to access the third-party (read: non-Microsoft) accounts you already use, from Windows Live.

If you think about it, this is a sneaky way to achieve the original goal of Windows Live ID. That is, since the world didn't come to Windows Live ID, Windows Live ID has instead come to the world. Using that single sign-on, you can simply access all those wonderful third-party services from Windows Live. All you need to do is create an account—though you may already have one—and then configure it to access other services.

Every Windows Phone user should take the time to configure a Windows Live ID. And this is true even if you have no interest in using any Windows Live services directly. By creating such an account and configuring it properly, you will be able to turn on your new phone on day one, sign on with your Windows Live ID, and watch it automatically populate with all of the information that's tied to that account. This means e-mail, contacts, and calendars. Photos and news feeds from you and your friends and family, no matter where they're found online. And, as you will soon find out, so much more. This is the key to a killer Windows Phone experience.

> **NOTE** Yes, you can use Windows Phone without having a Windows Live ID, but I don't recommend it. And while this book does document how to configure your phone with other account types, I am assuming that you have a Windows Live ID. It's that important. So please don't skip the Windows Live ID creation and configuration steps if you want to get the most out of your Windows Phone.

Creating a New Windows Live ID

If you don't have a Windows Live ID, you will need to create one. Note, however, that you may already have such an account. Any e-mail address ending in hotmail.com, msn.com, or live.com is a Windows Live ID, for example. If you've created an Xbox Live account or a Zune account, that's a Windows Live ID too. So if you have such an account, skip ahead to the next section. If not, it's time to make one.

> **NOTE** It's possible for any e-mail address to be used as a Windows Live ID, so if you don't want to be stuck with one of Microsoft's domain names, you can also use your own (including competitor accounts from Gmail, Yahoo!, and elsewhere). Many educational institutions also use Windows Live services on the back end, so if you're a student, it's possible you have a Live ID already as well.

There are many avenues for reaching Microsoft's Windows Live ID sign up page, but the easiest, perhaps, is to just navigate to live.com. When you do so, you'll see the screen shown in Figure 1-1.

▶ If the Windows Live ID field on the right of this page is already filled out, this means you could already have an active Windows Live ID. So make sure you really intend to create a new account.

FIGURE 1-1: Here, you can begin your new online life with Windows Live.

Click the Sign Up button to continue. The Create Your Windows Live ID page will appear. As shown in Figure 1-2, you will need to fill out a form listing information about yourself and pick a Windows Live ID, which will take the form of *name@live.com* or *name@hotmail.com*. This ID will also be used for a Hotmail e-mail address.

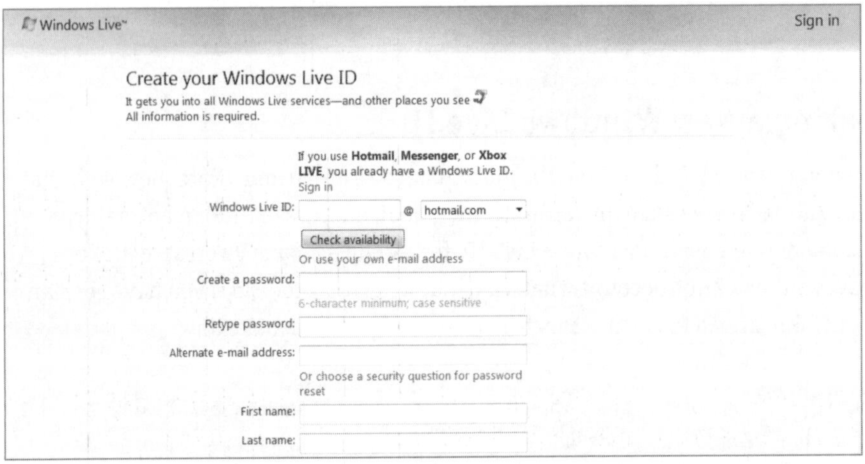

FIGURE 1-2: You can check the availability of the name you want before proceeding.

In the Windows Live ID field, experiment with different ID names to find one that is available. Note that common names, such as *Paul*, were taken long ago, so you may need to get creative. The form will make suggestions or provide an advanced search box, shown in Figure 1-3, if you pick an ID that's already taken.

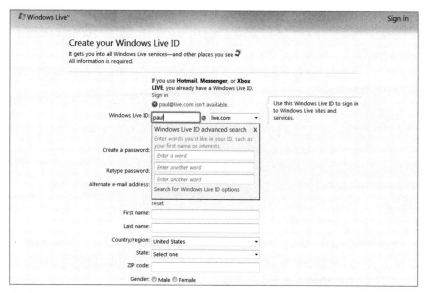

FIGURE 1-3: Windows Live will help you find a good ID.

When you find an acceptable ID, the form will tell you that it's available and you can proceed (see Figure 1-4).

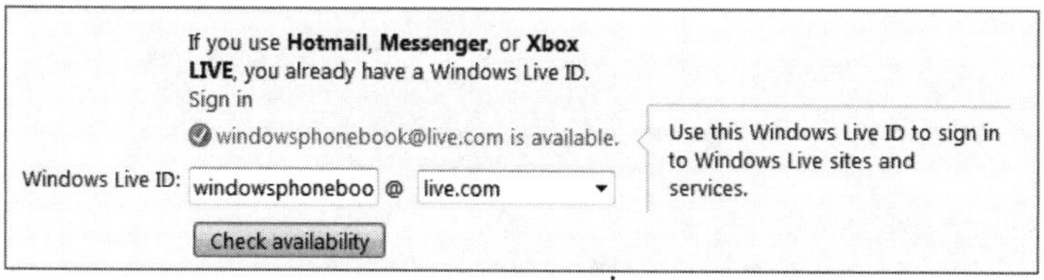

FIGURE 1-4: Once you find a name you like, you can move on.

ALREADY HAVE A NON-MICROSOFT E-MAIL ACCOUNT?

If you already have an e-mail account with a different company, you can turn that into a Windows Live ID as well. There is one important difference between using a preexisting e-mail address and creating a new one with Windows Live, however: You won't be able to use Hotmail for e-mail, contacts, or calendar management. Note, too, that when you configure an existing e-mail account as a Windows Live ID, you will need to create a password for this ID that is *separate* from the password you use to access e-mail from that account. I recommend just creating a standalone Windows Live ID and not using an existing e-mail account because it's very easy with Windows Phone to access multiple accounts in a seamless way.

Fill out the rest of the form, paying particular attention to the password, which should be complex if possible and rated "strong" by the form. (It will rate your password as you type.) According to Microsoft, a strong password contains 7–16 characters, does not include common words or names, and combines uppercase letters, lowercase letters, numbers, and symbols.

> **TIP** There are some excellent tools online to help you create complex passwords for web services. I use and recommend a free tool called Last Pass (lastpass.com), which provides a plug-in for all major PC-based web browsers (IE, Firefox, Chrome, and Safari), allowing you to securely create, store, and manage the passwords for all of the services you use online.

When you're done, click the button labeled I Accept. Windows Live will work for a bit and then display the Windows Live Home page (live.com), this time logged on with your new ID. This is shown in Figure 1-5.

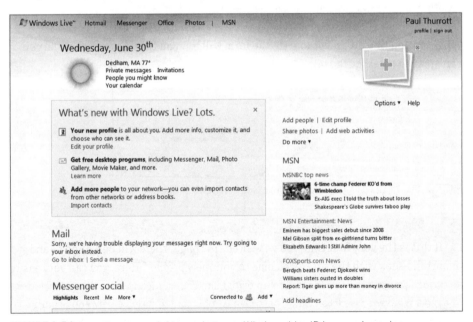

FIGURE 1-5: It's pretty sparse right now, but your Windows Live ID is up and running.

As initially configured, there's not much going on with your new Windows Live ID. But that's easy enough to rectify, and there are a number of things you can do to make this ID more valuable. You can start with the basics: initial Windows Live ID configuration.

Initial Windows Live ID Configuration

On that initial Windows Live Home page, you should see a link titled Edit Your Profile. Click that, or, if it's not present, click the Profile link in the upper right of the page. Either way, you'll be brought to your Windows Live Profile page, where you can configure your new ID. This is shown in Figure 1-6.

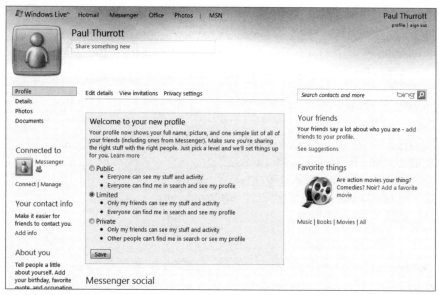

FIGURE 1-6: Windows Live Profile.

> **TIP** You can return to your Windows Live Profile at any time by visiting profile.live.com.

If this is the very first time you've visited this page, there will be a handy—and important—box with the title "Welcome to your new profile." Here, you can very easily configure your privacy settings for Windows Live. You can of course change this later, but I recommend taking a moment to get this right before proceeding. Fortunately, Microsoft has made it simple with just three basic choices:

▶ **Public:** Everything you do—what Microsoft calls your activities—is available publicly on Windows Live, even to those people with whom you have no formal relationship. Furthermore, anyone can find you by searching on Windows Live and can view your profile. I'm not a privacy nut, but I don't recommend choosing this setting, unless, of course, you're a reverse voyeur. (They're out there.)

▶ **Limited:** This is the default setting and the least restrictive option I think you should consider. Configured this way, only your friends—those people you've explicitly "friended" on Windows Live—can see what you're doing via the service. But as with the Public setting, anyone can find you by searching on Windows Live and can view your profile. This is the setting to choose if you are concerned about privacy but do want others to be able to find you online.

▶ **Private:** With this most restrictive setting—and, for whatever it's worth, the one I use—only your friends can view what you're doing online, and only your friends can search for you or view your profile. This is the option you'll want to pick if you're concerned about privacy and don't want other people to find you.

Once you've chosen a setting, click Save.

> **WARNING**   If you are at all concerned about your privacy online—and you should be—this isn't enough. Please be sure to visit the Windows Live advanced privacy page (`profile.live.com/Privacy`) and then click the Advanced link to see a comprehensive form for really fine-tuning your privacy settings, as shown in Figure 1-7.

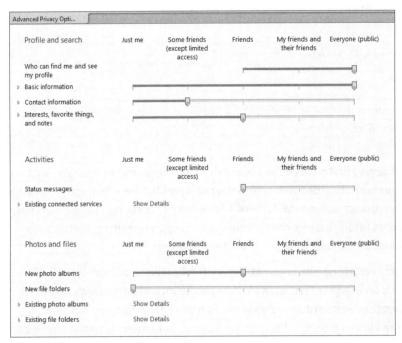

FIGURE 1-7: Spend the time to get your privacy settings exactly right. You can't be too careful online.

From here, there are a wide range of options you can configure for your Windows Live ID. (Or not. Remember, it's your choice.) Some of the more important ones include:

▶ **Personal information:** Click the Details link on the left side of your Profile page to access a page where you can edit your personal information, including your name, personal photo, contact information, work information, general information (gender, occupation, location, interests, and more), social information (relationship status, relationship interests, hometown, places lived, humor, fashion, and favorite quote), and education information.

▶ **Status:** At the top of the Profile page is a conversation balloon with the text, "Share something new." This is where you can type a personal note, similar to a Twitter post (or "tweet") or Facebook status post.

Importing Contacts from Other Services

After you've completed filling out your Windows Live ID, you may want to import contacts from other services, especially if you intend to use this account for e-mail or to communicate with others using Windows Live services and applications such as Windows Live Photos (photo sharing), Windows Live Spaces (blogging), or Windows Live Messenger. To do so, click the Add Friends to Your Profile link on the Profile page. (Or just navigate to profile.live.com/connect.) From this page, shown in Figure 1-8, you can add individual people to your contact list or import them from other e-mail accounts and online services.

▶ *You can also update your status on Windows Live with Microsoft's instant messaging (IM) application, Windows Live Messenger. This app works as a front end of sorts to Windows Live on Windows-based PCs.*

FIGURE 1-8: Windows Live helps you import contacts from other services.

While adding single contacts at a time is pretty straightforward, it's also monotonous, so I want to focus on importing. After all, you probably have contacts elsewhere, in an e-mail application (like Outlook), on a competing e-mail service like Gmail or AOL, or on other online services such as Facebook or MySpace.

To import contacts, click the appropriate service or application. While the options vary slightly depending on which one you pick, there are three basic types of integration here:

▶ **Facebook and MySpace:** Thanks to deep integration with Windows Live, Facebook and MySpace contacts importing works quite differently from the other choices. In fact, these services are so special that I'm going to examine them separately in the next section, so hang tight. (Or skip ahead.)

▶ **Manual import:** Many of the other services, including LinkedIn, AOL Mail, Hyves, Google (Gmail), Hi5, and Tagged require you to log on to that service before you can import contacts. So when you select one of these options, you'll see a page created by that service where you can log on in order to authorize the contacts copying. A typical screen of this type is shown in Figure 1-9.

▶ Windows Phone works natively only with online accounts, like Windows Live, Gmail, and Facebook. You will not be able to sync information from a desktop e-mail client like Outlook to Windows Phone.

FIGURE 1-9: Services such as Gmail require you to log on so you can transfer information to Windows Live.

▶ **Outlook and another Windows Live account:** To import contacts from Microsoft's corporate-oriented e-mail and personal information management application, or from Windows Live, you will need to first export them in a format Windows Live can understand.

> **NOTE** Interestingly, these options can be used to import contacts from Outlook Express (Windows XP), Windows Contacts (Windows Vista), Windows Live Hotmail, Yahoo! Mail, and Gmail as well, as shown in Figure 1-10. Note that in any of these cases, you will need to have exported your contacts into an acceptable format first.

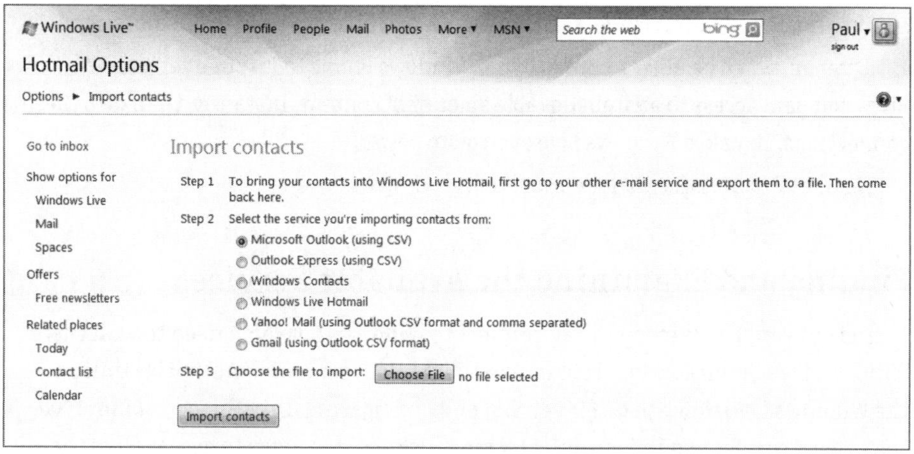

FIGURE 1-10: Hidden under the Outlook and Windows Live options are other import choices.

▶ Don't see your e-mail provider listed? Or maybe you just want a more seamless way to import contacts from your current e-mail provider. If so, visit the Windows Live TrueSwitch site (secure5.trueswitch .com/winlive/) and fill out the form. Voila!

USING WINDOWS LIVE ID TO ACCESS YOUR SOCIAL NETWORKS AND OTHER SERVICES

Once your Windows Live ID is properly configured, you can begin connecting it to the other online services you're already using.

▶ This is, in my humble opinion, the coolest feature Microsoft offers in Windows Live and indisputably the single smartest thing you can do in order to later have the best possible experience with Windows Phone.

Unless you've been living under a rock, you're probably familiar with the fact that there are very popular services online, most of which aren't made by Microsoft. (I know, it's shocking.) In fact, you almost certainly use many of these services yourself: Facebook or MySpace for social networking; Pandora for music; Hulu for online TV shows; Flickr for photos; and many more.

There are literally dozens of valuable online services, but they all exist, in isolation, separate from each other. Each requires its own username and password, and to access content from each service, you need to manually visit each separately.

That's where Windows Live comes in. Yes, some parts of Windows Live compete with some of these other services. Windows Live Photos is a direct competitor with Flickr, for example. But by making Windows Live open and extensible to other services, Microsoft has also made it possible for Windows Live users to utilize the service as a hub, of sorts, for their other services. It gives you a single place to access information from Facebook, Flickr, and Pandora (or whatever), without having to manually visit each place separately. And you can access not just *your* information, but also the information of your contacts—that is, your friends, family, and other acquaintances—from those services.

Later on, you'll be able to connect your Windows Phone to just one service—Windows Live—but gain access to an unbelievable amount of content, instantly, thanks to these connections. It makes Windows Live even more powerful.

Neat, eh? Okay, time to get connected.

Finding and Examining the Available Services

To find out which services you can connect to Windows Live, you need to visit the Windows Live Services page. You do so by clicking the Add Web Activities link on the Windows Live Home page (`live.com`) or by navigating directly to `profile.live.com/services`. Shown in Figure 1-11, this page provides a way to access all of the online services which you can connect to Windows Live.

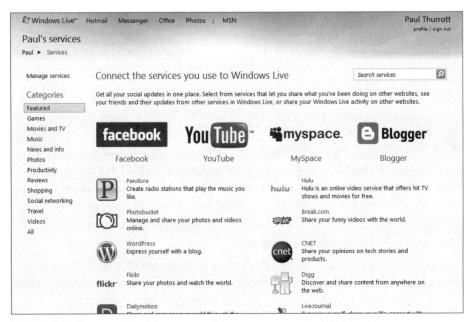

FIGURE 1-11: Here, you'll find the services that you can connect to Windows Live.

If you find the list too intimidating—it gets bigger all the time as more partners come on board—then you can use the Categories list on the left to filter it down. For example, you can click Movies and TV to only see video services.

Connecting an Online Service to Windows Live

For most of these services, you need to be a member—that is, have a user account at that service—in order to connect it to Windows Live. I'll use the Flickr photo sharing site as an example of such a service since it's very popular, but you can and should of course connect with whatever services you use.

To select Flickr, click Photos in the Categories list and then click the link for Flickr. You're presented with a screen explaining what it means to connect to Flickr, as shown in Figure 1-12.

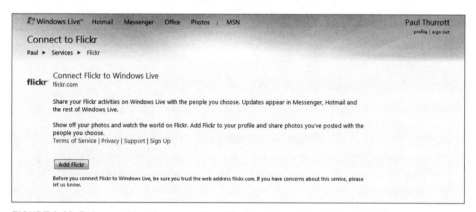

FIGURE 1-12: Before making the connection, Windows Live will explain what doing so means.

When you click the Add Flickr button, you'll navigate to the Flickr web site and be prompted for your Flickr credentials. When you log on, the browser returns you to Windows Live, notes that you're connected, and explains what the privacy settings are. (You can click the Change link to change this, of course.) Click the Connect button to complete the connection.

You're returned to the Windows Live Services page, where you can pick another service to connect.

You'll do that in a moment, but for now, return to Windows Live Home (live.com). You'll see a note about the connection in your Messenger social feed—a list of "What's new" items that carries across all connected services—and, if there are any new photos posted to Flickr, a link to that new content as well. This is shown in Figure 1-13.

FIGURE 1-13: As soon as you connect to a service from Windows Live, content from that service appears in your Messenger social feed.

> **NOTE** Messenger social used to be called What's New. I still think that was a better and more descriptive name. Microsoft renamed it to Messenger Social because this list is also available via Windows Live Messenger, the company's IM application for Windows.

▶ *Technically speaking the Blog RSS Feed connection works with both RSS and Atom feeds. They work similarly.*

Okay, time to add one more service, and this time you'll use a different type of connection. While most of the services you can connect to Windows Live require you to be a member, some do not. For example, you may have a favorite web site that provides regular updates. These types of sites typically use an RSS feed to alert people about updates, and Windows Live supports connecting to any RSS feed via a generic Blog RSS Feed connection. You can find this option at the bottom of the main Services page.

You'll need the web site's RSS URL (uniform resource locator, essentially its web address) in order to make the connection. While each browser does this is a bit differently, most work similarly. In Internet Explorer, navigate to the web site and notice that the Feeds icon in the Command Bar turns orange, indicating that a feed is available. To view the feed, click the button. IE will now display the feed provided by the web site, as shown in Figure 1-14.

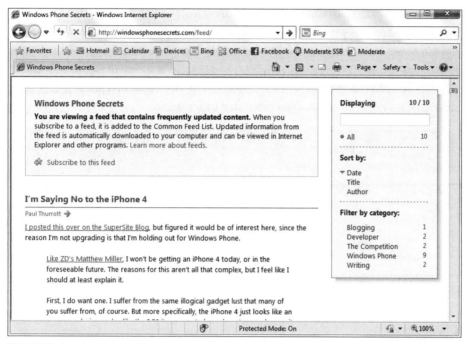

FIGURE 1-14: Web browsers can display RSS feeds, which you can connect to Windows Live.

The RSS URL, or address, can be found in the browser's Address Bar. Select this text and copy it to the clipboard (Ctrl+C works nicely). Then, paste it into the Blog URL on Windows Live's Connect Blog RSS Feed to Windows Live page and click Connect. After a bit of churning, the web site's feed will be added to your Messenger social feed as well.

GETTING AROUND THE BLOG RSS FEED'S BIG LIMITATION

The Blog RSS Feed connection has one very serious limitation: You can only connect it to one web site. That is, despite the fact that you probably have multiple sites for which you'd like to receive updates, Windows Live only lets you connect with one RSS (or Atom) feed. This is, of course, ridiculous. Is there a way around this? Yes, but it's a bit convoluted. Using an RSS aggregator service such as Friendfeed (`friendfeed.com`), you can connect to all the web site RSS feeds you want, and then connect Windows Live to your Friendfeed RSS feed. Silly? You bet.

Be sure to spend some time and connect to each of the services you already use. You can view and edit your connected services via the Connected Services page, which you can access by clicking the Manage Services link on the Services page. (Or navigate directly to profile.live.com/Services/?view=manage.) As shown in Figure 1-15, this page lets you edit the settings for each connected service, including privacy, or remove individual services you're no longer interested in accessing.

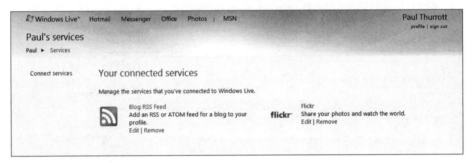

FIGURE 1-15: Manage connected services.

Viewing and Interacting with Content in the Messenger Social Feed

Once you've connected with all of your favorite services, it's time to see why this is so powerful. If you navigate to Windows Live Home (live.com), you'll see updates from all of your connected services appear in the Messenger social list. And that list could be quite voluminous, especially if you connect to some of the "chattier" online services, like Facebook.

What's neat about this is that this list isn't read-only. You can also perform certain actions on each update without having to go visit the service from which it came. So if you see a Facebook post, or a Flickr photoset, or whatever else you'd like to comment on, you can do so, right from Windows Live.

To comment on an update, click the Comment link that appears next to the update. When you do so, a new Comment interface opens up, as shown in Figure 1-16. You can type your comment and then add it to whatever service it originated from.

You can also perform other actions. If you mouse over one of the updates, a small gear icon will appear, as shown in Figure 1-17.

Click this gear and you'll see a small pop-up menu (Figure 1-18). This menu lets you mark the update's poster as a Favorite—which I'll explain in just a bit—or hide updates from the service from which the update originated.

FIGURE 1-16: You can comment on updates from other services directly from Windows Live.

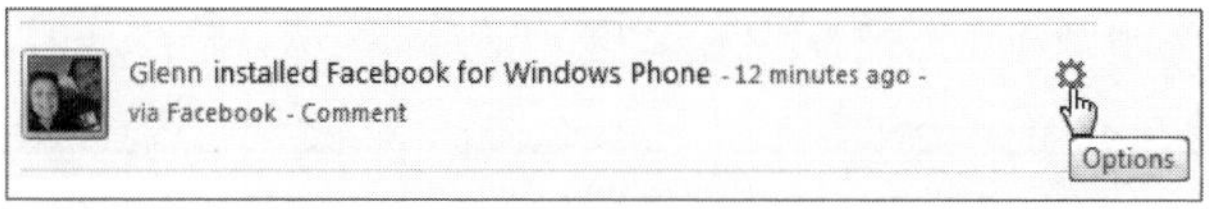

FIGURE 1-17: A small options icon appears when you mouse over individual updates.

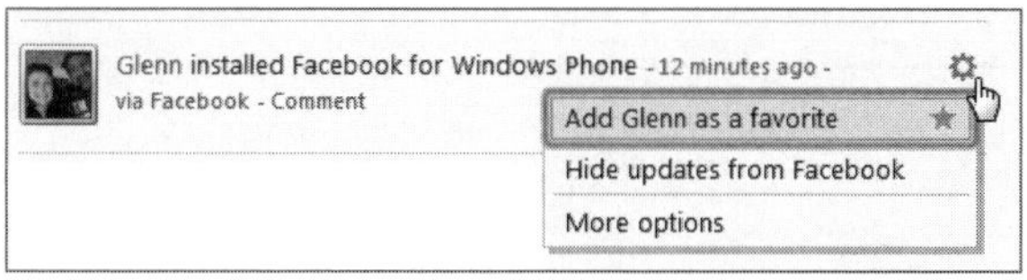

FIGURE 1-18: Click the icon and a small menu appears with more options.

There's also a More Options link that brings you to a very interesting page where you can manage the social updates from your friends or, more accurately, determine which Windows Live services will appear in your Messenger social feed. (You can manually navigate to this page by visiting profile.live.com/whatsnewsettings.) This page, shown in Figure 1-19, also lets you hide individual users, which can be very convenient. (Hey, we all have one of *those* friends, right?)

Perhaps by now the power of this system is obvious. But the real beauty of Windows Live, and its connections to the outside services you already use, is that once you do get a Windows Phone, you will simply log on to your Windows Live account, and all this stuff will propagate around the phone as makes sense. So your Windows Live Hotmail-based e-mail, contacts, and calendars will of course appear in the device's Mail, Contacts, and Calendar interfaces. But updates from your connected photo services will also appear in the phone's Pictures UI. And your Messenger social feed will show up in the phone's People experience. And all you have to do is sign in once.

FIGURE 1-19: Selectively remove users and Windows Live services updates from this page.

> **TIP** There is a lot more going on with Windows Live, of course. And while it doesn't have all that much to do with Windows Phone, I do recommend that you download and install Windows Live Essentials (`get.live.com`), a set of useful and fun Windows applications that includes, among other things, the Windows Live Messenger application that also provides access to your Messenger social feed. It's shown in Figure 1-20.

Music Lovers: Connecting to Zune Social

While setting up a Windows Live ID and connecting it to the third-party online services you care about is absolutely critical for anyone interested in Windows Phone, there are a few Microsoft online services that are particularly interesting and relevant as well. And since these online services are tied to your Windows Live ID, and can be used to populate your phone with content, it makes sense to get them set up now, before you get your Windows Phone.

FIGURE 1-20: Windows Live Messenger provides PC-based access to your Messenger social feed.

The first is Microsoft Zune. If you haven't heard of Zune, or simply have never tried it, you may be in for a very happy surprise. Zune is an elegant and powerful digital media platform that encompasses a number of interesting components. These include:

▶ **Zune PC software:** This software can be used to organize and play digital media content, including music, videos, and photos, and to sync this content with various portable devices, including, yes, Windows Phones.

▶ **Zune Pass:** This subscription service allows you to browse, stream, and download all of the music you want, from Microsoft's voluminous online collection for a flat monthly fee. With Windows Phone, you can even perform these activities, over the air, right to the phone, with no PC required.

▶ **Zune Social:** This online community provides a way to share your favorite and new music with friends, family, and others. (And yes, of course it links up to the Messenger social feed so you can share via your Windows Phone.)

▶ **Zune portable devices:** Before there were Windows Phone devices, Microsoft made dedicated digital media players, including the Zune HD, which could harness the power of Zune on the go.

▶ **Zune Marketplace:** This is Microsoft's online store for music, TV shows, movies, podcasts, and more. It's available from the Zune PC software (on Windows-based PCs), on the Xbox 360 (more on this later in the chapter), and, yes, on your Windows Phone as well.

▶ **Xbox 360:** Microsoft's video game console includes Zune software for media playback, including Zune Pass streaming, and can interact with portable devices, including Zune players.

▶ **Bing music playback:** Using Microsoft's search engine (at bing.com), you can find out more about your favorite musical artists. And thanks to an integrated Zune player, you can even play entire songs by these artists as you search around for more information. (If you have a Zune Pass, you get unlimited streaming too.)

If this seems like a lot of information, well, it is. But that's why I discuss much of this in much more detail later in the book.

CROSSREF Check out Chapter 6 to see how you can use the Zune PC software with your Windows Phone. This chapter also includes a look at how the Windows Phone's Zune software works right on the device.

For now, you can get started by connecting your Windows Live ID to a Zune account. You'll use exactly the same underlying Windows Live ID, so it's easy.

First, open your PC's web browser, browse to zune.net, and click the Sign In link at the top of the page. Since you already have a Windows Live ID, you can sign in using that ID. And when you do, you'll be prompted to create your Zune account, which will be connected to that ID. It will look something like the screen shown in Figure 1-21.

One of the options you'll need to decide on right up front is whether you want to be part of the Zune Social. As noted previously, this is Microsoft's online community for music lovers, and it provides you with a way to share your musical likes and dislikes with others online. If you're unsure about this, just select Don't Share; you can always join the Zune Social later. The point now is just to get your Windows Live ID connected to a Zune account.

When you complete this first part of the form, you'll be prompted to create a Zune Tag. This is a name that will identify you to others in the Zune Social and, if you join Xbox Live as described in the next section, it's the same name you'll use for gaming endeavors as well.

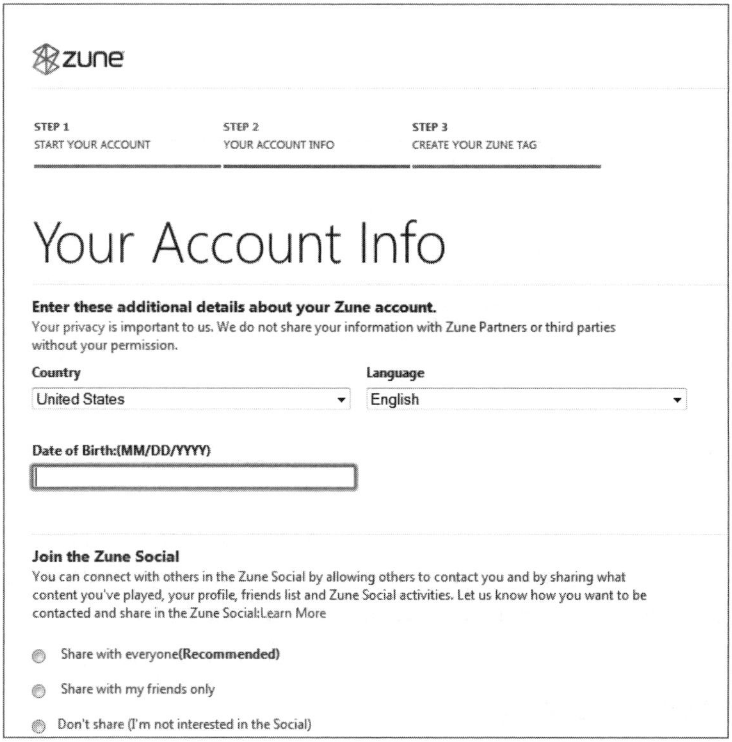

FIGURE 1-21: Here, you connect your Windows Live ID to a Zune account.

THINK IT OVER

I recommend not getting cute here. While many people create nonsensical Zune Tags, remember that this is the name you'll use when you communicate with others. So rather than be known as Flatulent Fred or whatever, try to pick something that you won't be embarrassed by later on.

A Zune Tag can consist of letters (A–Z, a–z), numbers (0–9), and single spaces. But it can't start with a number. And it can be up to 15 characters long, maximum.

My Zune Tag, incidentally, is *Paul Thurrott*. Yeah, it's boring. But people instantly know it's me.

As with your Windows Live ID, your Zune Tag must be unique. That means you can't pick a Zune Tag that's already in use by someone else. So *Paul Thurrott*, obviously, is taken. So, too, I'd imagine, are names like Bob Smith. The sign-up wizard will let you know if the name you want is available, as shown in Figure 1-22.

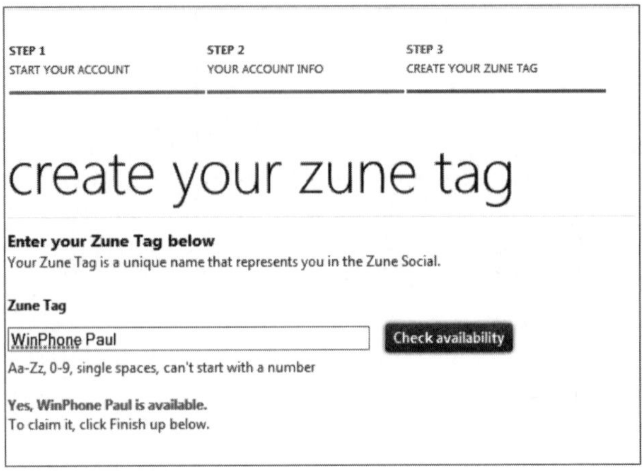

STEP 1
START YOUR ACCOUNT

STEP 2
YOUR ACCOUNT INFO

STEP 3
CREATE YOUR ZUNE TAG

create your zune tag

Enter your Zune Tag below
Your Zune Tag is a unique name that represents you in the Zune Social.

Zune Tag

WinPhone Paul   **Check availability**

Aa-Zz, 0-9, single spaces, can't start with a number

Yes, WinPhone Paul is available.
To claim it, click Finish up below.

FIGURE 1-22: And another classic Zune Tag is created.

When you're done creating the Zune account, you can download the Zune PC software, join Zune Pass, or discover some of the other interesting and unique features of the Zune platform, which I discuss in more detail in Chapters 6 and 16.

Gamers: Connect to Xbox Live

If you're a video gamer, chances are that you've already heard of Microsoft's Xbox, which is known far and wide as the most powerful and capable video game platform on earth. As with Zune, Xbox consists of a number of components. These include:

▶ **Xbox 360:** The premier video game console features HD graphics, surround sound, and the best library of video games available anywhere. It also connects to an ever-growing library of online services, including Zune (music and video), Netflix (TV and movies), Last.fm (music), Facebook and Twitter (social networking), and more. The Xbox 360 isn't just a video game console; it's also a central hub for entertainment and communications.

▶ **Xbox Live:** In addition to making a killer console, Microsoft also supplies the most popular video game service on earth. Xbox Live is available in a free version called Xbox Live Silver, and a paid version called Xbox Live Gold. Both provide access to free game demo downloads, HD movies and TV shows (via Zune), downloadable Xbox Live Arcade games, game add-ons, avatars (mini cartoon characters that represent you online), in-game voice and text chat, and photo sharing. But the Gold subscription adds online gameplay with friends, Netflix streaming (though you must also have a Netflix subscription),

▶ Xbox Live Gold costs $50 per year per account. But you can also purchase a Family Pack for $100 that provides up to four Xbox players with a year of access and supplies critical parental controls functionality.

Xbox Live Parties, video chat, Facebook, Twitter, and Last.fm access, and some other unique features.

> **TIP** Microsoft also has a related service called Games for Windows – LIVE. This awkwardly named service is essentially Xbox Live for Windows PCs, so it uses the exact same Windows Live ID that you use for Windows Live, Zune, Xbox Live, or Windows Phone. You can find out more at **gamesforwindows.com/live**.

▶ **Xbox Live Marketplace:** Microsoft's online store for gamers provides a way to purchase full games electronically, Xbox Live Arcade games (which tend to be smaller than full games), as well as free game demos and other content, game add-ons, and more. It's analogous to Zune Marketplace, except that the focus here is gaming instead of digital media. (That said, the two stores are merging and a lot of Zune Marketplace content is available via Xbox Live Marketplace as well. As you can imagine, having a single ID to access all this content is pretty convenient.)

You don't have to be a hard-core gamer to appreciate Xbox. In addition to expanding the audience for its gaming wares with the Kinect add-on for Xbox 360 (which provides Nintendo Wii–like motion sensing controls as well as voice control and opens the door to a new generation of more casual games), Microsoft has brought its Xbox Live service to Windows Phone as well. So you don't even need an Xbox 360 to take advantage of Xbox Live. (I examine the Windows Phone gaming features in Chapter 7.)

To sign up for an Xbox Live account, visit xbox.com in your PC's web browser and click the Sign In link at the top of the page.

If you already signed up for a Zune account, you will simply need to accept a new Terms of Use agreement. That's because the Zune Tag you already created will be used as your unique Xbox Live identifier, which is called a *Gamertag*. (I discuss this more in just a bit.)

If you skipped the Zune account sign-up (and really, shame on you for that), you'll need to fill out a form and create what's known as your Gamer Profile. This is essentially your online game-playing persona.

This Gamer Profile consists of a number of attributes, some of which you'll need to specify right up front. These include:

▶ **Gamertag:** This is essentially the name that will identify you to others while you're playing games on Xbox Live. (And that's true whether you're playing games on the Xbox 360 console, a Windows-based PC, or via your Windows Phone.) This Gamertag is identical to your Zune account, so check out the previous section for information on the rules for creating this Gamertag and my suggestions for not getting too immature about it.

► **Gamer Picture:** Microsoft lets you use a small picture to graphically represent you to others online. There are a number of built-in pictures to choose from, and if you log on with the Xbox 360 console, there are more available (including some for purchase, believe it or not).

► **Gamer Zone:** Microsoft provides four general gamer types from which you can choose, including Recreation (casual gamers), Family (G-rated content only, please), Pro (hard core but polite), and Underground (hard core, no rules). I know you're dying to know where I fall in this list. You may be surprised to discover its Recreation. Don't worry. I'll still take you down online, given the chance.

Once you create an Xbox Live Gamer Profile, you can visit your Xbox home page, where you can view information about this profile. (It's at `live.xbox.com` if you can't figure it out.) Since you're just starting out, your home page is going to be pretty bare, as shown in Figure 1-23.

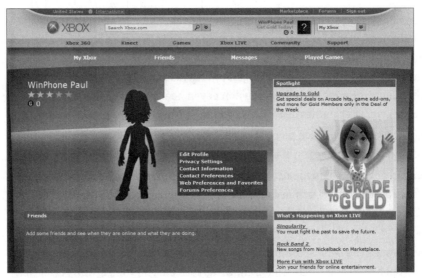

FIGURE 1-23: With your Xbox Live Gamer Profile created, it's time to get online and get beat up a bit.

There's a lot more you can do from here: Edit your profile, privacy settings, contact information, and other preferences, add friends, or sign up for an Xbox Live Gold account. (You are automatically given a Silver account when you create your profile.) But I examine gaming and the various Xbox Live features thoroughly in Chapter 7. For now, the important bit is just getting the account set up.

PICKING A PHONE

You may be surprised to discover that I consider properly configuring a Windows Live ID a far more important task than picking a phone. But it's true: We live in an age of throwaway smart phones, and while you may choose to replace your phone every year or two, your Windows Live ID will stay with you for many years to come. So it's important to get that right.

But you are eventually going to move on to the next phase in your Windows Phone adventure, and that involves picking the right phone. Of course, the phone that's right for you may not be the phone I'd pick, as we all have our own wants, needs, and requirements. And let's be clear: Just as with any smart phone platform, Windows Phone is going to evolve over time, and handset makers and wireless carriers will be coming out with new devices on a regular basis. So it doesn't make sense to recommend particular phones. Instead, what I'll do is highlight those features that will appear on all Windows Phone devices, and those that will be optional, so you can survey the market for available devices and make an educated decision when the time comes.

Understanding the Windows Phone Hardware Specifications

Microsoft's previous smart phone platform was called Windows Mobile, and while it did have a few things to recommend it, one of the problems with that platform was the almost limitless number of hardware types and form factors that shipped from a variety of device makers and wireless carriers. This diversification made the platform attractive to these companies for a while. But it also made it almost impossible for Microsoft to deliver software updates to customers, something it has been able to do more easily on Windows PCs via the Windows Update and Microsoft Update services.

Apple's wildly popular iPhone changed the smart phone market in many ways when it arrived in 2007. But one of the most important iPhone innovations was that it was Apple, and not the wireless carriers, that controlled software updating. And the result has been years of steady improvements, all of them absolutely free, giving customers new and exciting capabilities over time. As a result, the iPhone has evolved into a truly compelling smart phone, one so influential that it has transformed the way other companies approach this market as well. Witness the rise of Google Android, a more open iPhone copy of sorts.

As for Microsoft, the software giant wanted to retain the good bits from Windows Mobile but throw out the bad. So while it still allows multiple device makers and wireless

There were other reasons Microsoft couldn't deliver software updates to Windows Mobile customers. Primarily, wireless carriers didn't want users to get free software updates and preferred customers purchase new phones for fairly obvious reasons.

carriers to sell Windows Phones—diversity is good in some cases—it has also fleshed out a rigid set of hardware specifications for this platform. So if a device maker or wireless carrier wishes to sell Windows Phone devices, they must conform to the specs.

What's Included on Every Windows Phone

For now at least, these specs are liberating rather than confining, and at the time of Windows Phone's initial launch in late 2010, they together represent the makings of a very high-end smart phone indeed. According to Microsoft, every Windows Phone must include at least the following hardware:

- ▶ **Processor (CPU):** All Windows Phones must provide at least a 1 GHz ARMv7 Cortex/Scorpion or better processor. What this means to you is that all Windows Phone devices will be able performers: In the mobile device world, 1 GHz is still fairly uncommon beyond the very highest-end devices. And this positioning is important: Windows Phone is a premium smart phone platform.

- ▶ **Graphics:** Windows Phones will ship with a DirectX 9–capable graphics processing unit, or GPU. This provides your phone with exactly the same graphical capabilities—from a visual perspective—as is possible with Microsoft's Xbox 360 video game console. The result is stunning visuals and the possibility of seeing games ported from the console to the phone in full fidelity.

> **NOTE** All Windows Phones use ClearType "sub-pixel rendering" technologies for super-clear text displays. But Microsoft is only specifying a 16-bit color screen as the minimum, so some higher color (24-bit) images might have visual banding. If it's advertised this way, consider a Windows Phone with a 24-bit color screen for superior visuals.

- ▶ **RAM and storage:** Each Windows Phone must include at least 256MB of RAM (memory allotted for the operating system and running applications) and 8GB or more of Flash memory (storage for content, including applications, digital media, documents, and the like).

- ▶ **Hardware buttons:** Every Windows Phone comes with a dedicated set of hardware buttons positioned in a consistent way around the device. These include front-mounted Back, Home, and Search buttons (for navigating "back" as per a web browser, returning to the Home screen, and launching the Bing search experience, respectively); a dedicated camera button (with full and half press support for launching the camera application, auto-focusing, and taking photos); volume up and down; and power/sleep (with brief and full press support for dimming the screen, waking up the device, and so on).

THE BACK BUTTON

The Back button is particularly interesting and useful because it works in different ways throughout the phone. You can use it to go back within an application (to a previous screen or experience), go back between applications (return to the Home screen and then "go back" to the previously-used application), close an open virtual keyboard, menu, dialog, or search experience, navigate to a previous page, and more. This button, completely absent on the iPhone, is in fact one of Windows Phone's best features.

▶ **Camera:** While smart phone cameras haven't quite caught up to dedicated digital cameras from a quality perspective, your Windows Phone should come pretty close. Microsoft requires hardware makers to include at least a 5 megapixel camera with flash (and, as noted above, a dedicated camera button). You can already find devices that exceed these requirements.

TAKING WIDESCREEN PHOTOS AND VIDEO

The Windows Phone camera must take pictures in a 4:3 aspect ratio, which is non-widescreen. Some phone makers offer enhanced cameras with 16:9 or 16:10 widescreen photo (and video) capabilities. Some even ship devices with a second, front-mounted camera for video conferencing. Note, however, that this second camera is not natively supported by the Windows Phone OS, so the phone maker will need to ship special software for that purpose.

▶ **Capacitive multi-touch display with four or more contact points:** Like the iPhone, Windows Phones are primarily touch-based devices with virtual keyboards, or Soft Input Panels (SIPs), that work in both portrait and landscape modes. The screens offer touch and multi-touch, of course, with up to four contact points. That means you could theoretically place four fingers on the

▶ Hardware makers are free to optionally provide a hardware keyboard as well, and since some users still prefer these physical keyboards to onscreen virtual keyboards, that may be an interesting option for you.

screen, each doing something different, and the device could accurately process that information and act accordingly. The Windows Phone screen supports gestures as well. Of course, I will explain the use of this screen fully throughout the book.

▶ **Onscreen resolution:** Windows Phone supports two screen resolutions, 800 x 480 (WVGA) and 480 x 320 (HWVGA). The former is more common and more appropriate for what will likely prove to be the most popular Windows Phone configuration. But hardware makers are free to use the lower-resolution screen type, and will likely do so in smaller devices, including those with slide-out hardware keyboards.

▶ **Accelerometer:** First popularized by the iPhone, an accelerometer is an internal component that can measure acceleration along multiple axes. What this means to you is that a Windows Phone can detect, and respond to, the device being tilted in different directions. The accelerometer is used in ways both utilitarian—if you rotate the device, the display will rotate to accommodate the new orientation—and far less practical—in a racing game, for example, tilting the screen left to right as you play could steer the car.

▶ **Assisted GPS (A-GPS):** Windows Phones ship with this latest GPS (global positioning system) hardware, providing quicker startup and better accuracy, the latter of which is key to a U.S.-based requirement that will allow 911 dispatchers to find smart phone users in an emergency.

▶ **Compass:** Windows Phones ship with an internal compass, which works in concert with the GPS and other location sensors (including Wi-Fi and cellular connection) to accurately find your location and supply information about the direction you are facing.

> **NOTE** As originally delivered in late 2010, the compass hardware in Windows Phone works only with the built-in Bing Maps functionality. Microsoft will provide programming libraries to access the compass to developers later, however. So by the time you read this, it is possible that third-party access to the compass will have already arrived.

▶ **Light sensor:** Thanks to the built-in light sensor, the Windows Phone camera can accurately gauge illumination requirements for the flash and produce accurate and clear low-light photos.

▶ **Proximity sensor:** This sensor can detect how close other objects—such as your face or a table—are to the phone. So the phone can know when you're making a phone call or when you've placed the device on a table. It can also know that it's in a pocket and thus not respond to button taps.

▶ **FM radio tuner:** All Windows Phones ship with an FM radio tuner, providing free access to FM radio and, via bundled software, the ability to mark particular stations as favorites.

▶ Thanks to the inclusion of Zune software on the phone, you can also identify and even purchase songs you hear on the radio. I discuss this capability in Chapter 6.

NOTE These specs are what Microsoft calls its "Chassis-1" specs. Presumably, over time, there will be further updates to the requirements.

What's *Not* Included on Every Windows Phone

If you're an eagle-eyed technology follower, or are simply performing due diligence for your next 2-year commitment, you may have noticed that the Windows Phone hardware requirement list doesn't include some hardware features that you believe are important or even necessary in a modern smart phone. In some cases, these omissions are nothing to worry about: Hardware makers are free to exceed Microsoft's requirements and do bundle additional features with their phones. In other cases, however, the lack of certain features is a bit more troubling, because the underlying platform simply doesn't support this hardware.

Here are some features that Microsoft—good, bad, or indifferently—does not explicitly require its phone makers to include with a Windows Phone. When picking a Windows Phone, it's a good idea to understand which of these features are valuable to you and choose a device according to which features are included.

▶ **Wi-Fi:** Despite its absence from the hardware requirement list, you can expect virtually every Windows Phone to include 802.11g (Wi-Fi G) or 802.11n (Wi-Fi N) wireless networking capabilities.

▶ **Bluetooth:** Ditto for Bluetooth, a separate wireless networking standard that is most often used to connect portable devices with in-ear headsets, keyboards, in-car navigation systems, and other hardware.

NOTE If you're a Bluetooth fan, you'll be interested to know that Windows Phone explicitly supports the following Bluetooth profiles: BT 2.1 + EDR; HFP 1.5 – Hands-Free Profile; HSP – Headset Profile; A2DP 1.2 – Advanced Audio Distribution Profile; AVRCP 1.0 – A/V Remote Control Profile; and PBAP – Phone Book Access Profile.

▶ **Removable storage:** Most non-iPhone smart phones (and virtually all popular Android-based phones) ship with some kind of memory card slot so that you can inexpensively expand the device's internal storage (but not RAM). Today, these mini memory cards typically range from 2GB to 32GB of storage, but of course, technology improves as time marches on.

▶ **Ultra high resolution screens:** At the time of this writing, the iPhone 4 supports a resolution of 960 x 640, which exceeds the highest resolution supported by Windows Phone. While there is little doubt that the Windows Phone OS could handle higher resolutions, device makers are prohibited from selling such a device at this time. As Microsoft evolves the Windows Phone hardware requirements over time, this limitation will change.

▶ **Gyroscope:** While Windows Phone does support an accelerometer, it is lacking a gyroscope, a hardware component that is also found in the iPhone 4. Speaking simply—because, let's face it, this is complicated stuff—a gyroscope simply provides a more accurate, or more sensitive, measurement of how the device is being rotated in X, Y, or Z axis (or "directions"). Given the relatively non-subtle hand movements that will be typical in human/phone interaction, I do not feel that a gyroscope is a particularly important improvement over an accelerometer and that its loss will not impact the Windows Phone experience, gaming or otherwise.

In other words, don't skip out on Windows Phone because of this missing feature.

▶ **Video recording:** While Microsoft doesn't specify that the Windows Phone camera be able to record video, virtually all Windows Phones do, in fact, ship with this capability. Expect VGA (640p) or HD (720p) or better video recording capabilities.

▶ **Geo-tagging:** Another neat camera feature, geo-tagging allows your camera to optionally "tag" each photo with location data so that you can later discover exactly where the photo was taken on a map. This capability is absolutely possible with Windows Phone, thanks to its built-in GPS and other location sensors, and is in fact a feature of the built-in camera software. So no worries here.

▶ **Headphone jack, microphone, and external speaker:** While Microsoft does not require Windows Phone hardware makers to include a standard headphone jack, microphone, or external speaker(s) on their devices, most of course will do so. Be sure to look for these features, however.

▶ **USB connection:** While all Windows Phones will need to provide some way to charge the device, Microsoft does not specify the type of connection that will be used. The result is that different Windows Phones unfortunately will use different power/charge connections, most of which are some variation of USB. In conjunction with a compatible cable, you can charge your phone via a PC, or with a USB power adapter, via a standard wall receptacle.

NOTE One useful feature that Microsoft is not supporting, let alone requiring, is the Zune dock connector that the company previously used on its line of Zune portable media players. This connector worked exactly like Apple's popular dock connector, which provides iPod, iPad, and iPhone users with a standard connector type. You will not find a Windows Phone with a Zune dock connector.

You get the idea: Microsoft specifies some of the more important Windows Phone hardware features in order to provide a consistent experience for users. But Windows Phone also leaves a lot up to the device makers, so there will still be some variation between Windows Phones and, unfortunately, even some areas where Windows Phones simply fall short, at least until Microsoft adds support for certain missing functionality.

MORE SUBTLE CRAPWARE

With Microsoft's previous mobile platform, Windows Mobile, device makers and wireless carriers were able to further differentiate their wares by adding custom software solutions or by actually replacing the tired Windows Mobile user interface with a UI "shell" such as HTC Sense. Microsoft does not allow this level of customization in Windows Phone, part of its effort to exert more control over the platform and ensure that customers have a consistent experience, regardless of which device they get. However, device makers and wireless carriers are allowed to offer far more subtle customizations via software applications, or apps, which run under Windows Phone. Except in rare instances, these apps should not be considered true differentiators, and can instead be ignored.

SUMMARY

If you're as excited by Windows Phone as I am, you're going to want to spend a bit of time preparing for your new phone before you rush out to the store and spend your money. There are two key things to do before buying a phone. First, you should establish a Windows Live ID and connect it with all of the online services to which you belong, providing a central hub for your connections and relationships. Then, you should understand which Windows Phone hardware features are required and optional, allowing you to make a more educated buying decision. With these tasks out of the way, you're ready to head out to your local wireless carrier store or electronics retailer and purchase your new Windows Phone. The next chapter explains how to best configure this phone when you first take it out of the box.

CHAPTER 2

Unboxing and Getting Started

It's that magic day! You've shopped around, taken the plunge, and selected a Windows Phone of your very own. This chapter covers the "Day One" experience: The unboxing of your new device, the first time you turn it on and run through the initial configuration, and some details about the new multi-touch interactions you'll need to know to use the phone.

It's exciting, I know. But you should also plan to work methodically through this first day and make sure you configure the phone properly and familiarize yourself with what is quite definitely the most innovative smart phone interface to come down the pipes in years. After this chapter, I'll assume you know the basics.

There's a lot going on here, and how well you navigate through the various Day One tasks will go a long way toward guaranteeing future successes. So take a deep breath, relax, and pull that shiny new box over in front of you. It's time to take a look at your new phone.

UNBOXING YOUR WINDOWS PHONE

While every Windows Phone will be slightly different, you should find a set of similar components inside the box with every device (Figure 2-1).

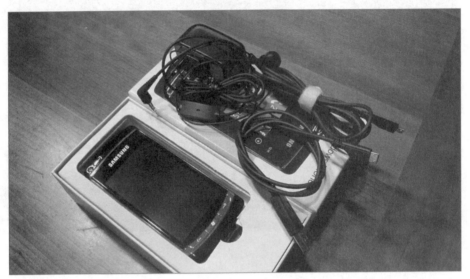

FIGURE 2-1: The Unboxing: A Windows Phone in the box, with all the goodies.

These will include:

▶ **Windows Phone:** The actual phone (Figure 2-2) is shipped inside the box sans battery and, for those on GSM-type networks, without a SIM card installed.

FIGURE 2-2: No prototype Windows Phones were harmed in the writing of this book.

GSM OR CDMA?

GSM (Global System for Mobile Communications; originally Groupe Spécial Mobile) is an international wireless standard and the most popular wireless network type in the world. In the United States, both AT&T and T-Mobile use GSM while Sprint, Verizon, and most smaller carriers utilize a wireless technology called CDMA. There are many differences between the two systems, but for purposes of this discussion, GSM-based phones require the use of a SIM (Subscriber Identity Module) smart card, which includes the customer's subscription information. (On older, pre-smart phone–type phones, the SIM card also contained contacts information.) CDMA-based phones, meanwhile, encode this information directly into the device.

▶ **Battery:** The removable battery, shown in Figure 2-3, is shipped detached from the phone and will need to be inserted before the phone can be used.

FIGURE 2-3: Windows Phones typically include a removable battery.

▶ **SIM card:** On GSM-type phones (see sidebar), your wireless carrier will need to give you a SIM card, which is shown in Figure 2-4. This card is typically inserted into the phone for you at the place of purchase, but you can do so yourself very easily, as I'll describe in just a moment. (The SIM card slides into a thin slot inside the phone, usually near the battery.)

FIGURE 2-4: SIM cards contain a smart chip and need to be punched out of a larger card before they can be inserted in the phone.

▶ **USB sync cable:** This short cable allows you to connect your phone to the PC for synchronization purposes. With Windows Phone, all of this activity takes place through the Zune PC software (version 4.7 or higher), which you can download from the Web at zune.net. Note that the phone's battery will also charge while it is plugged into a PC using the USB sync cable, which is shown in Figure 2-5.

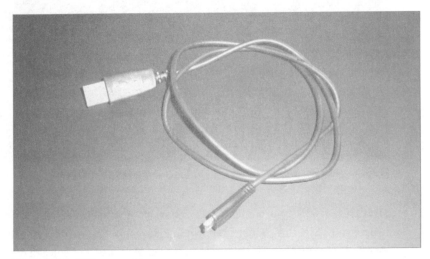

FIGURE 2-5: USB sync cable.

► **Charging cable:** This dedicated charging cable connects your phone to a power outlet for charging purposes. Generally speaking, the phone will charge faster when attached to the wall than it will when attached to the PC using a USB sync cable. The small tip end plugs into the USB connector on the phone, as shown in Figure 2-6.

FIGURE 2-6: The charging cable utilizes the same small USB port as the sync cable.

► **Headphones:** Most Windows Phones will ship with at least a basic pair of wired stereo headphones. Some will include an integrated microphone, such as the pair shown in Figure 2-7, so you can use this set for both music playback and phone. Note that most bundled headphones are usually middling quality at best. My advice is to investigate higher-quality third-party offerings. If you make a lot of phone calls, you might also want to look into a Bluetooth-based hands-free headset.

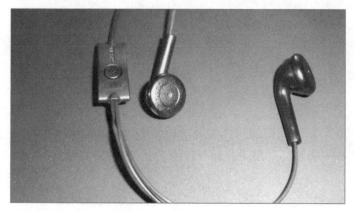

FIGURE 2-7: This bundled pair of headphones is low-end but does include an inline microphone for phone use.

▶ **Documentation:** While most electronic devices these days do not ship with much in the way of paper-based documentation, you should receive some documentation, if only with basic information. Please refer to the web site for your phone's maker for complete documentation, including, usually, PDF-based documentation that you can read on your PC, or print if required.

Putting It All Together

Before you can get started using Windows Phone, you'll need to insert the SIM card, if you're using a GSM-based phone and if that wasn't already done for you at the store. Then, you'll need to insert the battery and charge the phone. Here's how.

First, referring to the instructions that came with the phone, remove the back panel if required to expose where the battery and, optionally, the SIM card need to be inserted. If these are in the same bay, you will usually need to insert the SIM card first. Pop the SIM card out of the larger card in which it is contained, being careful not to bend or split the card in any way.

Then, locate the SIM slot on your phone. A SIM card can only be fully inserted correctly if it's oriented correctly, and there will generally be a diagram on the phone near the SIM slot indicating which way this is. (One corner of the SIM card is "dog-eared" to help with this orientation.) Carefully slide the SIM card into the SIM card slot, as shown in Figure 2-8.

FIGURE 2-8: SIM cards can be inserted only in one orientation, like the SD card in a digital camera.

Be sure to insert the SIM card all the way. A correctly-inserted SIM card will not stick out of the SIM card slot but will instead be flush with the outside edge of the slot. This is shown in Figure 2-9.

FIGURE 2-9: A correctly inserted SIM card will not hang out of the SIM card slot.

Once this is complete, or if you don't need to insert a SIM card for some reason, you can plug the battery into the phone. As with the SIM card, the battery can be inserted only one way correctly, and you will typically see a pair of metal connectors, as in Figure 2-10, which will help you determine which end is which: Just match the connector pins on the battery with the similar pins in the battery bay.

FIGURE 2-10: The battery can also be installed correctly in only one orientation.

Now you can reapply the back cover to the phone, sealing off the battery and SIM card (Figure 2-11).

FIGURE 2-11: After the internal components are plugged in, you can seal the case and get busy.

At this point, you're probably excited to turn the phone on and start playing. You can do this, but be sure to plug the phone into a wall outlet using the bundled charging cable so that you can get the phone fully charged as well. There's no need to wait for the phone to be charged to start. Go ahead: Turn it on.

Initial Configuration

The first time you turn on Windows Phone, the device may quickly flash some basic phone configuration information, but it will quickly move ahead to the white boot screen shown in Figure 2-12.

> **NOTE** This boot screen is your first peek at a common Windows Phone feature, though it may not be obvious: In the center of the screen, you can see a series of five dots move horizontally from left to right. These dots are an animated progress indicator, similar to a progress bar on a PC, and they indicate that the phone is doing something. You'll see this kind of progress indicator throughout Windows Phone, though once you begin using the phone, they will appear at the very top of the screen, and are thus more subtle.

FIGURE 2-12: The Windows Phone boot screen.

Windows Phone will quickly complete booting and then begin stepping you through the out-of-box experience (OOBE), or what Microsoft now calls the Day One experience.

1. It begins with the simple Welcome screen shown in Figure 2-13, which will be customized a bit by the device maker.

   Here, you have two options. You can make an emergency phone call only— no other calls are allowed until you've completed the sign-up process—or you can tap Get Started and continue. I assume you want to do the latter, so tap Get Started.

FIGURE 2-13: Step one of the Day One experience: the Welcome screen.

NOTE Windows Phone is fully optimized for multi-touch displays, so the interface assumes you're going to be tapping the screen with your finger. For basic buttons like Emergency Call or Get Started, all you need to do is literally tap the screen with the tip of a finger.

2. In the next step of this wizard, you must choose from between the five basic languages that are available, as shown in Figure 2-14. (It's possible that Microsoft will add support for more languages by the time you read this.)

FIGURE 2-14: The Choose a Language screen.

Choose the appropriate language—I'll assume English (United States) for the purposes of this walkthrough—by tapping that choice on the screen. The currently selected choice in this list will be highlighted in blue, which is the default accent color used across the system (though you can change that later). Chances are, the correct choice is already selected, and thus already colored blue. When you're done, tap the Next button to continue.

3. In the next screen, shown in Figure 2-15, you must accept the Windows Phone terms of use, which consists of Microsoft's end-user license agreement (EULA) for the software system found on your device as well as the company's privacy statement. These documents are actually pretty important, but I don't expect most people to actually pay attention to them. And let's face it, who's going to get this far and not keep going?

Tap Accept.

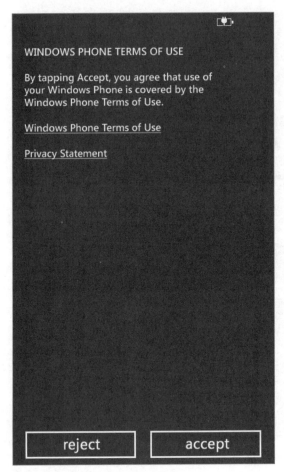

FIGURE 2-15: Windows Phone Terms of Use.

4. In the next screen, shown in Figure 2-16, you have an important choice to make. You can accept Microsoft's recommended default settings for Windows Phone or you can step through a slightly longer customization process where you fine-tune each option to your liking.

My advice here is the same as it is for the similar screen in desktop versions of Windows or any other Microsoft software: Always choose the Custom option. The reasoning is that you'll never be able to easily go back and do this again, you want to get it right, and going the custom route doesn't actually take that much more time anyway. Because of these reasons, I'm going to assume you tap Custom and continue. I know you want to do the right thing.

FIGURE 2-16: Windows Phone Settings. You will choose wisely.

5. In the next step, you'll see two options, only one of which is checked by default (Figure 2-17).

These are:

▷ **Allow cellular data usage on your phone:** Checked by default, this is typically the correct configuration. However, in the rare instance in which you may be using Windows Phone without a data plan, or via a very limited data plan, you may want to uncheck this option.

▷ **Send information to help improve Windows Phones:** Maybe I'm just a sap, but I think it's important to always provide anonymous and automatic feedback to Microsoft, because I know the company does in fact use this data to make their products better. But this option is unchecked by default. So do the right thing and select it.

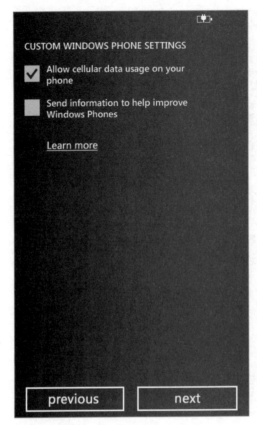

FIGURE 2-17: Custom Windows Phone Settings.

By the way, this screen in the wizard features a new UI object, or *control*, called the check box. It works just as it does in desktop versions of Windows and is used to toggle a choice between two states, enabled and disabled. A check box that is checked is said to be enabled, while one that is unchecked (or empty) is disabled.

Tap Next when you've made your choices.

6. In the next screen, shown in Figure 2-18, you choose the time zone in which you live (or currently are).

This screen works just like the Choose a Language screen, though there are many more choices. Windows Phone will generally pick the correct time zone automatically, and the currently selected choice will be highlighted in the default blue accent color. But if the correct time zone isn't chosen, you can of course tap the correct choice in the list.

FIGURE 2-18: The Choose Time Zone screen.

Because the time zone list is so long, however, it extends off both the top and bottom of the screen. And as you would in a traditional PC interface, you can scroll up or down in this list. However, this is a touch-based interface. So scrolling doesn't require tapping on arrows or other controls, as with a PC. Instead, you simply flick the screen up or down. Flicking in a downward motion will cause the list to scroll down, thus moving you higher up in the list. Likewise, flicking in an upward motion will cause the list to scroll up, thus moving you lower in the list.

These flicking gestures are dynamic, too. So if you flick the screen harder, it will scroll more quickly. And if you flick it gently, it will scroll slowly. It's also worth mentioning that you can stop the scrolling at any time by tapping the screen.

When you're done picking a time zone—and playing with the incredibly responsive screen—tap Next.

7. In the next screen, you're prompted to sign in with your Windows Live ID, as shown in Figure 2-19.

FIGURE 2-19: Sign in with a Windows Live ID.

Now, if you've been following along since page one, you've already set up your Windows Live ID, which involves not just creating the ID but also configuring it properly to work with all of the social networks and online services that you already use. If you have not done this, please go back and read Chapter 1 first. It's incredibly important that you at least set up a basic Windows Live ID before logging on to the phone for the first time. Yes, you can use Windows Phone, sort of, without doing so. But I don't recommend this, even if your primary account is at Google or elsewhere.

But you've done the right thing. So tap Sign In to continue.

8. In the next screen (Figure 2-20), you're prompted to enter your Windows Live ID and associated password. As important, perhaps, you'll get your first experience with the Windows Phone virtual keyboard.

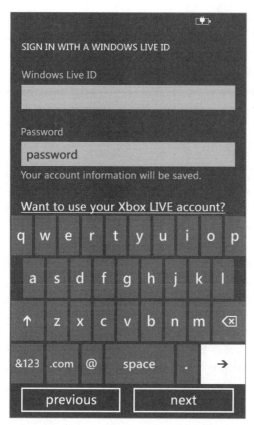

FIGURE 2-20: Sign in with a Windows Live ID and check out the Windows Live virtual keyboard for the first time.

TURNS OUT THE KEYBOARD IS SMART, TOO

This won't be obvious even after you've used the phone for a while but Windows Phone actually utilizes several, mostly subtly different, virtual keyboards, each of which is optimized for different conditions. The keyboard you see here is optimized for typing in Internet information, and it includes a dedicated **.com** key as well as an **@** key. Likewise, it doesn't assume an initial capital letter, since Internet information, such as the e-mail address you're about to enter, is generally all lowercase.

Some keyboard basics to consider. First, the Windows Phone virtual keyboard is laid out in a standard QWERTY layout by default, so if you're not a touch typist, you soon will be (if only with your thumbs). It supports sub-layouts, too, for access to other characters. To type one or more numbers, or another non-letter character, for example, tap the **&123** key. (And from within this other keyboard layout, you can use the More key—a right-pointing arrow—to access even more characters.) To use an uppercase character, tap the Shift (up arrow) key.

You can navigate between the Windows Live ID and Password fields in different ways, but the easiest (and quickest) is to simply tap the Password text field after you've completed entering your e-mail address. If you tap outside of the text input fields, the virtual keyboard will disappear. Fear not: It will return as soon as you tap within one of the text entry fields again.

Finally, the Windows Phone virtual keyboard supports some simple editing. Say you need to type your Windows Live ID, which is *thurrott@live.com*. (It's not, of course, as that's *my* Windows Live ID. But this is just an example.) By mistake, however, you've typed *thurtott@live.com* without realizing the error until you reached the end. Now what?

To change that middle "t" to an "r," tap and hold on the Windows Live ID text field. Eventually, you'll notice that a little blue I-beam cursor appears above the text box, as shown in Figure 2-21.

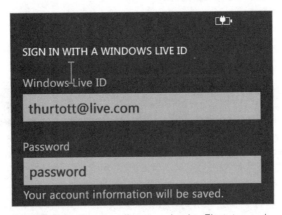

SIGN IN WITH A WINDOWS LIVE ID

Windows Live ID

thurtott@live.com

Password

password

Your account information will be saved.

FIGURE 2-21: Time to edit out a mistake. First, tap and hold to get the I-beam cursor.

Now, slide your finger down the screen so that it's below the text box. As you do so, the I-beam cursor will slip into the text box and move between two of the entered characters. While continuing to press down on the screen, move left or right to position that I-beam cursor so that it is after the spurious letter ("t" in this case), as shown in Figure 2-22.

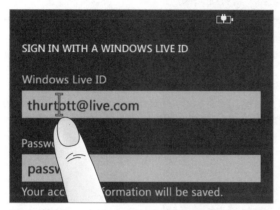

FIGURE 2-22: As you slide your finger left and right, the I-beam cursor moves with you.

When the cursor is properly positioned lift your finger off the screen. The I-beam cursor will disappear, replaced by the normal cursor (which looks like a thin vertical line). Now, tap the Backspace key (it looks like an X inside a left-pointing arrow)—this will delete the incorrect character ("t")—and tap the correct character ("r"). You're good to go, and it's easy to see other how similar edits might be handled. This style of editing is available throughout Windows Phone, and you'll quickly become used to it after you've done it a few times.

When you're ready to log on, tap Next.

9. The virtual keyboard will disappear and the message "Connecting to Windows Live . . ." will appear near the top of the screen. Likewise, if you look closely, you'll see some blue progress dots animate across the very top of the screen, another indication that the phone is doing something. (In this case, it's con-necting to the Internet over your phone's wireless data connection.) When it has made the connection and correctly logged on to your account, you'll see the fun message shown in Figure 2-23.

Tap Done to complete the sign-in process. After a moment, the default blue Windows Phone user interface will appear. And now you can actually use your new phone.

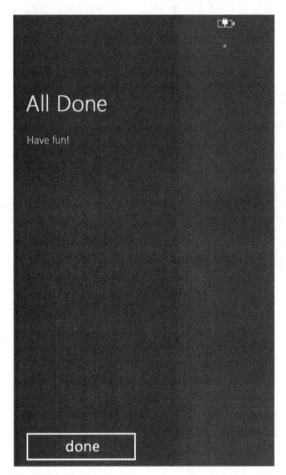

FIGURE 2-23: Have fun!

WINDOWS PHONE USAGE

When you complete the out-of-box experience, you'll be presented with the Windows Phone Start screen, shown in Figure 2-24. This screen is a scrollable list of live tiles, each representing a separate Windows Phone application or other experience. You scroll up and down this screen as you did the various lists you ran into during the sign-in phase.

There are a few basic things going on here. You can tap a live tile to launch individual applications, and much of the rest of this book is dedicated to describing each of the applications Microsoft includes with this system.

FIGURE 2-24: The Windows Phone Start screen.

At any time in Windows Phone, you can tap the device's Back button, found below the screen, to return to a previous experience or "go back" in other ways. So if you launch an application and want to return to the Start screen, just tap the Back button, and you will go back (in this case, to the Start screen).

You can also scroll from left to right from this Start screen (or tap the right arrow button) to display the All Programs screen. This screen, shown in Figure 2-25, differs from the Start screen in that it's an uglier, text-based list, it's in alphabetical order, and it includes links to every single application on the phone, as well as Settings and some other features. It's also not customizable in any meaningful way.

You can flick to the left to return to the Start screen. Or tap the left arrow button. Or, you guessed it, tap Back.

FIGURE 2-25: The All Programs screen.

Of course, there are a few things you need to do before you dive too deeply into your new phone. In fact, a few of these things will present themselves to you automatically. When you first exit the out-of-box experience, you may notice a small blue band appear at the top of the screen, as shown in Figure 2-26. This is actually a notification pop-up, or *toast* in Microsoft-speak.

If you tap this notification toast, the Messaging app will appear displaying the full welcome message from Microsoft (Figure 2-27). This is a read-only message, so you can't reply to it.

CROSSREF If you want to know more about Messaging, check out Chapter 14, where that application is fully documented.

FIGURE 2-26: Microsoft welcomes you to Windows
Phone with a pop-up notification.

If you're within range of a Wi-Fi network, say at work or at home, Windows Phone
will also display a notification toast indicating that it has found one or more wireless networks. Tap this notification, and you'll be presented with the Wi-Fi Settings
screen, shown in Figure 2-28. You can configure your phone to access a wireless network from this screen, of course, including typing in a password if required.

As noted previously, this book is largely concerned with the various software
interfaces that Microsoft provides in Windows Phone, so much of what you'll read in
the pages ahead will focus on the different applications, settings, and other interfaces that you'll see on every Windows Phone. Before moving ahead to these topics,
however, it's important to understand a few Windows Phone basics. And these include
both usage models—based largely around the multi-touch display—and common user
interface elements that you'll run into time and again.

So I examine these next.

Interacting with Your Phone

In the walkthrough of the first day experience described earlier in the chapter, I
touched on a number of basic ways in which you interact with the multi-touch screen
such as that found on all Windows Phones. Here, I want formalize that concept a bit
and briefly discuss each of the touch-based input methods that are supported on
Windows Phone.

▶ If you have a
Wi-Fi network,
configure
Windows Phone
to use it. Wi-Fi
networks offer
much better
bandwidth and
performance than
cellular networks.
Windows Phone
will use the better
performing
network, so it will
use Wi-Fi over
cellular when
possible.

FIGURE 2-27: The complete welcome message.   **FIGURE 2-28:** The Wi-Fi Settings screen.

TOUCH/TAP/SINGLE TOUCH

Windows Phone is a next-generation software system that supports multiple input models, including a number of natural user interface interactions based on touch and multi-touch. The most basic of these, of course, is *touch* or, as it's sometimes called, *single touch*. When you touch the screen of your phone with your finger, a process I will refer to as a "tap" throughout this book, you're using the single touch interaction method. You tap the screen (Figure 2-29) for many reasons, including selecting text, pressing a button or other control (including a key on the virtual keyboard), and so on.

TAP AND HOLD

If you're familiar with desktop versions of Windows, you know that right-clicking an object is often the key to finding out more about that object and triggering additional, hidden actions. Tap and hold—where you tap the screen but don't immediately let go—works just like that and is demonstrated in Figure 2-30. In most cases, it will trigger a pop-up menu listing actions you can perform on the selected object. Occasionally, you'll tap and hold on an object and nothing will happen. In such cases, the object simply doesn't have any pertinent actions to offer.

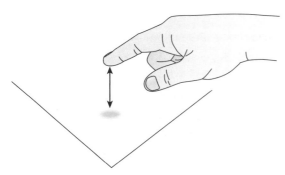

FIGURE 2-29: Tap.

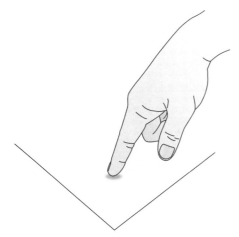

FIGURE 2-30: Tap and hold.

GESTURES

Windows Phone also supports single-touch gestures. The most obvious of these is scrolling, which can be performed in an up and down motion, as through lists, or in a left and right motion, as through panoramic experiences. In either case, you're essentially flicking the screen (Figure 2-31).

You can also *pan*, which is like scrolling except that instead of flicking the screen, you actually press and hold and move your finger in any direction. This is most frequently used in editing situations, such as when you need to position the text entry cursor somewhere specific within a block of previously entered text.

DOUBLE-TAP

In many Windows Phone UIs, double-tapping an object, akin to double-clicking a mouse in desktop Windows versions, can perform special actions. The most common is to zoom. For example, if you are browsing the Web and wish to zoom the browser's view into a certain text column, you can double-tap that column to do so. Double-tap it again to zoom back out to the previous view. This double-tap zoom action also works in the Maps app and in other Windows Phone applications.

PINCH AND STRETCH

Likewise, Windows Phone supports multi-touch gestures as well. The most common is to pinch the screen to zoom in on the current view. Or, conversely, you can "reverse-pinch" (or stretch your fingers apart onscreen) to zoom out. Pinch to zoom is shown in Figure 2-32.

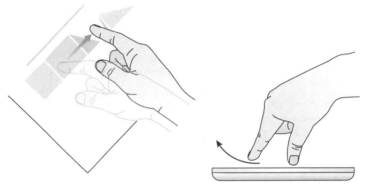

FIGURE 2-31: Flicking the screen to scroll.

FIGURE 2-32: Pinch to zoom. It's okay, your phone won't mind.

> **NOTE** The Windows Phone screen actually supports four or more touch points, so it's possible that you could run an application that could independently target four different onscreen taps at the same time. There aren't many scenarios for that kind of interaction on such small devices, but there are some games that could offer this kind of thing, including such titles as four player air hockey, where each player could independently control their own onscreen player.

Hardware Interfaces

Windows Phone also supports a number of non-touch user interfaces, though not all will be found on every phone. Every phone will, however, include a certain set of hardware buttons and other features. These include:

- **Power button:** This surprisingly versatile button behaves differently depending on what's going on with the phone. If the phone is completely powered down, you can use this button to turn it on. If the phone is powered up and on, you can tap this button to lock the phone (and turn off the screen). And if you need to hard reset the phone, just hold down the power button for 8 seconds: You'll get a jaunty "Good-bye!" message and the phone will shut down.

- **Back button:** This button is used to navigate back to the previous experience. This works both between applications and the OS, as well as within applications. (For example, Internet Explorer uses the Back button as a browser Back button, navigating you to the previously visited web page.) It can also be used to close menus, dialogs, and virtual keyboards.

- **Start button:** This button is very simple: It navigates the phone immediately to the Start screen.

- **Search button:** This button launches the Bing search experience in most cases, but it's also used in certain applications to perform in-application searches.

- **Camera button:** The dedicated camera button launches the Camera application, allowing you to take still pictures and videos. This button is enabled even if the device is off and locked; just hold down for two seconds.

- **Volume Up and Down buttons:** These buttons can be used to adjust the system volume, as well as in-call conversations (when the phone is active), media playback, and so on.

- **Microphone:** Every Windows Phone includes at least one microphone for making phone calls.

- **Sensors:** Every Windows Phone includes a number of sensors, which are used to improve the overall phone experience. These include an accelerometer, GPS (really assisted GPS, or A-GPS), proximity sensor, camera, compass, and a light sensor.

- **Output hardware:** All Windows Phone devices include an audio output jack, an in-device speaker (or speakers), a screen, and vibration functionality. Additionally, each Windows Phone includes an FM radio receiver.

▶ The Back button is surprisingly versatile. One thing it doesn't do, however, is emulate the Backspace key on the keyboard.

▶ If you press and hold on the Start button, Windows Phone's secret voice command system starts up.

▶ If you receive a call and the ringer is annoying just tap a volume button to mute the ringer.

Some hardware devices are optional. The most obvious is a hardware keyboard, shown in Figure 2-33, which will be offered by some phone makers on some Windows

Phone models. My expectation is that keyboard-less Windows Phone devices will be far more popular than those with hardware keyboards.

FIGURE 2-33: A Windows Phone hardware keyboard.

Common UIs

Looking at the software interfaces generally, there are a few common user interfaces that you'll see throughout Windows Phone. These include the following:

STATUS BAR

At the top of virtually every Windows Phone screen—except, perhaps, in most games— you'll see a thin band called the Status Bar that provides a quick glance at vital phone statistics like the battery gauge and time. This is the default Status Bar view, and it's shown in Figure 2-34.

Tap anywhere near the top of the screen and a fuller Status Bar will appear with additional status information, including the strength of your cellular signal and, if available, Wi-Fi signal. This is shown in Figure 2-35.

FIGURE 2-34: The default Status Bar.

FIGURE 2-35: A Status Bar with more information.

The Status Bar can actually provide a surprising wealth of information. Some of the available status icons you may see include, from left to right, cellular signal strength, data connection type, call forwarding status, roaming, Wi-Fi signal strength, Bluetooth status, ring mode, input status (shifted keyboard or not), battery gauge, and time. The complete range of icons is shown in Figure 2-36.

FIGURE 2-36: A complete Status Bar.

APPLICATION BAR

Many standard (one-screen) Windows Phone applications will include a simple toolbar, called the Application Bar, which runs along the bottom of the screen and provides access to one to four round buttons, which represent commonly-used tasks. A typical Application Bar is shown in Figure 2-37.

FIGURE 2-37: An Application Bar.

To access more tasks, you can access the Application Menu by tapping the special More button, which appears as three dots at the end of the Application Bar. This expands the Application Bar up, providing access to those additional tasks, as shown in Figure 2-38.

▶ When you tap the More button, you also get to see the name of each Application Bar button, which can be handy. Some of the buttons aren't obvious.

LANDSCAPE AND PORTRAIT VIEWS

When you hold the phone normally, it's said to be in *portrait view*, where the height of the device is longer than its width. Virtually all Windows Phone applications work in this default portrait view, and indeed many applications only work in portrait view. Thanks to an internal accelerometer, however, you can rotate the device left or right and view the screen in a horizontal, or *landscape*, view. In this view, the Application Bar moves to the left or right edge of the screen, and the Status Bar moves to the other side, depending on which way you turned it, as shown in Figure 2-39.

The problem with landscape view is that it's not supported in all Windows Phone applications, including some—like Maps and Excel—where a wider display would in fact be desirable.

FIGURE 2-38: An Application Bar with exposed Application Menu.

FIGURE 2-39: A Windows Phone application in landscape view.

SINGLE-SCREEN APPLICATIONS AND PANORAMIC HUBS

While there will be some differentiation between different Windows Phone applications, Microsoft is supporting two main application types: standard, single-screen applications and panoramic experiences, or hubs.

Applications are generally single-screen experiences, though they also often feature a pivot control so that the user can swipe between different sections, or columns, of information. They are usually standalone experiences (like the built-in Calculator and Alarms utilities) and derive content from a single source. They're not usually extensible by third-party developers. Applications, or apps, can be very rich (like a game) or utilize the stock Windows Phone "Metro" UI for a clean, simple look. A typical single-screen app is shown in Figure 2-40.

Hubs, sometimes called panoramic experiences, are one of Windows Phone's strongest selling points. These super applications appear to visually extend far beyond the confines of the Windows Phone screen, and to view the entire experience, you need to scroll, or flick, horizontally. Conceptually speaking, a typical hub resembles Figure 2-41, not all of which will appear on the device's screen at once.

FIGURE 2-40: The Alarms utility is a simple, single-screen application.

FIGURE 2-41: A Windows Phone panoramic experience, or hub, extends far beyond the confines of the device's screen.

Hubs differ from single-screen apps in a few important ways. These include:

1. They're panoramic. Hubs typically extend across two or more screen widths, because they provide more information than can fit on a single screen.

2. The content contained in a hub is typically derived from multiple sources. These can be online sources (Windows Live, Facebook, and so on), on-device sources (local photo galleries and the like), or any combination of those.

3. They're extensible. Developers can add on to the built-in hubs and add their own features. For example, Last.FM and Pandora could (and will) extend the built-in Music + Videos hub. And third parties will write Flickr and Google Picasa Web add-ins for the Pictures hub. The possibilities are endless.

> **NOTE** This, of course, is just a short overview. I examine the various Windows Phone applications and hubs in much more detail throughout this book.

SUMMARY

Properly configuring your new Windows Phone from day one will ensure a good experience going forward, and set you up to discover the other user interfaces, applications, and services I discuss throughout the rest of the book. And there's a lot to learn, especially if you've never before owned or used a multi-touch device like Windows Phone.

Now you're ready for a deeper exploration of the innovative new Windows Phone interface, called Metro. Not surprisingly, this is the very next topic I'll examine.

CHAPTER 3

Understanding the Windows Phone User Interface

Microsoft designed the Windows Phone user experience— code named "Metro"—as the key differentiator between this new generation of devices and the competition. To date, all smart phones, including Apple's stunning and innovative iPhone, Google's me-too Android, RIM's business-oriented Blackberry, and others, have been designed to work like miniaturized PCs. That is, they run applications. And when you want to perform some common task—such as make a phone call, view pictures, or check your schedule—you have to think in terms of the application you must run in order to accomplish that task.

Windows Phone does not work that way, and that's exactly why it's so exciting. Instead, Microsoft has engineered this new platform to work the way you do, with a set of integrated experiences that blend content from a variety of locations, putting what's important to you right up front and center. In this chapter, you'll dive deep into Metro, discovering how it works, of course, but also why it works the way it does.

You'll also take a quick spin around the Metro UI, exploring the various available hubs and apps, setting up the deeper explorations that occur later in the book. Once you're done with this chapter, you should "get" Windows Phone: Not just the where and how, but the *why*.

THE WAY WE WERE: HOW MICROSOFT SCREWED UP MOBILE SO BAD IT HAD TO START OVER FROM SCRATCH

Way back in 1995, Microsoft began testing a new type of Windows that would run on consumer electronics (CE) devices instead of PCs. Called Windows CE, this system looked a lot like the Windows 95 OS that was popular on the PCs of the day, and it offered programmers a similar experience for developing applications. But underneath the hood, Windows CE was different: It was aimed at a non-PC hardware platform that was appropriate for the mobile devices that were coming to market at the time, could run with minimal RAM and storage, and utilized a stylus as a pointing device instead of a mouse.

> **NOTE**   The original version of Windows CE, which I beta tested in 1995-1996, was code named "Pegasus."

Pre-Phone: Windows CE, Palm PC, Palm-Sized PC, and Pocket PC

The original version of Windows CE was designed for a short-lived range of miniature PC-like devices called Handheld PCs. (See Figure 3-1.) These devices looked like mini-laptop computers, but were awkwardly sized: They were too big to fit in a pocket and too small to use comfortably. (Today, Apple sells such a device. It's called an iPad.)

Windows CE and the first awkward Handheld PCs also had the misfortune to ship in the same year as Palm's innovative Pilot. This tiny, palm-sized PDA (personal digital assistant) was an instant smash hit, offering users a device that was pocket-sized, useful, and also fun. (Fun fact: Palm had to drop the Palm Pilot name after Pilot Pen Corp. sued.)

Struggling to keep up with Palm in the suddenly-hot PDA market, Microsoft melded its Windows CE system to work on a palm-sized device and with the resulting loss of onscreen real estate. Unfortunately, it decided to brand this new product as the Palm PC, causing Palm to sue for trademark infringement. (And you know, it really *was* a bald-faced predatory move on Microsoft's part.) After some grandstanding, Microsoft backed down, renamed the product to Palm-Sized PC, and held its collective breath.

FIGURE 3-1: One of the original Windows CE devices.

Palm didn't sue again, but then it didn't need to: The Palm-Sized PC was a dud, and consumers didn't respond to devices that used a desktop Windows interface (this time with the Start button moved to the top of the screen) on a device that actually could fit in your hand.

Microsoft kept trying. They renamed the system, yet again, this time to Pocket PC. (A typical Pocket PC device is shown in Figure 3-2.) And over the course of a few years there, Microsoft actually did pretty well given the relatively small size of the PDA market. But the most important change to come during the Pocket PC era was the development of a version of this OS that would work on a new generation of PDAs with phone functionality. Over time, these devices became known as smart phones for what I assume are obvious reasons. And Microsoft was uniquely positioned to enter and perhaps even dominate this then-nascent market.

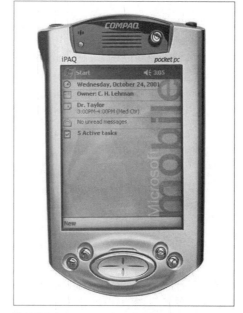

A smart phone is generally considered to be a portable phone that has PC-like functionality. But Microsoft approached this product line from the opposite angle. It had the PC-like PDA platform first and added phone functionality to it after the fact.

FIGURE 3-2: Microsoft did find some success with the Pocket PC.

The Phone Era Begins

Microsoft's first smart phones were developed as an adjunct to the Pocket PC line, where one version of the OS would serve the PDA platform and the other would serve

PDA phones, adding phone-specific features such as a numeric keyboard, dialer, and contacts integration. In 2003, the software giant renamed this product line, again, this time to Windows Mobile, and it released a confusing number of product editions, including two aimed at phones, Windows Mobile 2003 for Smartphone and Windows Mobile 2003 for Pocket PC Phone Edition.

> **NOTE** Why this differentiation? Smart phones, at the time, were seen as very small devices with tiny screens, whereas Pocket PC Phones would have larger touch- and stylus-based screens that more closely resembled the previous generation PDA devices. This distinction eventually disappeared.

Over time, Windows Mobile grew more powerful and functional, but it also suffered at the hands of its more aggressive competitors. First came Research in Motion, or RIM, a Canadian company that grew to great success on the back of its "push" e-mail functionality. Push allows users of RIM's Blackberry smart phones to access their e-mail (and contacts and calendar and tasks) over-the-air, directly, and not via synchronization, which is slower and requires a wired connection between the device and the user's PC. Microsoft responded to RIM by adding push functionality to Windows Mobile, but by then it was too late: RIM began dominating the corporate market for smart phones, especially in the United States, a position it has yet to relinquish. A typical Blackberry is shown in Figure 3-3.

And then the world *really* changed. In 2007, Apple announced and then released its iPhone smart phone (Figure 3-4). By targeting consumers rather than business users, and focusing on functionality such as media playback and Internet browsing, Apple opened up smart phones to a whole new market. It didn't hurt that the iPhone, along with its software, was beautiful to look at, fun to use, and featured advanced multi-touch technology that the competition struggled to duplicate for years.

The iPhone took off for good once Apple opened up the device to third-party development and established a thriving Apps Store from which users could download and, for paid apps, purchase selections from an ever-growing collection of apps. Today, no modern smart phone platform—including Windows Phone—is considered complete without such a store.

FIGURE 3-3: A RIM Blackberry smart phone.

Microsoft, like the competition, has spent years trying to match Apple in the smart phone market. It developed new versions of Windows Mobile to no avail, and lost market share over the next 3 years. It developed, but never released, a Windows Mobile 7 product that would have basically copied the iPhone design, morphing it on top of the old Windows Mobile foundation that, quite frankly, hadn't changed appreciably since that very first version of Windows CE.

One thing is clear: If Microsoft continued down this path, Windows Mobile would have been driven into the ground by RIM in the business market and by Apple in the consumer market. It is at moments like this that companies typically do one of two things. They can fail to see what's happening and become slowly more irrelevant over time. Or they can simply start over.

Guess which one Microsoft chose?

FIGURE 3-4: Apple's innovative iPhone.

A NEW BEGINNING: METRO

In 2009, examining both the marketplace and the work it had done toward a new version of Windows Mobile, Microsoft hit the reset button. It jettisoned years of work, over a decade of technological history, and simply decided to start over from scratch. Well, not entirely from scratch. As it turns out, other groups within Microsoft had been laying the groundwork for what would become the company's next-generation phone platform.

This work started with a project called Freestyle, which became Windows Media Center, a TV-friendly interface for digital media. Aside from some obvious graphical niceties and functional excellence, the big deal with Media Center, in retrospect, is that it pushed Microsoft to start thinking about nontraditional (that is, non-mouse and keyboard) PC interaction, in this case a TV-based remote control.

As Media Center evolved over the lifetimes of Windows XP, Vista, and then 7, it was adapted to work with other nontraditional interfaces, including the pen/stylus interface from Tablet PCs, and, later, touch and multi-touch. (In fact, it's very likely that more people interact with Media Center via touch screens today than with a remote control, something that Microsoft could not have foreseen back in 2001.) Windows Media Center is shown in Figure 3-5.

FIGURE 3-5: By the time Windows 7 appeared, Media Center had evolved to work with HDTV displays and multi-touch.

Media Center didn't stand alone, of course. Microsoft pushed this interface to mobile devices as well, first via its short-lived Portable Media Center platform and then with the "Origami" interfaces it created for the Ultra-Mobile PC (UMPC, shown in Figure 3-6). Both of these products were failures from a sales perspective, but they provided Microsoft with valuable experience in melding very visual user interfaces and touch capabilities into highly portable form factors.

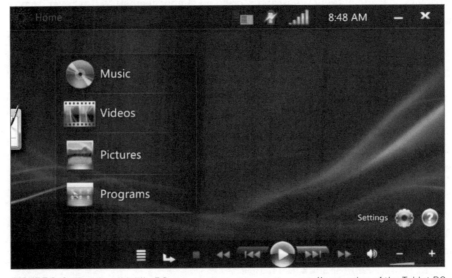

FIGURE 3-6: The Ultra-Mobile PC was an attempt to create a smaller version of the Tablet PC with touch capabilities.

And then came Zune. Microsoft's answer to the iPod hasn't exactly set the world on fire, but again, by iterating this portable media platform over four generations of devices, culminating with the Zune HD in late 2009, Microsoft gained still more experience. And it's work on the Zune HD (Figure 3-7) and the PC software that Zune users use to synchronize with PC-based digital media content, would lead directly to the Windows Phone platform.

FIGURE 3-7: We didn't realize it at the time, but the Zune HD included an early version of the Windows Phone user experience.

This platform has many components, and as you will discover, Windows Phone users, like Zune HD users, also use the Zune PC software—shown in Figure 3-8—to synchronize PC-based music, video, and photos to their devices. (You can find out more about this software in Chapter 6.) But the single biggest influence that the Zune platform has on Windows Phone, of course, is the user interface (or "user experience"). And on Windows Phone, this highly evolved UI is now called Metro.

There are many ways to describe and explain Metro, but perhaps the most obvious is to examine how Microsoft describes this user experience internally. I'm not interested in regurgitating marketing documentation, however. Instead, let's see how Microsoft's view of Metro stands in the harsh cold light of reality. Then, I'll jump right into the software and give you a tour.

Key Metro Themes

According to Microsoft, which tends to be fond of nauseating marketing drivel, Metro is the Windows Phone design language. It's called Metro because it's modern and clean. It's fast and in motion. It's about content and typography. And it's entirely authentic.

FIGURE 3-8: The Zune PC software also features elements of the interaction model that Microsoft uses in Metro.

Once you get over your gag reflex—don't worry, it's normal—and really examine these claims in the light of what Microsoft has actually accomplished with Windows Phone, some interesting trends emerge. I'll examine them very briefly.

▶ **Modern and clean:** The Metro user experience breaks with conventional thinking in the smart phone space and provides a UI that is modern and clean, or as I like to think of it, a UI that "gets out of the way." If you've been around the tech space for a while, you know that this is how Mac fans describe Mac OS X and make the inevitable comparison with the busier Windows. This time, however, the tables are reversed, and it is Microsoft, not Apple, with the cleaner, less busy design.

So the Metro user experience is simple by design. It features a lot of white space, or larger than expected areas of onscreen real estate that are left devoid of onscreen controls, in a nod to design simplicity. Microsoft says that Windows Phone has undergone a "fierce reduction of unnecessary elements" in the user interface. This is not a busy UI by any stretch of the imagination.

This focus drives home Microsoft's point that a Windows Phone is not a tiny PC, as were all previous Windows Mobile, Pocket PC, and Windows CE devices. It is instead something else, something unique given its size and form factor. And this way of thinking differentiates Windows Phone from the iPhone and Android competition: Those phones work very much like mini-PCs, offering an application-based experience where you must dive in and out of separate, siloed experiences.

▶ **Fast and in motion:** While the iPhone and other smart phones offer some modicum of animation and mini-design flourishes that resemble a page turning or flipping up from the corner—*how gauche!*—Windows Phone deeply integrates animation and motion into the user experience, providing visual cues and feedback about the actions you make. And these animations and motion move at a rapid clip, thanks to the underlying power of the device's CPU and GPU (graphics processing unit).

There are transition animations as you launch applications, move between screens, or accomplish tasks. Considering the Spartan nature of the Windows Phone user experience, these transitions play an important role, because they provide context for what you are doing, and where you are navigating within the UI.

You can see motion and animation in the live tiles on the Windows Phone Start screen as well. These tiles provide animations as a tease for what you'll see if you should tap them. The People tile animates with a moving kaleidoscope of your contacts' photos, for example. As Microsoft says, "live tiles use motion to engage the user, to pull them in."

Motion and animation, of course, are hard to capture in the static screenshots found in this book. For this reason, I recommend getting your hands on a Windows Phone so you can see it in person. A Windows Phone feels alive and vibrant, ready for action, whereas your typical smart phone—I'm looking at you, iPhone and Android—provides just a boring, static grid of icons; a UI that requires you to do all the work. With Windows Phone, you'll feel compelled to explore. It's an entirely different kind of experience.

▶ **Content and typography:** In keeping with the use of white space noted previously, Windows Phone further differentiates itself from other smart phones by putting content front and center. Microsoft contends, correctly, I think, that a phone is a personal, intimate device; a life companion. So instead of designing the Metro UI with applications at the forefront, Windows Phone lets content be the interface. You no longer have to think about which application to launch when you want to access a favorite photo. Instead, you just access the Pictures experience, which combines photos and images from any number of applications and online services. That these locations contain not just your own photos, but photos from your friends and family too, is just the icing on the cake.

In pushing the content that most matters to you to the forefront, Microsoft has also de-emphasized the traditional user interface "chrome" that can clutter up other smart phone UIs. The Windows Phone chrome consists of window and screen frames, borders, toolbars, and so on—UI features that are found by default in the user experience. The content *is* the UI, and you interact directly with that content. Thus, the phone works the way you think, instead of forcing you to think about the way the device organizes things—as the iPhone does.

Of course, you can't just push common UI elements off to the side without making some trade-off. After all, this isn't a user experience for toddlers. So Microsoft has based the Metro user experience, heavily, on nicely typographic text, or type. And while the notion of textual menus and UI elements as beautiful may sound illogical—what is this, DOS?—in use, the Windows Phone user experience—like that of the Zune HD before it—is elegant, expressive, and attractive. As important, it's highly usable.

▶ **Authentic:** This bit is, perhaps, the hardest to swallow. It seems that Microsoft is pushing perhaps a bit too hard to establish its new user experience model as not just a viable alternative to the competition, but as a completely superior way of doing things.

If I were in charge of Windows Phone marketing, I would simply state this as, "It's a phone, stupid." Or, as Microsoft *has* noted, "It's a phone, not a PC." The point being that while Windows may make plenty of sense on a PC, it doesn't make a heck of a lot of sense on a device with a 4-inch screen. So Windows Phone is authentic, or true, to the device. The hardware is simple and modern by design, as is the software. There's no decoration and no ornamentation on either, and no need for it.

What Sets Metro Apart

To separate Windows Phone from the competition, Microsoft has come up with a list of seven areas of differentiation. Again, I'm not so interested in marketing here. But these areas do provide insights into the design of the system, and where Microsoft feels that it has the advantage. To that end, they're worth discussing.

These areas of differentiation are:

▶ **The Start Experience:** On any smart phone, the so-called "start experience" is what happens when you turn the device on at the beginning of the day and start interacting with it. It's literally the starting point for your interactions with the device.

Windows Phone provides two start experiences. The first is the default Start screen, which provides a handy "glance and go" view consisting of a customizable grid of live tiles, which access underlying hubs (panoramic experiences) and applications. This view is brand new to Windows Phone, and unlike anything on other smart phones or, for that matter, other Microsoft products.

What's neat about these live tiles is that they can provide rich notification information, allowing you to discover, at a glance, what's going on without having to manually navigate to the underlying application. Consider something basic like the calendar. On the iPhone, the Calendar icon, like any other iPhone icon, can provide only textual notifications. So you can glance at that icon and see that you have one or two pending items in your schedule, but to find out more you have to launch the application. On Windows Phone, the Calendar tile comes alive with information about your next pending schedule item. There's no need to dive into the application. You can just glance and go.

These rich notifications can work on any live tile. The People tile animates with each contact's picture. The Pictures tile—which spans across the width of the screen, occupying twice the space of lesser tiles—will show photos stored on the device as well as those from various online services. The Xbox Live tile displays your avatar. And so on. Third parties, too, can create their own customized live tiles. Glance and go. Glance and go.

Windows Phone also offers a second start experience. This one will be more familiar to those of you with experience with other smart phones, because it presents a simple list of every single application installed on the device. Where the default Start screen is "glance and go," this secondary screen—accessed by tapping the small arrow icon on the right side of the start screen—is "get me there."

Here, you'll find a scrollable list, similar to what was available previously in Windows Mobile 6.5 but formatted a bit differently, of every single app on the device.

I'll discuss the Start screen and live tiles in more detail later in this chapter.

YOU CAN'T REPLACE THE START SCREEN

While some power users may prefer to swap out the Start screen for the more static apps list as the default UI, there is no way to do so, sorry. But even if there was, I'd caution against doing so: The visual, live tile–based Start screen is, I think, one of Windows Phone's strongest selling points and is both useful and attractive.

▶ **Social Communications:** If you're familiar with the iPhone or other modern smart phones, you know that there's a separate app (in many cases, many separate apps) for each social networking and online service out there. So if you want to access Facebook, you find and launch the Facebook application. Twitter? Find and launch the Twitter app. MySpace? LinkedIn? You get the drill.

Jumping in and out of apps is possible on Windows Phone. In fact, all of the major social networking and online services are or soon will be available as discrete apps on Windows Phone just as they are on other smart phones. But Windows Phone offers a better way— one that works the way you think instead of requiring you to think the way the phone works.

To this end, Microsoft combines these apps into single, integrated views— called *hubs*, or panoramic experiences—that allow you to keep track of the family, friends, and others you care about without having to move from app to app to make it happen. The software giant calls this the "here and now" and it's exposed throughout the Windows Phone user experience in various ways.

One obvious example is the People hub and its associated live tile. Instead of providing just a rote contacts list, the People hub provides a visual way to access the people you've recently interacted with, all of your contacts (across various services), and a cross-service "What's new" feed (derived from the web-based Windows Live Messenger Social feed). It's the central aggregation point for all of the services you've joined, and connected via Windows Live (as discussed in Chapter 1).

There are a couple of advantages to this approach.

▷ First, you only have to connect the services you care about to your Windows Live ID once.

▷ And second, you don't have to manage or navigate in and out of different apps all the time (as you do on the iPhone, Android, and other smart phones). What you get with Windows Phone is a more seamless experience, one that is focused on the relationships that matter to you, not on discrete apps, one for each service.

More conceptually, the Windows Phone approach puts your contacts at the forefront of your social communications, where they should be. That is, the people you care about most are the focal point. And because Windows Phone pays attention to the connections you've made, the most recent people you've phoned, messaged, or contacted otherwise are available right at the start of the People hub. And if you really care about someone, you can even pin them to the Windows Phone Start screen, giving them a place of honor—one that you can quickly access at any time.

CROSSREF You'll see a bit more of the People hub later in this chapter. For a more detailed explanation of this user experience, see Chapter 4.

Try creating a shortcut to your wife or best friend to your iPhone's Start screen. (Go ahead, I'll wait.)

▶ **Hardware Choices:** As I discussed in Chapter 1, Microsoft has decided to make rigid but important hardware requirements of companies wishing to create Windows Phones. But Windows Phone customers will still get plenty of choice. The devices will be made by numerous hardware manufacturers and sold via all major wireless carriers around the world (compared to the iPhone, which at the time of this writing, is still available for sale in the U.S. via only one wireless carrier, AT&T).

Microsoft has also taken control of the Windows Phone software update process. So instead of relying on wireless carriers to determine which software updates can make their way to users' phones (that is, virtually none of them since they're more interested in selling new phones than in providing free software updates), Microsoft is now in charge. And if you're familiar with how Windows Update works in PC-based versions of Windows, you know that the company offers a wealth of functional updates as well as bug fixes and security updates.

CROSSREF Microsoft's Windows Phone hardware requirements—as well as a list of optional hardware components—can be found in Chapter 1.

▶ **Photos:** As with other social experiences, Microsoft is righting the wrongs of photo viewing and sharing on Windows Phone. So instead of requiring users to install, manage, and launch multiple apps in order to view their photos as well as photos from their friends, Microsoft is providing a single Pictures hub that aggregates all of this content in a single place.

To understand why this is so desirable, we once again need to beat up on the iPhone. On Apple's device, you are required to use multiple, disconnected applications and to manage them manually. You need to think in terms of the apps you have installed. Local photos—those taken with the iPhone's camera or synced from the PC—are found in the Photos apps. Facebook photos can be accessed from the Facebook app. Other photos will be found in whatever other apps you've installed. And if you use a service that doesn't provide its own app, you can navigate to different web sites using the Safari browser app. On the iPhone, the photos you want to see are all over the place.

On Windows Phone, the Pictures hub provides an extensible front end to the photos stored directly on the phone and those found on an unlimited number of online services. These photos—located in different places, potentially all over the world—are all presented in a single cohesive, panoramic user interface. So instead of thinking about which app you need to launch to view which photos, you can just make the one-to-one connection between the pictures you want to see and the Pictures hub. It really is that easy.

> **CROSSREF** See Chapter 5 for more information about the Pictures panoramic experience.

> ▶ **Location Aware Search:** Defending the apps-based approach of the iPhone in mid-2010, Apple CEO Steve Jobs said that, while search was popular on desktop-based PCs, his iPhone customers instead used discrete apps to find things locally. This comment was both self-serving and erroneous: It was a shot across the bow of his competition at Google, which makes both the dominant search engine and the Android smart phone platform.
>
> But even on the iPhone, search rules. And if you think about it, smart phones are natural conduits for local search, since you take them with you when you're out and about, and they contain integrated GPS hardware that can locate you precisely and help onboard apps find local services.
>
> Windows Phone isn't the first smart phone to offer integrated searching capabilities, but it is the first to offer truly contextual search that works differently depending on where you are in the user interface and on which app you're using. The underlying service, of course, is Bing, Microsoft's search engine. And thanks to the dedicated Search button on the front of each Windows Phone, getting help when you need it is literally as quick as tapping a button.
>
> Contextual search means that the built-in search functionality understands what you're doing and thus acts accordingly. If you're in the e-mail application and tap search, Windows Phone knows you want to search e-mail. If you're in the browser, it will search the Web using the built-in Bing app.
>
> Contextual search also applies to the kind of search you're doing. Search for "restaurant" in Bing, and the app will assume you want to find a restaurant that is local to you at the time of the search. But if you search for, say, "pasta," it will assume you want to find out more about pasta on the Web.

What's nice about the Bing search experience is that it features the same multi-column interface found in many other Windows Phone experiences, making it easy to transition between Web, local, news, and other search types, without having to type in the search query again.

CROSSREF You can learn more about Bing and location-aware search in Chapter 9.

▶ **Gaming:** While Microsoft previously provided its Xbox Live service to Windows users via the lackluster Games for Windows - LIVE, Windows Phone marks the first time this service has made its way to the mobile space. So you can access the Xbox Live Spotlight feed (essentially the Xbox Live "What's new" feed), your Xbox Live avatar, Gamerscore, and other Gamer information, game requests (which are specific to the phone), Xbox Live games for Windows Phone, and more. To do so, Windows Phone provides a Games hub that functions much like other panoramic experiences on the device.

What's interesting about this game support is that Microsoft is providing developers with a rich and familiar video game development environment that, get this, is compatible with both Windows and the Xbox 360. So in addition to getting a nice collection of Windows Phone–specific games to choose from, it's possible and even likely that we'll see games that are written for all three platforms. And that you may in fact be able to start a game on, say, the Xbox 360 and the finish it on the way to work on your Windows Phone.

Also possible, but much less likely, are games in which Windows Phone gamers could compete in real time against gamers on Windows or Xbox Live.

To me, however, the exciting bit here is that Windows Phone opens up the Xbox Live service—which is excellent and full-featured—to a whole new class of device. And whether you're an Xbox 360 gamer or not, access to this service on Windows Phone makes these devices all the more interesting. If you were waiting for Microsoft to create a portable Xbox, wait no more: Windows Phone is it.

CROSSREF The Windows Phone gaming functionality is fully discussed in Chapter 7. Don't worry, I researched this one extensively so you don't have to.

▶ **Best in Business:** While Windows Phone is designed in large part for Microsoft to catch up in the consumer space, the software giant hasn't forgotten its business roots. And while some esoteric enterprise features won't happen until a future software revision, the initial shipping version of Windows Phone arrives with thorough, and in some cases quite unique, business functionality.

So yes, you get the expected e-mail, contacts, and calendaring solutions, and yes, Windows Phone can connect to multiple Exchange (and Exchange-type) accounts. As with the iPhone or Android, Windows Phone is a first-class business solution.

Where Windows Phone leaps ahead of the competition is in its bundling of full-featured Microsoft Office solutions. Each Windows Phone comes with fairly decent (given the form factor limitations) versions of Microsoft Word, Excel, and PowerPoint, and a truly first-class version of OneNote, Microsoft's note-taking solution. In addition, Windows Phone can seamlessly access SharePoint-based document repositories (assuming your workplace has upgraded to SharePoint 2010) via a SharePoint Workspace Mobile client, providing secure, over-the-air connectivity.

CROSSREF The productivity features in Windows Phone are discussed in Chapters 10, 11 and 12, which deal with e-mail, calendaring, and Office, respectively.

Metro's Guiding Principles

According to Microsoft's internal documentation, the software giant has three guiding principles, or what it calls "red threads," for Windows Phone. That is, Windows Phone should be personal, relevant, and connected. It's that simple.

NOTE The term "red threads" refers to an ancient Asian myth (common to both China and Japan) called the *red thread of destiny*. In this myth, those who are destined to be soul mates are tied together at the ankles with invisible red thread. You know, kind of like you and your phone.

Because these principles are by definition high level, I don't want to waste too much time on them here. I do think, however, that each is worth a (very) short discussion because, as with the previously-discussed themes and differentiators, they establish what it is that Microsoft is trying to accomplish here and what we, as users of this platform, can expect to experience.

▶ **Personal.** Look at today's popular smart phones—the iPhone and Android, primarily—and you see devices that look and function like mini-PCs. They provide an OS with a user interface, and you launch apps to get things done. When you want to do something else, you exit the current app and find and then launch another one.

The thing is, phones *aren't* PCs. And it's not just because they're smaller. They're also more intimate. You carry them with you at all times, so they're there when you're making memories, either explicitly with the built-in camera, or implicitly, when you're using social networking services, messaging, or e-mail to discover what others are doing and tell them what you're up to. Phones are personal. They should be customizable in ways that make them special to you, and not constricted to work the way some megalomaniac in Cupertino dictates.

To move beyond the PC usage metaphor, Windows Phone focuses not on apps but on the user and the things that matter most to them. Microsoft calls this usage model "Your day, your way." And since Windows Phone contains your life, it is as unique as you are. Sure, the phone is a tool. But it's hard not to get all warm and fuzzy just thinking about how it conforms to the way you do things, and not the reverse.

▶ **Relevant.** Simply making the phone more personal will make it more relevant to users. Relevancy takes several guises, including the Start screen that eschews an unimaginative static grid of icons (that you see on the iPhone), for a highly customized grid of live tiles that provide live updates about those things that are most important to you.

Put more simply, Windows Phone is task-centric, not app-centric. It lets you organize your life around the things you want to do, not force you to think in terms of which apps do what.

Microsoft calls this "Your people, your location." The phone exposes information about the people and things you care about most via live tiles and hubs. It uses the phone's GPS capabilities to ensure that the information you receive isn't just timely but is also relevant to where you are physically. It's relevant.

▶ **Connected.** Smart phones are, by definition, connected to the outside world. And it is this connection that drives the personal and relevant connections discussed previously. The difference between Windows Phone and other smart phones, of course, is that it provides a deep connection not just to social networking and online services, but to people. People want to be connected, not just with services, but with each other.

Microsoft calls this "Your stuff, your mind." Thanks to Windows Phone's unique approach to connectivity—via live tiles and panoramic hubs—you can be updated about the activities of your family, friends, and other contacts in real time. As they do things in the real world and update their social networking status, play games online, and e-mail and send text messages, the phone is updating itself automatically, providing you with an ever-evolving view of those things that are important to you. And, again, it's doing so in ways that make sense for people, not requiring you to work the way the phone does.

You get the Windows Phone religion yet? Good, because it's time to jump into some real-world, hands-on experience.

REAL-WORLD METRO: A WHIRLWIND TOUR OF THE UI

From the time you turn on your phone, you understand that it provides something different from the stagnant competition in the smart phone market. Sure, Windows Phone and its Metro UI hit all the high points, with touch and multi-touch gesture support, responsive hardware, and all the standard apps you expect. But it's so much more than just the basics. In this section, I'll examine the different parts of Metro, and see how this system really works.

FIGURE 3-9: The Windows Phone lock screen isn't just about security: It's customizable and features information at a glance.

Lock Screen and Customization

When you turn on your Windows Phone, you'll be presented with a lock screen like that shown in Figure 3-9.

This lock screen not only performs the basic task of protecting your phone and its valuable data from thieves—assuming you've configured it with a password—but it also provides a first glimpse at Windows Phone personalization and its ability to provide you with valuable at-a-glance info how and where you want it.

By default, the Windows Phone lock screen displays an image of some kind, but you can customize this with your own photo, perhaps a cute family snapshot or a picture from a meaningful event or trip.

The lock screen also provides information at a glance, via a line of small icons at the bottom, about such things as missed calls, voicemails, unread e-mails, and so on. You can't jump directly to any of the related UIs from this screen, but you can glance and very quickly tell if something important is going on.

Start Screen and Customization

Once you've gotten past the lock screen, you can focus on Windows Phone's Start screen, the grid of large, rectangular blocks called *live tiles* that provides access to your most commonly needed applications, hubs, contacts, web pages, and other information. The Start screen, shown in Figure 3-10, is typically taller than the height of your phone's display, so you may need to scroll down to see all of the available live tiles. You do this by simply flicking your finger across the screen, from bottom to top. (Conversely, to scroll back up, you flick a finger top to bottom on the screen.)

As with the lock screen, you can (and should) customize the Start screen to your heart's content. You can *add*, or pin, new items to the Start screen, and this is accomplished throughout the Windows Phone UI using a *tap and hold* action that is the phone's version of the right mouse click. Among the many items you can add to the Start screen are shortcuts to applications and hubs, e-mail accounts, individual contacts (including yourself), individual web pages, individual musical artists (or albums, or genres, or even a single song), and more. Figure 3-11 shows the pop-up menu that appears when you tap and hold on an album in the Music + Videos interface, providing you with a way to pin that item right to your Start screen.

FIGURE 3-10: The Windows Phone Start screen contains live tiles for the information you need the most.

> You can—and should—add a password to your Windows Phone through the Settings interface. Swipe right on the Start screen to display the All Programs list. Then, scroll down to Settings and navigate down the System list to Lock & Wallpaper.

What's further interesting about the Start screen is that it will auto-customize itself, thanks to the dynamic nature of various live tiles. The People tile, for example, will animate between various images of your contacts. The Phone tile will display the number of missed calls, and whether there are any voice messages. The Messaging tile will display the number of unread MMS and SMS text messages. E-mail tiles will display the number of unread e-mails. Calendar will tell you the date and what your next appointment is. On the Pictures tile, you'll see a thumbnail of the background image used in the Pictures hub, an image you can of course customize with your own picture.

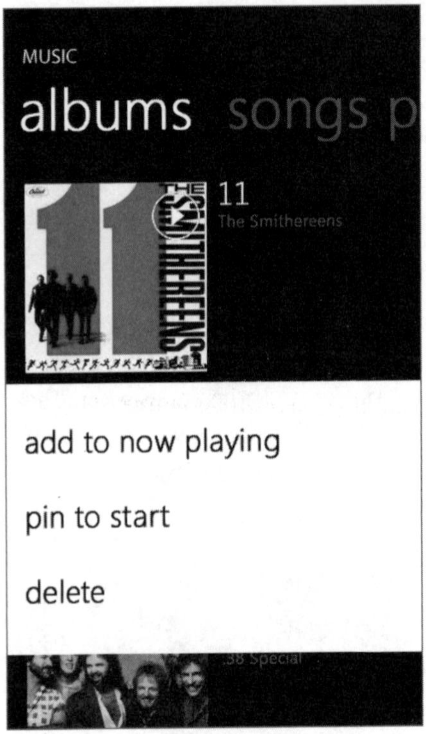

On and on it goes. Live tiles are what they sound like—alive—animating where appropriate and providing live updates about what's going on.

You can rearrange and delete live tiles, too. To do so, tap and hold on any live tile. When you do, the tile will appear to visually rise to the front, indicating that you can now move it by dragging it to a new

FIGURE 3-11: Many items can be pinned to the Windows Phone Start screen.

▶ *Unpinning a live tile does not delete the underlying item. It only removes the shortcut to that item from the Start screen.*

position, or tap the little Unpin badge in the upper-right corner of the tile to remove, or unpin, that tile from the Start screen.

> **NOTE** If you tap and hold on a live tile and enter this special edit mode but then don't do anything, Windows Phone will eventually "let go" of the item and return your Start screen to its normal orientation.

All Programs List

The Start screen is designed to contain only those items that you access most frequently. But your phone is full of other content, of course, and if you want to find all of the applications stored on your phone, as well as related items such as all configured e-mail accounts and settings, you'll need to visit the All Programs list. And to do that, you just need to swipe from right to left on the Windows Phone Start screen. When you do, you'll see the screen shown in Figure 3-12.

I'm going to quickly examine the available built-in applications (and special applications called *hubs*) in the next section. But you can find out more about e-mail accounts in Chapter 10, and about the many possibilities in the Settings interface in Chapter 15.

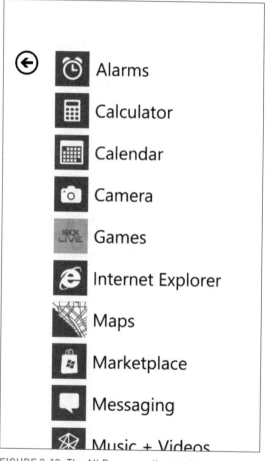

FIGURE 3-12: The All Programs list provides a list of all of the applications installed on your phone, not just the ones you've configured to appear on the Start screen.

HUBS AND APPLICATIONS

Smart phones existed before the iPhone, and they even ran applications, or apps, before there was an iPhone. But give Apple some credit: Its creation of an Apps Store and a formal application development process turned the iPhone from a successful product into a bona fide blockbuster. It became so popular that the competition, including Palm and Google, simply aped Apple's apps-based computing model in their own smart phone platforms, webOS and Android.

Microsoft could have done the same thing. But as explained previously, it instead created Windows Phone, a smart phone platform so innovative it makes the iPhone and its many copycat competitors look sad and tired by comparison.

The key to Windows Phone's central advantage is that this platform provides a completely new interactive model, where users don't have to repeatedly dive in and out of applications. On the iPhone, if you want to do anything, you need to first con-sider which application solves the problem. So you can't do something general such as "check up on your friends." Instead, you need to manually launch apps for such things as e-mail, Facebook, Twitter, photo sharing services, and so on. You do all the hard work, remembering which application does what.

Windows Phone thinks like you do. And the key to this revolution is the introduction of the *hub*, something akin to a super application. These hubs provide a way to aggregate content from a variety of sources, so you can view this disparate information all from a single, panoramic experience.

Yes, Windows Phone has regular apps too, and you will indeed interact with them from time to time, and you could even download new apps from an online apps store, called the Windows Phone Marketplace. So Windows Phone gives you the best of both worlds. Now it's time to examine hubs and apps and how they work together to make Windows Phone the best smart phone platform yet invented.

Hubs Are Super Applications

On Windows Phone, there are two kinds of apps, "normal" apps and hubs. First, I'll examine hubs, since these new interfaces are a prime differentiator between Windows Phone and the competition. And as you will soon see, they're also one of the coolest reasons to own a Windows Phone.

Under the hood, a hub is just an application. That is, from a technical perspec-tive, looking at the source code and comparing how these things really work, a hub is indeed an application. The difference comes with *integration*. Where a standard

Windows Phone does just one thing—provide an interface to a single e-mail account, for example, or play a game—a hub is designed to integrate services from numerous places and present them in a cohesive, single interface.

Hubs are also visually differentiated from "normal" applications. That is, hubs are designed as multiscreen, panoramic experiences instead of single screens, as is typical with normal apps. But since your Windows Phone can only display a single screen of information at once—it does have just one, statically-sized screen, after all—you can't see all of a hub at once. Instead, you view it one screen, or *section*, at a time. And you can move horizontally across the available sections by scrolling from left to right.

Consider Figure 3-13. Here, you can see a panoramic hub as it really looks, a widescreen landscape with multiple sections, each of which can be viewed one at a time. Overlaid on top of the hub is a phone, so you can see how only part of the hub is visible via the phone at any given time.

FIGURE 3-13: A hub is a panoramic experience where only part of the full UI is visible at any time.

Scroll to the right and the next section is visible. As you keep scrolling to the right, you'll uncover new sections, until you reach the end of the hub. Then, when you scroll right, the hub will flip around, like a repeating cartoon backdrop, and you'll start back at the beginning again.

The most obvious example of a hub is Pictures. This hub includes three sections by default: Galleries, a text list from which you can access various local (on-device) and online photo galleries; an automatically promoted gallery section, from which you can see pictures from a randomly selected local photo gallery; and the What's New section, which provides a list of photo-based social networking updates from your families, friends, and other contacts. The Pictures hub is shown in Figure 3-14, again with a phone overlaid on top so you can gain an appreciation of its layout.

FIGURE 3-14: The Pictures hub is, perhaps, the most obvious example of why this UI type is such a good idea.

Three things make Pictures a hub.

1. First, there's the panoramic UI, which is so obviously evident.

2. Second, though Pictures presents you, the user, with a single user interface, it can derive the content it presents from many different places. The All item in the Galleries section, for example, provides access to photos you've taken with the device's camera, photos you've synced from your PC, pictures you've saved from the Web, photo galleries stored online in the Windows Live Photos service, and, optionally, photos from your Facebook account. The What's New section, meanwhile, is populated solely with photos that have been posted online by others. It's a constantly updating, dynamic view of what's going on in your life, in pictures.

3. Not good enough? There's a third advantage to hubs, and what I've listed previously is just what you get out of the box. Hubs are also *extensible*. This means that third-party developers can build additional functionality onto the Pictures hub, as well as to other hubs in Windows Phone, and make these interfaces even more powerful. In the case of the Pictures hub, it's not hard to imagine third-party developers opening up the hub to popular online photo sharing services such as Flickr or Google's Picasa Web Album. Someone could write a photo editing solution that could provide in-hub editing of photos, or perhaps a way to sync full-sized pictures from the phone to the Web. The possibilities, as they say, are endless. And over time, Windows Phone is only going to get better. Many of those improvements are going to come via hub extensibility.

Applications Are Super, Too

In addition to hubs, Windows Phone also supports single-screen standalone applications, or apps. Of course it does. A number of these apps come built in to Windows Phone, running the gamut from simple utilities like Alarms and Calculator (Figure 3-15) to full-featured productivity solutions like Calendar or Internet Explorer, Windows Phone's web browser.

In addition to the apps you'll find on your phone when you bring it home, you'll also able to download a growing number of free, trial, and paid apps from the Windows Phone Marketplace, and these include every app type imaginable including, yes, full-screen, 3-D action games (Figure 3-16). Don't worry, not everything in Windows Phone is an integrated experience. Sometimes you just want to do something very specific, or play a game. There are plenty of solutions—with more on the way—for these situations.

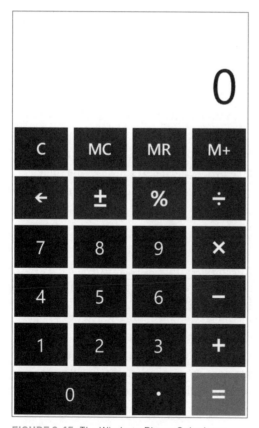

FIGURE 3-15: The Windows Phone Calculator.

FIGURE 3-16: A 3-D action game running in Windows Phone.

Hubs and Applications That Are Included with Windows Phone

With the understanding that these applications and hubs will be covered in more depth throughout this book, here's a quick preview of what's available, at minimum, on every Windows Phone. Note that Microsoft may augment this list over time, and that your phone maker and/or wireless carrier will almost certainly provide some custom applications (and live tiles) of their own as well. So what you see on your own phone should be a superset of this list.

HUBS

The following hubs can be found in Windows Phone:

- ▶ **Games:** This hub connects to your Xbox Live account and provides a third way—after the Xbox 360 video game console and Windows-based PCs—to play video games interactively with others online. The Games hub (Figure 3-17) lets you game via your wireless connection, send and receive game requests, buy and try new games, and find out more about what's going on with the Xbox Live game service. If you've ever experienced mobile gaming before, the Games hub will show you how it's supposed to be done.

CROSSREF You can find out more about the Games hub in Chapter 7.

FIGURE 3-17: The Games hub.

▶ **Marketplace:** Microsoft is working to converge its various online stores, which currently consist of the Zune Marketplace (music, TV shows, media), Xbox Marketplace (video games and related content), and the Windows Phone Marketplace (mobile apps) into a single, integrated experience. The Marketplace app on Windows Phone —shown in Figure 3-18—comes pretty close. It provides a single location to purchase apps and games, and Zune-based music, out of the gate. I expect Microsoft to open it up to more content types (including podcasts, TV shows, and movies) over time.

FIGURE 3-18: Windows Phone Marketplace.

CROSSREF Over-the-air access to the music content on Marketplace is covered in Chapter 6. Information about game browsing and purchasing can be found in Chapter 7. And app browsing and purchasing is discussed in Chapter 16.

▶ **Music + Videos:** This integrated experience provides a handy front end to all of your multimedia needs, including listening to music and podcasts and FM radio, watching TV shows and movies, and accessing third-party media services like Last.FM and Pandora. You can also access the Zune Marketplace's music collection over the air and, if you have a Zune Pass subscription, stream or download any music content from that service to your phone. It's all available from the Music + Videos hub, shown in Figure 3-19.

CROSSREF You can find out about the Music + Videos hub in Chapter 6.

FIGURE 3-19: The Music + Videos hub.

▶ **Office 2010:** The Office hub, based on the technologies found in the desktop version of Microsoft Office 2010, provides five impressive office productivity solutions: OneNote Mobile (note-taking with cloud synchronization), Word Mobile (word processing), Excel Mobile (spreadsheets), PowerPoint Mobile (presentations), and SharePoint Workspace Mobile (over-the-air document repository integration). This is the most powerful mobile Office solution available anywhere, presented as a single, panoramic Office hub (Figure 3-20).

CROSSREF The Office hub is thoroughly documented in Chapter 12.

FIGURE 3-20: The Office hub.

▶ **People:** Windows Phone provides a single interface for managing contacts from multiple accounts, all in a single view. Called the People hub, this interface lets you find phone numbers, e-mail addresses, maps, and other data related to your contacts, and helps you stay up to date with your contacts, via their social networking feeds. It's shown in Figure 3-21.

FIGURE 3-21: The People hub.

CROSSREF In Chapter 4, you'll get a full look at the People hub and how you can use it to manage your own digital persona as well as your contacts.

▶ **Pictures:** As noted previously, this hub provides a single location to access all of your own digital photos, as well as pictures shared by your family, friends, and other contacts. A screenshot of this hub can be found back in Figure 3-14.

CROSSREF The Pictures hub is thoroughly described in Chapter 5.

APPLICATIONS

The following applications can be found in Windows Phone:

▶ **Alarms:** The Alarms app, shown in Figure 3-22, lets you create one or more alarms, each with its own custom alarm sound and name, so you can use your Windows Phone as an alarm clock while on the go.

FIGURE 3-22: Alarms.

► **Bing:** Available exclusively from Windows Phone's dedicated Search button, the Bing app (Figure 3-23) provides Web, local, and news searches as well as context-sensitive searching within other Windows Phone applications. In many ways, it's the ultimate integrated experience.

FIGURE 3-23: Bing.

CROSSREF Bing and searching are the topics taken up in Chapter 9.

► **Calculator:** The Calculator app (see Figure 3-15) is exactly what it sounds like, no bells or whistles.

▶ **Calendar:** This well-designed application can aggregate appointments from multiple calendars and present them all in a single, simple interface. Calendar is shown in Figure 3-24.

CROSSREF   Calendar is covered in Chapter 11.

▶ **Camera:** Microsoft specifies some pretty aggressive hardware requirements for all Windows Phones, and part of those requirements include specific camera features. As a result, the Windows Phone Camera experience (Figure 3-25) is excellent.

▶ The Camera app can be used even when the phone is asleep and locked.

FIGURE 3-24: Calendar.

FIGURE 3-25: The Windows Phone Camera app.

CROSSREF The Camera app is covered in Chapter 5.

▶ **Internet Explorer:** The mobile web browser in Windows Phone is a decent
entry and is based on desktop Internet Explorer technologies. Called Internet
Explorer Mobile, this browser lets you browse the Web using multiple tabs,
access and save your favorite Web sites, and interact with online services.
Internet Explorer is shown in Figure 3-26.

CROSSREF Internet Explorer is the sole subject of Chapter 8.

▶ **Mail:** Windows Phone handles e-mail a bit differently than it does other
account data like contacts and calendars. Instead of connecting multiple
accounts into a single unified inbox, it instead provides a different Mail app
for each e-mail account you configure. That said, Mail is an excellent mobile
e-mail solution, and as shown in Figure 3-27, it comes with a highly efficient,
text-based UI.

FIGURE 3-26: Internet Explorer.

FIGURE 3-27: Mail.

CROSSREF Mail is the subject of Chapter 10.

▶ **Maps:** Based on Microsoft's Bing Maps service, Windows Phone Maps (Figure 3-28) is available either via Bing, automatically, as when a search result includes a map, or via a dedicated Maps app. Either way, you get directions, auto-location, and turn-by-turn navigation.

CROSSREF Because it's technically part of Bing, Maps is covered in Chapter 9 alongside Bing.

▶ **Messaging:** As a modern smart phone platform, Windows Phone supports both text-based (SMS) and multimedia (MMS) messaging. You can see this simple app in Figure 3-29.

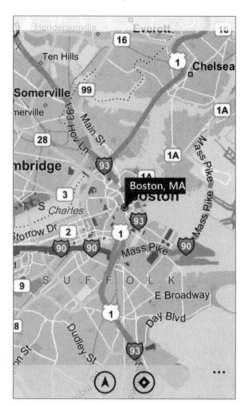

FIGURE 3-28: Maps.

FIGURE 3-29: Messaging.

CROSSREF For more on Messaging, check out Chapter 14.

▶ **Phone:** Windows Phone does so much, it's easy to forget that it's a phone too. But don't worry, Windows Phone offers tremendous phone capabilities, including integrated voicemail support. The Phone app is shown in Figure 3-30.

CROSSREF The phone and voicemail capabilities of Windows Phone are examined in Chapter 13.

▶ **Settings:** Windows Phone offers a tremendous amount of customization functionality, for both the built-in services and onboard apps. You can find this all in the Settings interface, available in the All Programs list. Settings is shown in Figure 3-31.

FIGURE 3-30: Phone.

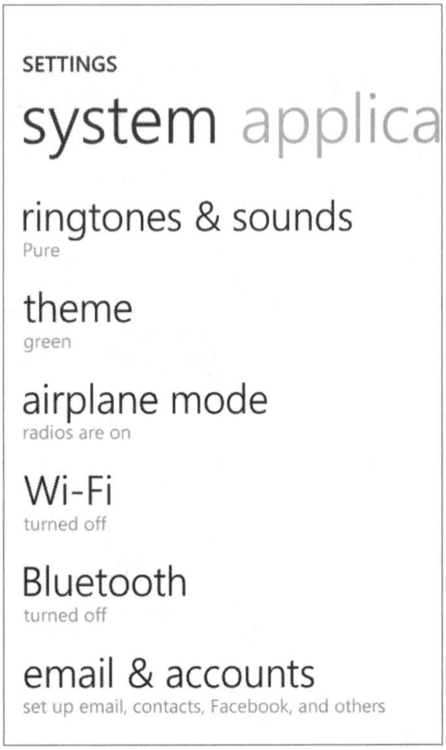

FIGURE 3-31: Settings.

> **CROSSREF** Settings is important enough that I dedicate an entire chapter to it, Chapter 15. But I discuss various Settings screens as needed throughout the book as well.

SUMMARY

Windows Phone is the result of years of Microsoft's mobile industry. But rather than rely on the past as it has so often, Microsoft this time started over from scratch and came up with something I think you'll agree is both different *and* better than the competition. The key to this success is the Metro user interface, which is designed to get out of the way and let you focus on the content that matters to you. This content can be highly visual—as in the Pictures or Music + Videos hubs—or text based, such as in productivity solutions like Mail and Calendar.

As part of its goal to provide users with a complete solution out of the box, Microsoft also provides Windows Phone with a full suite of hubs—or super applications—and apps, so you can get up and running on day one. But you will also be able to find other unique solutions for your phone from your wireless carrier and from extensive apps, music and media, and game marketplaces, which are available directly in Windows Phone, or via your PC.

Understanding what comes with Windows Phone, and why it is the way it is, is key to enjoying what comes next. Throughout the rest of this book, I'll build on the information you discovered here.

CHAPTER 4

You and Your Friends: How to Connect with Others, Connect to the World

IN THIS CHAPTER

▶ Managing you and your online contacts with the People hub

▶ Viewing and editing your own digital persona

▶ Finding and interacting with contacts

▶ Linking and unlinking contacts

▶ Finding out what's new with the people you care about

▶ Accessing recent contacts

▶ Pinning contacts to the Windows Phone Start screen

Windows Phone allows you to configure any number of online accounts and access them all from your device. A big part of this functionality is wrapped up in the People hub, which works as a sort of superpowered address book, aggregating the contacts lists from multiple accounts and providing a single view into them all.

If that's all it did, the People hub would be quite useful. But what's more interesting, perhaps, is that this user experience can also work in powerful ways across your accounts. It provides the ability to link and unlink contacts from different accounts. You can edit these accounts and customize them with new photos, ringtones, and more.

Most amazingly, you can view a single aggregated feed listing all of the activities that your contacts are doing online. This feed consists of whatever online services you've configured through Windows Live, and it can include Facebook updates as well.

Finally, you can also use the People hub to view and edit your own online persona, which is the way other people view you out in the world. And since this is in many ways the most basic People functionality, I'll start right there.

MANAGING YOUR DIGITAL PERSONA

Look in the mirror. Go ahead, I won't tell anyone. See that person staring back at you? That's who we're going to focus on in this section. You. Or as you might refer to yourself—this is about you after all—*me*.

Windows Phone approaches the relationship it has with its device owner a little bit differently than other smart phones. That's because you are at the center of the Windows Phone experience, and everything the phone does and can do is tuned to be useful to you, the user.

Compare this way of doing things to app-driven smart phones such as the Apple iPhone and Google Android, where you are forced to think like the device and know which applications do which things. Windows Phone doesn't do that. It understands that you have a life, and that you have certain people, events, places, and things that are important to you. As a result, the Windows Phone user interface has been constructed to make it as easy as possible for you to get things done.

The key to this change, of course, is an underlying understanding of what it is that makes up a Windows Phone user, knowing where that person will look to discover information about, and interact with, family and friends. In technical terms, this is your *digital persona*, your online account or accounts that establish you as an entity that can perform tasks and establish relationships with others.

It sounds technical and perhaps even a little bit scary. But the reality is that setting up a digital persona is easy, happens quickly, and pays enormous dividends down the road. In fact, assuming you paid attention to my advice in Chapter 1, you've already done all the hard work already. So here, I'll show you how correctly managing your digital persona will turn that lump of metal and plastic into not just a phone, but *your* phone.

Viewing Your Digital Persona

Windows Phone provides two main interfaces for accessing your own personal information. The first is a Me tile that appears on your Windows Phone Start screen, animating between four different displays. One is a full-tile image featuring the personal picture you configured as part of your Windows Live ID's profile. The second is a half-sized version of that photo, with the text *Me* on top. And there's a blank version of the tile with the text *Me* in the corner. And finally, there's a quick peek at your latest social networking update. These four displays are shown in Figure 4-1.

The second is via the People hub. We discuss this hub in more detail later in the chapter, but if you tap the People tile on the Start screen, you'll be transported to the People hub, shown in Figure 4-2, where you can see a quick link to your own profile right from the top of the main view.

Tap this and you'll be brought into your own contact card. (This card is also displayed when you tap the Me tile on the Start screen.) Your own contact card, or "Me," is shown in Figure 4-3.

FIGURE 4-1: The Me tile, seen in various possible states.

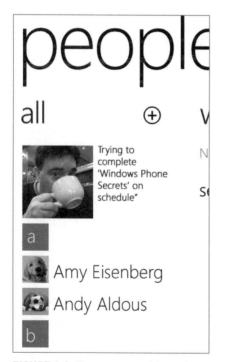

FIGURE 4-2: There you are, right at the top of the People hub.

FIGURE 4-3: It's me! No, really. It is.

▶ Next to each of these posts is a Comment ("+") button, which allows you to comment on your own posts (or reply to others' comments).

This card contains a number of elements, many interactive. And much of what's available here isn't obvious. From top to bottom, of course, you can see your current Me photo, and your latest social networking update next to that photo, and then a list of social networking updates, culled from the Windows Live Messenger Feed and, if configured, Facebook.

Editing Your Digital Persona

The Me card is a single-screen user interface, in that you cannot swipe left or right to see additional information. Everything there is to see is right here on this single screen, though of course you may have to scroll down—and tap the Get Older Posts link—to see it all.

There are, however, a number of actions you can take from this screen, and only one of them is obvious.

REFRESHING THE VIEW

To preserve battery life, Windows Phone doesn't constantly poll your social networking feeds. Instead, it performs these updates on a set schedule that depends on a number of factors such as your connectivity type, the existing battery life if the device isn't plugged in, and so forth. So depending on the situation, you may want to occasionally manually refresh your own feeds to see recent updates that were made elsewhere.

To refresh the view, tap and hold on your profile picture or on any of the posts you see on the screen. A small pop-up menu will appear with just one item: Refresh. Tap that item to refresh the view.

CHANGING YOUR PHOTO

▶ Web-based pictures cannot be used. If you'd like to use a picture you found online, you must first save it to the phone.

You may also want to change the photo used to represent your digital persona. To do so, tap your picture. Windows Phone will display a Choose Picture screen from which you can select any photo stored on the phone or, in a nice touch, use the internal camera to take a new photo.

COMMENTING ON A POST OR REPLYING TO A COMMENT

The beauty of social networking services such as Windows Live and Facebook is that you can post information about yourself, or multimedia such as photos, and that others you know can comment on those posts, thus striking up a virtual watercooler conversation. This works in reverse too: Using Windows Phone and various web-based tools, you can keep up with your family, friends, and other contacts via social networking services as well. And when you see something you want to comment on, doing so is easy.

With regards to your own posts, you can see whether others are commenting via your Me page. On the right side of the screen, next to each of your posts, is a Comment button. If this button has a "+" sign in it, no one has yet commented on that post. But you are welcome to leave your own comment—you know, if you're lonely, or are starting up a Norman Bates–style internal conversation.

If someone *has* commented, you will instead see a number inside the Comment button. This number (Figure 4-4) indicates how many comments you've gotten.

Messenger 13 minutes ago
"Trying to complete 'Windows Phone Secrets' on schedule"

2

FIGURE 4-4: The Comments button changes to indicate how many comments you've received on an individual post.

To view the comments, tap the Comment button (and not the actual post). Windows Phone will then display a screen like that shown in Figure 4-5.

Paul Thurrott

Messenger about an hour ago
"Trying to complete 'Windows Phone Secrets' on schedule"

Paul Thurrott
thanks
13 minutes ago

David Abbott
Good Luck
15 minutes ago

add a comment

FIGURE 4-5: You can view comments to your own post without leaving the People hub.

Obviously, you can also continue the conversation from this screen as well. Just tap the Comments box to start typing your own comment.

> **NOTE** Oddly, you cannot refresh the conversation from this view. So if you'd like to update the list of comments, you have to tap the phone's Back button and then tap on the comment box for the correct post again; Windows Phone will reload the post and all of the comments, including any that have been left since you last looked.

BEING A PEOPLE PERSON: MANAGING YOUR FAMILY, FRIENDS, AND OTHER CONTACTS

You can only manage your own online persona for so long. Eventually, you're going to want to spend a bit of time connecting with the people you really care about. This is generally done via the People hub referenced briefly in the previous section, but before I dive too far into that, it will be instructive to step back a bit and consider how it is that these people came to be on your phone in the first place.

You can add multiple accounts to your phone. Not just your default Windows Live ID, which is important of course, but also accounts of different types: Outlook/Exchange accounts, Google accounts, Yahoo! Mail accounts, Facebook accounts, and so on. Virtually any kind of account imaginable can be added to Windows Phone, assuming it offers some form of standards-based e-mail, contacts, and/or calendar support.

> **CROSSREF** I examine the different supported account types in more detail in Chapter 15.

That last bit is key because different account types provide access to different services. And because the People hub operates with, well, people, what this chapter is concerned with, of course, are those account types that allow you to synchronize a contacts list between an online service and your phone.

Those account types are Windows Live, Facebook, Outlook, and Google. That's it.

If you configure an account type of, say, Yahoo! Mail, you'll be able to access your Yahoo!-based e-mail from Windows Phone, no problem. But what you won't be able to do is access your Yahoo!-based contacts list (or, as it turns out, your Yahoo! calendar). At least not from the phone's People interface.

For some account types—Windows Live (secondary accounts only), Outlook, and Google—you can specify which services are synced to the phone. So you could theoretically sync contacts only from Outlook, if you wanted, and only the calendar from Google. Or vice versa. Or any combination you desire. (And let's not get into the complication of having multiple accounts of the same type, which is also possible.)

For one account type—Facebook—you get no meaningful configuration options at all. If you choose to sync with Facebook, your Facebook-based contacts, photos, and feeds are all going to sync to the phone. You can't pick and choose.

Ditto for your primary Windows Live account. This account will sync contacts, calendar (though you can manually turn this off through the Calendar app), photos,

▶ *Well, they're not all going to sync to the phone. Instead, only those Facebook contacts that have configured a phone number of some kind will sync to Windows Phone.*

and feeds, no matter what. (But you *can* manually enable or disable e-mail syncing; that one is your explicit choice.)

To view and, where possible, edit these account settings, you will need to visit the Email & Accounts configuration screen in Settings. Taking a look at Figure 4-6, you can see that I have multiple accounts configured. And three of them—Windows Live, Facebook, and Outlook—are configured to sync contacts with the phone.

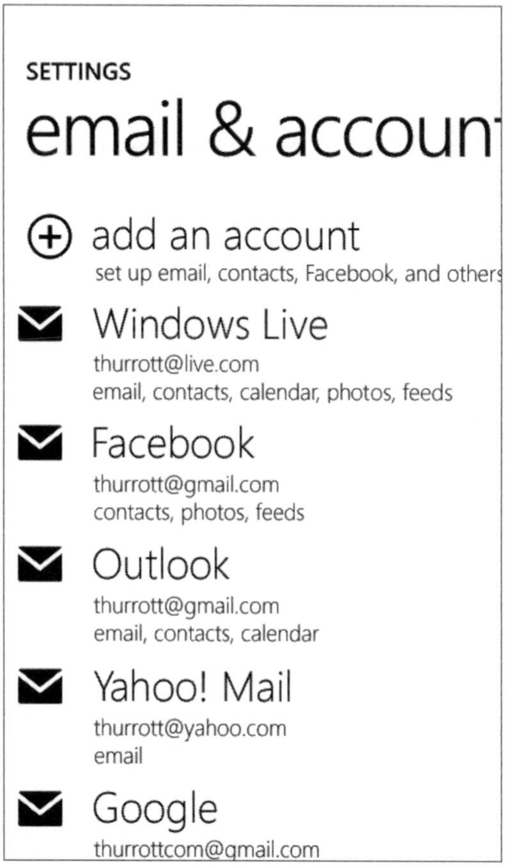

SETTINGS
email & accoun⌐

⊕ add an account
set up email, contacts, Facebook, and others

✉ Windows Live
thurrott@live.com
email, contacts, calendar, photos, feeds

✉ Facebook
thurrott@gmail.com
contacts, photos, feeds

✉ Outlook
thurrott@gmail.com
email, contacts, calendar

✉ Yahoo! Mail
thurrott@yahoo.com
email

✉ Google
thurrottcom@gmail.com

FIGURE 4-6: Hopefully, you won't configure this many accounts on your own phone, since this gets complicated quickly.

As you'll discover in Chapter 10, Microsoft curiously doesn't provide a unified inbox for e-mail. Instead, every single account you configure on the phone for e-mail access will have its own e-mail application (and Start screen live tile). They're kept separate.

Even more curiously, this is not how Windows Phone handles contacts (or calendars). In fact, it's done in exactly the opposite way. No matter how many accounts you configure for contacts access, Windows Phone will aggregate them into a single view, with a single list of contacts. And there's absolutely no way to visually or logically separate these contacts, on the phone, by account type.

It's not odd to do things this way. It is, however, odd to handle e-mail and contacts in such different fashions. But, that's the situation you have, so it's the situation you have to deal with. And that aggregation of contacts into a single mega-list you can access from a single view? It's called the People hub. And it's time to see what it looks like.

Using the People Hub

This view could consist of contacts from many different places.

The People hub, shown again in Figure 4-7, provides an aggregated view of all of the contacts contained in all of the applicable accounts you've configured on Windows Phone. At the very least, this list will consist of contacts from your primary Windows Live account, which you learned how to configure all the way back in Chapter 1. But many people will configure other accounts on the phone as well.

FIGURE 4-7: The People hub.

The hub consists of three sections, All, What's New, and Recent.

▶ The **All** list is exactly what it sounds like: a list of all of your contacts.

▶ The **What's New** list provides an aggregated feed of all of your contact's online activities, as determined by how well you configured your Windows Live ID (again, described back in Chapter 1). (If you've configured a Facebook account on Windows Phone, those updates will appear in this list as well.)

▶ The **Recent** list, meanwhile, provides a quick way to access the contacts you've most recently interacted with.

I want to look at the All list first, since this is the primary interface for finding and viewing information about your contacts.

Finding and Interacting with Your Contacts

To find individual contacts, you can scroll down through the list as you would any other Windows Phone list, by flicking your finger vertically across the screen. This works fine, but if you have a lot of contacts as I do, you may find it quicker to use a cool Windows Phone shortcut. Just tap one of the colored letter boxes, instead of a contact. When you do, you'll be transported to the screen shown in Figure 4-8.

From this grid, simply select the first letter of the first name of the person you're looking for. The contacts list will jump immediately to that location.

If you know exactly who you're looking for, you can also bypass this list by searching instead. While looking at your list of contacts, simply tap the Search button on your phone. A search box will appear over the contacts list, as will a virtual keyboard. This lets you type in the name of the contact for which you're looking. As you type, the list is whittled down to only those names that match your search criteria. This is shown in Figure 4-9.

To view an individual contact, simply tap on that person's name. This name can appear in the All list, in a contacts search results list, or in the Recent list. When you do so, you'll see something like the screen in Figure 4-10. This screen is called a *contact card*.

From this card, you can access an astonishing array of information, though of course most of the contact cards you see will probably only expose a small percentage of what's possible.

▶ By default, contacts in the People hub are sorted by First name, Last name, rather than Last name, First name. So, to find someone named Paul Thurrott, you would tap P, not T. You can change this sorting as I'll show you later in the chapter.

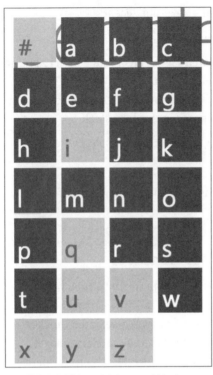

FIGURE 4-8: This quick jump grid helps you move quickly through a long list.

FIGURE 4-9: You can also search for specific contacts if you'd like.

The following fields are available on each contact card:

► **Photo:** You can associate a photo with each contact.

► **Name:** The name field is really two fields, First Name and Last Name, combined into a single, more readable entry. You can also optionally specify Middle Name, Nickname, Title, Company, and Suffix fields as part of the name.

► **Phone number(s):** Every contact can have multiple phone numbers associated with it, including one mobile phone, two home phones, two work phones, and phone numbers for company, pager, home fax, and work fax.

► **E-mail:** Likewise, each contact can be configured with multiple e-mail addresses, including those for personal, work, and other.

► **Ringtone:** You can assign a custom ringtone to any contact. This is a nice way to customize the phone, since you can tell who's calling based on which ringtone sounds.

► Note that some contacts may already have photos associated with their cards, because this was configured by them on a connected service (like Facebook), or because a photo was otherwise configured for that contact elsewhere.

▶ **Address:** This field is really an aggregation of several separate fields, including Street, City, State/Province, ZIP/Postal Code, Country/Region, and Address Type (Home, Work, or Other). You can configure multiple addresses.

▶ **Website:** This field can contain the URL, or web address, of that contact's web site, like www.winsupersite.com.

▶ **Birthday:** You can configure one birthday for each contact, with month, day, and year information.

▶ **Notes:** This text field can hold arbitrary information about the contact.

▶ **Anniversary:** You can configure one anniversary date for each contact, with month, day, and year information.

FIGURE 4-10: A contact card provides information about an individual contact.

▶ **Significant Other:** This lets you specify the husband, wife, or other partner of the current contact. But it's really just a text field, and isn't connected in any way to an actual, separate contact.

▶ **Children:** Ditto for the Children field: You can add any text here you'd like.

▶ **Office Location:** Another text field. You can add any text here you'd like.

▶ **Job Title:** And, you guessed it, another text field. You can add any text here you'd like.

Additionally, contact cards are associated with an account (Windows Live, Google, whatever). Interestingly, you can link two or more contacts into a single contact card, which can be handy when you have duplicate contacts across multiple services. (For example, I have separate contacts for my wife in both Facebook and my primary e-mail account.) You'll get a chance to look at that in just a bit.

EDITING A CONTACT CARD

To edit the information on a contact card, tap the Edit button in the contact card toolbar.

If the contact is unlinked—that is, the contact is a unique contact that exists in only one account—you will see a screen like that in Figure 4-11. From here, you can edit any of the fields associated with the contact, adding or changing information and saving it back to the original account.

To edit one of the fields, simply tap on it. A typical edit field screen is shown in Figure 4-12. The edit process is pretty straightforward: Select the field you want to edit and make changes using the virtual keyboard. (Some fields, of course, use custom controls, such as date fields.)

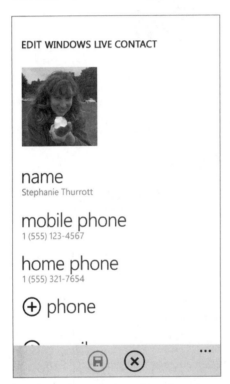

FIGURE 4-11: A contact card in edit mode.

FIGURE 4-12: Editing a field in a contact card.

When you're happy with the changes, tap the Save button. For this type of contact card, changes will be saved back to the original contact on whatever service the contact is hosted. So if you access this contact later from the full Web on your PC, or from your Windows-based e-mail application, or whatever, you'll see the changes you made here.

More important, perhaps, these changes will live "outside" of the phone. They're not just being made to the contacts list on your Windows Phone.

EDITING A LINKED CONTACT CARD

Some contact cards are *linked*, however. This means that you have two (or more) contacts, on different accounts, which in fact represent the same person. If Windows Phone can detect enough duplicated information between these contact cards, it will automatically link them for you. The advantages to this are clear: Rather than have two (or more) contacts in your People hub with the same name, linking these contacts together is more representative of the real world.

There are some issues around linked contacts, however. For example, if you want to edit some information on a linked contact card, you will need to specify which account you intend to edit. Fortunately, this is easy.

When you tap the Edit button in the toolbar for a linked contact, you'll be presented with a screen like that shown in Figure 4-13. From here, you can choose which account to edit by tapping one of the appropriate links (Edit Windows Live, Edit Outlook, and so on).

From there, you just edit normally.

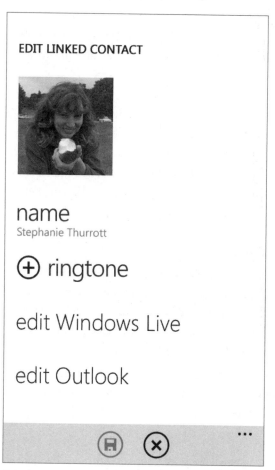

FIGURE 4-13: Editing a linked contact requires just one additional step.

EDITING A FACEBOOK CONTACT CARD

There is one other special case. If you try to edit a Facebook-based contact, Windows Phone will alert you with the following text: "You can't change Facebook contact info on your phone, but you can edit details that will appear on the contact card." If you click the Add button, you're brought to what appears to be a pretty normal contact edit experience. But there is one very important difference.

Instead of editing the information in Facebook, Windows Phone will instead create a new contact, in the account of your choice (as long as your choice is Windows Live or Outlook), and link that account to the Facebook account. Any edits you make will go into that new, linked, account, and will not be reflected on Facebook. But at least it provides a way to create or edit account info that will live on past your phone.

LINKING AND UNLINKING CONTACTS

I mentioned linked contacts a few times already, but it's worth also mentioning that you can manually link any contacts Windows Phone missed. You can also unlink any linked contacts you'd rather see remain separate.

To link a contact to another contact, open their contact card. Then, tap the Link toolbar button. Windows Phone will provide a list of suggested links (based on similarity), or you can tap a Choose a Contact link to choose any contact.

Unlinking is also pretty straightforward. This time, open a linked contact card and tap the Link toolbar button. You'll see a list of linked profiles. To remove one of the profiles from the link, tap it. You'll be asked to confirm the unlinking before it proceeds.

INTERACTING WITH A CONTACT CARD

If your contacts are properly configured, each should have some combination of phone numbers, e-mail addresses, physical street addresses, and other information. Not surprisingly, you can interact with this information and trigger other phone activities. I examine these activities throughout the book, but what the heck, since you are looking at contacts already, it's worth spending a moment seeing what's possible.

> ► **Call them on the phone:** If you tap a contact's phone number, which will be denoted by "Call Mobile," "Call Home," or similar, the phone application will launch and give them a call (Figure 4-14).

CROSSREF Windows Phone's telephone capabilities are discussed in Chapter 13.

FIGURE 4-14: Tap a phone number and start a phone call.

▶ **Send a text message:** Choose Text Mobile, and you can send a text message using the Windows Phone Messaging app.

CROSSREF Messaging is explained in Chapter 14.

▶ **Trigger an e-mail:** If you tap a Send Email link, Windows Phone will prompt you to choose an account, if needed, and then launch the New Mail screen so you can specify the subject line and body of a new e-mail.

CROSSREF E-mail is covered in Chapter 10.

▶ **View their location on a map:** Contacts with physical (street) addresses can be mapped using the built-in Maps application, which is part of Bing. Just tap the Map Home Address (or similar) link, and Maps will open up and navigate to the tapped location, as shown in Figure 4-15. From there, you can use Maps to find directions from your current location to the address you tapped.

CROSSREF Maps is covered in Chapter 9.

IMPORTING YOUR OLD CONTACTS

Here's a neat trick: You can also use Windows Phone to import the contacts from your old phone. To do so, you must first insert your old SIM card into your new Windows Phone. Then, in Windows Phone, visit All Programs, Settings, Applications, and then People. Tap Import SIM Contacts.

Finding Out What's New with Your Contacts

Remember, you can configure your Windows Live account to seamlessly access multiple online services.

In addition to functioning as a superpowered address book, the People hub also provides a What's New feed that aggregates content from your Messenger Social feed (formerly called What's New) and, if configured, your Facebook account. It's a one-stop shop where you can find out what's going on with your contacts, no matter where they're posting information. (Well, almost. Windows Live doesn't connect to *every* online service.) The What's New section is shown in Figure 4-16.

FIGURE 4-15: Addresses can be mapped directly from the People hub.

FIGURE 4-16: The What's New section provides a way to easily keep up with your friends and other contacts' activities.

You can scroll down the list to see what's up, tap the Get Older Posts link at the bottom if you need to know more, and tap and hold anywhere in this section to choose a Refresh item that will update the feed with the very latest posts. It all works very much as expected.

One of the neatest things you can do, of course, is interact with your peeps by leaving comments to their posts. To do this, find a post you like then tap the comment box over on the right. This box will either have a plus sign ("+") in it, or a number indicating how many comments they've already received. When you do so, the post opens with a Comment box, shown in Figure 4-17, where you can type your own message.

> You can also "like" Facebook posts and post items to your friends' Facebook "walls" from this interface.

FIGURE 4-17: Commenting on one of your contact's posts, in this case from Facebook.

Using the Recent List

On the far right of the People hub is a third section called Recent. This is straightforward: It provides a list of those contacts you've most recently interacted with, in reverse chronological order. The Recent section is shown in Figure 4-18.

Pinning People to the Start Screen

Most of us have someone who is so important to us that we need to call, message, or otherwise get in contact with him or her on a regular basis. It could be your husband or wife, brother or sister, best friend, whoever.

People you've accessed most recently show up in the Recent section of the People hub, with the most recently accessed contact at the tip. But with a truly special person, it might be even more convenient to

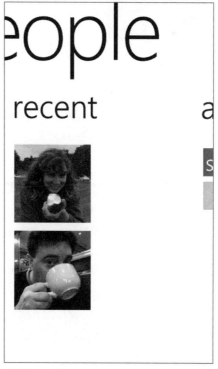

FIGURE 4-18: The Recent section provides a list of recently-accessed contacts.

simply pin that person's contact card right on the Windows Phone Start screen. That way, they'll be accessible with just one click.

To pin someone to the Start screen, locate his or her contact card in the Recent or All section of the People hub. But instead of tapping it once to view more information, tap and hold on that person's entry. In the pop-up menu that appears, choose Pin to Start. When you do, Windows Phone will navigate to the Start screen, so you can see that that person's contact card is now pinned as a live tile (Figure 4-19).

FIGURE 4-19: You can pin favorite people right to the Start screen.

From here, you can reposition the live tile or delete it. Either way, you'll need to tap and hold on the tile first.

CONFIGURING THE PEOPLE HUB

The People hub offers only a few customization options, which are available in the Settings interface. To find this interface, navigate to All Programs, Settings, Applications, and then People. As you can see in Figure 4-20, only a few options are available.

▶ **Sort list by:** With this option, you can determine if names in the People hub's All list are sorted by First name (the default) or Last name.

▶ **Display names by:** Here, you can determine the display order of names in the People hub's All list. The default is First, Last but you may prefer Last, First. (I do.)

▶ **Import SIM contacts:** If your previous phone was a GSM-type device such as those sold by AT&T in the United States (and most locales internationally), it will have used a subscriber identity module, or SIM card. On pre-smart-phone–type devices, these SIM cards were often used to store contacts, and you can use this option to import such contacts.

▶ **Add an account:** Click this link to start a wizard to create a new account.

▶ **Accounts list:** Here, you'll find a list of whatever accounts are configured on the phone along with which services (contacts, e-mail, calendar, and so on) they provide.

▶ CDMA-type phones, most common on U.S. carriers such as Verizon Wireless, do not utilize SIM cards.

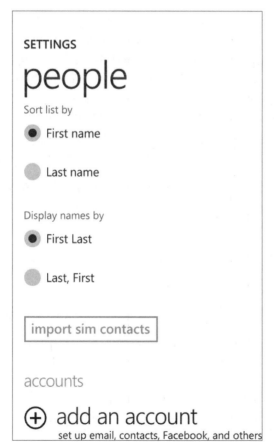

FIGURE 4-20: People hub settings.

SUMMARY

The People hub delivers on Microsoft's promise to provide a single place from which you can manage your own online persona as well as all of your contacts, no matter where they're from. In this way, it is a classic Windows Phone hub because it brings in information from disparate and disconnected places and allows you to view them and interact with them, all from a single, attractive view.

The People hub provides a lot of useful functionality, and it's the place you'll go to start phone calls, new e-mails, SMS and MMS messages, and even to get directions to someone's house.

It's also the place you'll go to keep up with your friends and other contacts. So instead of visiting numerous web sites to find out what's going on, you can use the single What's New feed in the People hub to catch up with others and comment on their activities. Meanwhile, you can also see who's commented on your own activities and respond in kind.

There are many areas in the initial shipping version of Windows Phone where Microsoft did a great job on the basics but missed out on some of the deeper, more complex functionality. The People hub is not such an area: Here, the company has done integration and aggregation right.

CHAPTER 5

Digital Memories: Using the Pictures Hub and Camera

Windows Phone is a wonderful smart phone platform with useful capabilities, innovative interactions, and the modern technical chops you expect of a leading edge product. But if I had to pick the one aspect of this phone that just puts it head and shoulders over the competition, it would be the way it allows you to enjoy digital photos. This functionality is so well designed, so perfectly connected to the content that matters the most, it just makes me smile every time I see it.

Yes, Windows Phone devices offer up the requisite digital camera, which lets you take digital still photos and videos, store them on the phone, and share them with others online and via your PC. We expect that. And yes, there is a way to view those pictures on the phone. Of course, there is. That's the baseline.

Where Windows Phone blows past all other mobile photo experiences is with its Pictures hub, which lets you view both your own pictures as well as those that are shared by friends and family, and it does so seamlessly. It lets you customize this hub with your own imagery, using a picture that will also automatically show up on the device's Start screen.

And that's when the smiles start. This is *your* phone, with your pictures, as well as pictures from those you care about most. And those pictures surface in surprising and entertaining ways, giving you a chance to enjoy memories and interact with those who are making memories of their own.

USING THE PICTURES HUB

The Pictures hub is one of the most wonderful visual experiences on Windows Phone, but it is also the simplest to understand. Here, you can manage, view, and share photos, including those that you take with the phone's internal camera, those you sync to the phone via your PC, those you've shared online, and, perhaps most interestingly, those your family, friends, and other contacts have shared online as well.

Like other hubs, the Pictures hub is presented as a panoramic experience that can view one screen, or section, at a time (Figure 5-1). By default, you will see three sections from left to right: Galleries, which lists the default photo galleries; a featured gallery; and What's New, which presents a dynamic feed of your contacts' photo-related online posts.

FIGURE 5-1: The initial Windows Phone Pictures Hub, before any customization.

In the first section, you'll see three galleries called All, Date, and Favorites.

▶ The **All** Gallery, shown in Figure 5-2, lists all of your picture galleries, including galleries of locally stored pictures (like Camera Roll, Saved Pictures, and any synced pictures), as well as photos you are sharing from Windows Live and, if configured, Facebook.

FIGURE 5-2: The All gallery displays both local and web-based photo galleries.

▶ **Date**, meanwhile, organizes locally stored photos only, by date, and not according to folder.

▶ The **Favorites** view displays those locally stored photos you've marked as favorites. I explain this feature later in the chapter.

Within any given gallery, you will eventually reach a display of photo thumbnails, like the Date view shown in Figure 5-3. (The All view alone displays folders, not individual photos.)

To view an individual photo, simply tap on a thumbnail. The photo will fill the screen as well as it can given the aspect ratio differences between it and your phone's screen. (Note that you can rotate the screen to view landscape oriented pictures more naturally.) You navigate between individual photos using your standard Windows Phone skills: You can flick the screen to go back and forth, pinch and double-tap to zoom, and tap Back to exit.

You can also perform various actions on photos (and on photo thumbnails) using a tap-and-hold method. I discuss various tap-and-hold actions throughout this chapter.

Flicking over to the center of the Pictures hub display, you'll see that one of your locally-stored photo galleries has been surfaced up for quick access. There's no way to determine which gallery is displayed in this fashion. Instead, Windows Phone picks a gallery randomly.

Over at the far right of the Pictures hub is its more enigmatic feature, the What's New section, shown in Figure 5-4.

▶ *What you can't do, oddly, is trigger an automatic photo slideshow. If you want to look at pictures, you have to navigate between them manually.*

FIGURE 5-3: The Date view, like other photo galleries, displays a grid of thumbnails.

FIGURE 5-4: The What's New section.

This works like the What's New section in the People hub, but with an important difference. Instead of seeing all of your contacts' social networking updates, this feed presents only those updates that are related to photos. So you will see such things as Facebook and Windows Live–based shared photos, pictures shared on Flickr, and so on, depending on which services you've configured through Windows Live and which accounts you've configured on Windows Phone.

CROSSREF I explain how to configure your Windows Live account properly in Chapter 1.

There is one major problem with What's New. While this section does make it easy to find the photos your friends and other contacts have posted online, it doesn't let you view some of them from inside the hub. That is, Windows Live and Facebook-based photos can be viewed normally. But if you click on a photo from Flickr, or some other second tier service (from Windows Phone's perspective), Internet Explorer will load and navigate to the appropriate page on the Web. You can, however, comment on posted photos directly from the What's New section. And that's true of any photo, not just those shared from Windows Live or Facebook.

TAKING PICTURES AND VIDEOS WITH THE CAMERA

If you're used to the low-quality cameras found on many other smart phones, feature phones, and cell phones, the camera found in a typical Windows Phone will be a revelation. That's because these devices actually take great photos and videos, and provide forward-looking features like GPS location services. Depending on which phone you get, it's very possible that you'll never need to carry around another camera.

Understanding the Hardware Capabilities of the Windows Phone Camera

The key to this future is Microsoft's minimum hardware standards for Windows Phone. You may recall from Chapter 1 that Microsoft requires device makers to include a number of minimum hardware specifications for every Windows Phone. The camera, specifically, must offer at least 5 megapixels of resolution, flash, zoom, and auto-focus capabilities, and support both still pictures and video. And there must be a dedicated camera button on the side of every Windows Phone that supports both full and half presses, as you'll see in just a bit.

So what do these specs mean in real life? With regards to megapixels, people often confuse this measurement with overall picture quality, because it's not hard to understand that 5 megapixels is more than (and thus "better" than) 4 megapixels. But like so much in life, it's more nuanced than that. Pixel size, and thus "pixels per inch," is also an important measurement, and it's possible (and likely) that a camera that packs more pixels per inch will provide better pictures than one that does not. Optics quality is another factor, and there are of course good and bad camera components out there that react differently to different lighting, movement, and other situations.

That said, cameras today are typically measured in megapixels, much like PCs used to be measured by MHz (and, later, GHz) clock speeds. After a certain point, it's not the most accurate way to compare things. But it's what's happening.

The Windows Phone prototype device I used while writing this book can take still photos up to 2560 x 1920. Do the math, and that's 4,915,200 total pixels, which makes sense since 5 megapixels is roughly 5 million pixels. It's also well beyond the resolution of 1080p HD, which is 1920 x 1080. So pictures taken with this camera would fill an HD display. (In fact, they'd have to be downsized or cropped in some way.) That doesn't mean they're going to look any good, however. Again, "quality" and "resolution" aren't the same thing.

My test device can also take 640 x 480 video, which is what's called VGA resolution, after the old PC standard. 640 x 480 is sub-HD resolution, or what we call "standard definition" video. It's possible—highly likely, actually—that the camera on your own Windows Phone will take much higher resolution (and higher quality) video than does my current test unit. In fact, according to the device makers I've spoken with, some form of HD video capability will be quite common. Most Windows Phones will probably offer 720p HD, or 1280 x 720 pixel resolution video capabilities. So if video is a concern, shop around for a phone that meets those needs.

Looking at the zoom and auto-focus, expect some device makers to cut corners. All Windows Phone cameras will offer zooming capabilities, but many will likely ship with "digital zoom," not optical zoom, which is lower quality.

Software in the phone approximates how "real" (optical) zoom would work, leading to more blurring the more you zoom in. Likewise, any hand shake while taking a photo that is digitally zoomed can lead to further blurring of the image.

Auto-focus, too, is a nice feature. But it's possible that you will see Windows Phones with more advanced focusing capabilities, including the tap-to-focus functionality that Apple provides on its iPhone smart phones. This is not required by the Windows Phone minimum specifications, however.

Okay, it's time to take some pictures and videos and see how the camera works out in the real world.

Pocket to Picture: Windows Phone's Best Camera Feature

In mid-2010, I drove cross-country with my father in a Volkswagen convertible. When we arrived in Colorado, we saw a deer at the side of the road. "Quick!" my dad said, pulling over. "Take a picture!" I fumbled for my iPhone 3GS, yanking it up to capture the moment before the skittish animal bounded through the trees. Oh, right, the screen was locked, so I had to turn it on. But it was locked with a password, so I needed to correctly tap that in, an action that was complicated by the fact that I had recently changed the password for security reasons. Finally, I managed to arrive at the iPhone home screen, but not the screen with the camera. Frantically swiping right to left, I tried to navigate to where I thought that camera icon was located, lost in sea of icon-gridded iPhone home screens. Finally, I found it. So I tapped the icon, waited impatiently for the camera app to finally load, raised the phone to my eye, looked, and...

You guessed it. I snapped a blurry picture of the deer's tail and a slice of its hindquarters. In the time that elapsed while I was fighting the iPhone interface, the deer had simply walked away.

This will never happen to you with Windows Phone thanks to a new feature Microsoft calls "pocket to picture." If I had had a Windows Phone in this same situation, I could have simply taken out the phone, pressed the camera button, and taken the picture. And this would have worked even if the device was off at the time and locked with a password. That's because Windows Phone, unlike the iPhone, has an actual camera button. And the underlying camera works even if you're not logged onto the device.

Revolutionary? Maybe not in the strictest sense. But almost everyone who's ever struggled with a phone-based camera has experienced something similar to what I just described. And if you are (or were) an iPhone user, you know exactly what I'm talking about. This is a common and very frustrating occurrence.

Pocket to picture is simple. You just pick up the phone and press the camera button. It doesn't matter if the phone is off (and/or locked with a password), or if you're using it currently. Either way, it will switch, almost immediately, into the camera application, ready to take a picture. If the phone was off when you pressed the button, it should take about 2 seconds from the time you press the button to when the device is ready to take a picture, maximum. If the phone is already on, it will take even less time.

The only caveat here is the amount of pressing you'll need to do. To prevent in-pocket camera activation, you need to use a "full press"—hold down the button for about one second—in order to activate the camera, and you'll hear a tiny beep when it's on. If you're already using the phone, a half press will do, just a tap really.

▶ By the way if the phone was off and locked with a password, and you do take a picture with the camera, you can't just tap Start and bypass the phone's security lock. You'll be prompted to log on at the lock screen instead. That makes sense.

NOTE If you are coming to Windows Phone from iPhone and miss the old way of doing things, fear not: There's a Camera app in the Programs list you can use, and it works just like the iPhone camera app. In fact, if you're feeling really nostalgic, you can even pin the Camera app to your Windows Phone Start screen and fumble around for it every time you want to take a picture.

Taking Still Pictures

Taking a photo with Windows Phone is a snap (ahem). Simply enter the Camera app (Figure 5-5), via either the phone's Camera button or by launching the Camera app manually in the Programs list. Then, using the phone's screen as an electronic viewfinder, point the phone at the subject you wish to capture and press the camera button to take the shot. (You can use a half-press here.) The phone will emulate the sound of an old-school camera taking a picture and your photo will be saved to the phone's storage. Simple, right?

FIGURE 5-5: Windows Phone makes an excellent point-and-shoot camera.

Well, it can be that simple. But you really should take the time to master how the camera works. Not only can you do different things while taking a picture, but there are many still-picture-related options you can consider configuring.

> **NOTE** You may be interrupted by a pop-up screen that asks you whether you'd like to automatically share pictures online. If you're not yet familiar with this feature, see the discussion about sharing photos later in this chapter.

First, consider what you see onscreen when the Camera app is running.

When held in the normal landscape mode for picture taking, you will see some onscreen controls on the right side of the screen. (Of course, what's normal to me might be less so to you: Three controls are actually locked to what is traditionally the bottom of the Windows Phone screen when the device is held in portrait mode. That is, they're against the side of the screen that is next to the Back, Start, and Search hardware buttons. If you rotate the device around to different orientations, those controls will stay right there.)

These controls, from top to bottom, include a still picture/video toggle, zoom up and down, and settings. The still picture/video toggle switches the phone between still and video modes, and since the camera always comes up in still picture mode, you will have to tap this if you wish to take a video.

Zoom works as expected, though the quality of pictures taken while the camera is zoomed will vary according to the hardware capabilities of your device. In short, if your Windows Phone only supports digital (software) zoom, I recommend testing picture quality before using it to capture important memories.

I examine the Photo Camera Settings interface in just a moment. Before that, however, look over at the left side of the screen while the Camera application is running. You'll see the edge of... something. Something that is not part of the image you see through the camera's viewfinder. That's no mistake. Instead, it's a bit of graphical bleed-over, and what you're seeing there is the rightmost portion of the previous photo you captured with the camera. If you tap and swipe on this slice, you can start flipping through the previously captured pictures on your phone. So it's a nifty way to make sure that perfect shot was indeed perfect before you move on.

WINDOWS PHONE CAMERA AND BATTERY LIFE

One interesting tidbit about picture taking on Windows Phone—normally, Windows Phone is very aggressive about powering down the device to save battery life. But if you turn on the camera, you'll notice that the device stays powered up for a much longer time period. This is by design: Microsoft figures if you've enabled the camera, you intend to use it, and performance is faster if the device stays powered up. Of course, this occurs at the expense of battery life.

When you tap the Settings button, the Photo Camera Settings interface takes over most of the screen, as shown in Figure 5-6.

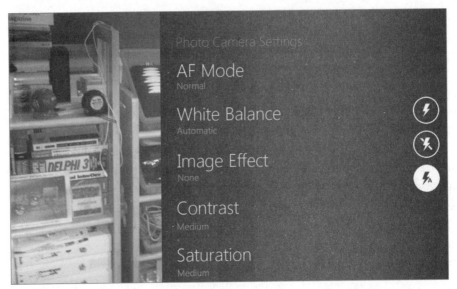

FIGURE 5-6: The Photo Camera Settings interface.

Photo Camera Settings offers a number of controls you can customize. These include flash controls (in round buttons on the right) and a bewildering list of settings. Most people will want to examine only a small number of these settings, so I'll discuss those first.

▶ **Flash controls:** Windows Phone offers three possible flash settings: On, Off, and Automatic. You will typically want to leave this on Automatic, but it can be handy in certain situations to manually enable or disable the flash, so it's important to know where these controls are located.

▶ **Photo quality:** Windows Phone provides three plain-English photo quality options: High (the default), Medium, and Low. Why you'd want to configure this to anything but High is unclear, but at least make sure it is set to High. Then, leave it alone.

▶ **Photo resolution:** Your Windows Phone will support different possible resolutions, depending on the hardware characteristics of its camera. On my test device, the available options here are VGA (640 x 480), 2M (2 megapixels, or 1600 x 1200), 3M (2048 x 1536), and 5M (2560 x 1920). Generally speaking, I prefer setting this on the highest possible resolution. But your needs may vary, so check this setting to ensure that it's on the optimal resolution.

Beyond these basic settings, Photo Camera Settings also lets you configure a number of advanced options. I don't recommend messing around in here unless you really know what you're doing or have time to experiment. Note that you can always use the Restore to Default link to undo any changes.

- ▶ **AF mode:** This option determines how the camera's auto-focus feature behaves. You can switch between normal, which is the default, and macro, which helps you focus on objects that are very small and very close to the camera (such as when you try to take a picture of a butterfly on a flower or a similar subject).

- ▶ **White balance:** This option can be used to compensate for the type of available light, since different lighting types can color photos incorrectly. The default value is automatic, where the camera will attempt to automatically compensate for different lighting types. Or you can manually choose between incandescent, fluorescent, daylight, and cloudy if you're not seeing the correct colors in your shots.

  What you're looking for, generally, is for white items in the real world to look white in your photos.

- ▶ **Image effect:** Normally, the Windows Phone camera won't apply any image effects to pictures you take with the camera, and in my opinion it never should: You can very easily apply any of these effects later using free PC-based software such as Windows Live Photo Gallery or Google Picasa, and do so without changing the original shot. That said, if you're in the mood for something quirky, Windows Phone will let you apply a mono(chromatic), negative, sepia, antique, green, or blue effect to any shot on the fly.

- ▶ **Contrast:** This option can help you compensate for problems with the phone's built-in camera where shots are either generally too washed-out (not enough contrast) or too dark (too much contrast). You can choose between a number of settings, including minimum, low, medium (the default), high, or maximum.

- ▶ **Saturation:** As with contrast, the saturation of colors in your photos could be off, and this control will help you digitally apply more or less saturation, using the same options seen with contrast. Again, the default is medium.

- ▶ **Sharpness:** This option also works like contrast, but refers to the sharpness of the pictures you take. Note that increasing the sharpness can also result in grainy, pixilated effects in your photos.

- ▶ **Exposure compensation:** Normally, the Windows Phone camera will automatically choose an exposure setting for each picture, on the fly (where exposure is a measurement of the amount of light allowed onto the camera's image sensor while the picture is being taken). However, you may find that pictures are too light or too dark in certain conditions. (The classic example is a low-light snow scene, which is hard to expose correctly.) Using this setting, you can adjust the automatically calculated exposure, in negative (minimum, low) or positive (high, maximum) steps. (The default setting is medium.) If you lower the exposure, you will lower the amount of light that is captured by the camera, and if you add exposure, you will add light to your photos.

▶ **ISO:** This is (basically) a measurement of the speed at which the camera takes a picture, where each number in the scale—which goes from 50 to 1600 on Windows Phone—is twice as fast as the one before it. If you're an old-timer like me, you may recall bringing different types of film with you on trips for different situations. You could use lower-ISO films, like 200 or 400 ISO, for outdoor shots and higher-ISO films, like 1600 for sporting events. By default, Windows Phone will automatically set ISO, and generally speaking you should let it do so. I've seen ISOs of 160 to 200 for indoor daytime shots, and ISOs as low as 40 for outdoor daytime shots.

▶ **Metering:** This setting determines how the camera determines the light level for the current shot. By default, it is set to Average, which is the most basic metering type and takes into account all of the light in the image area. Other choices include Weighted, which weights the image according to the light in the center of the image area, and Spot, which further fine-tunes the light level measurement to a smaller spot at the center of focus.

▶ **Wide dynamic range:** Backlighting—where most of the light in an image is coming from behind the subject—is one of the historic problems that has long dogged photographers both casual and professional. This option lets you automatically compensate for backlighting (like a window or bright sky) and get a more properly exposed, truer-to-life image. It can be on or off.

▶ *But if you're getting blurring in action shots, experiment with a higher, manual ISO setting.*

Taking Video

Video works a bit differently than taking still photos. First, you need to switch the camera into video mode by tapping the still picture/video toggle button. Then, to begin recording, simply tap the camera button. Windows Phone will beep and enter video mode. In this mode, zoom is disabled and a large counter ticks off the elapsed time, as shown in Figure 5-7. To stop recording, tap the camera button again.

> **TIP** Because you cannot change the zoom level while recording video, you will want to adjust this accordingly before you begin.

FIGURE 5-7: Windows Phone can also be used as a video camera.

As with the still camera, video recording has a number of options you can configure. In fact, if you tap the Settings button while in video mode, you'll see that the list of available settings has changed and is now specific to video.

Most of these options match up to the corresponding still picture setting. (So the Saturation option works similarly between both, for example. Video Quality, meanwhile, works like Photo Quality.) You can manually toggle the flash between on and off, which is nice. Note that when the flash is set to on, it will just stay on while you're shooting video.

I recommend leaving these options alone normally, unless you really know what you're doing. Just make sure that Video Quality is set to High.

By the way, videos are available from the quickie photo preview slideshow, which you can access by flicking from left to right across the screen while Camera is running. This display also shows the length of the video.

To play a video, just tap the giant Play button.

Finding Your Photos and Videos

After you've captured some photos and videos with the phone's camera, you may want to enjoy (or share) them later. Of course, to do so, you'll need to know where to look. Windows Phone stores these pictures in the Pictures hub, in a special folder called Camera Roll. To find this folder, open the Pictures hub and tap the All link.

Camera Roll is the first folder shown here, and will be in the top left of this gallery (Figure 5-8), next to and above other locally stored photos (like Saved Pictures and those photos you've synced from your PC), and above web-based photo folders from Windows Live Photos.

If you tap on the Camera Roll thumbnail, you will view the gallery of photos and videos contained within, as shown in Figure 5-9. You can tap on an individual photo or video to view it, or swipe across a photo you're looking at to navigate to the next photo.

FIGURE 5-8: Camera Roll can be found in the All gallery.

FIGURE 5-9: Photos and videos sit side by the side in the Camera Roll gallery.

MOVING PHOTOS BETWEEN THE PHONE AND YOUR PC

At some point, you're going to want to transfer photos between your Windows Phone and your PC. This works in both directions. There are photos on your phone, taken with the internal camera, or saved from the Web, that you may wish to back up in a high-resolution format, and the PC is ideal for this task. On the flipside, you may already have a collection of high-quality digital photos that you may enjoy carrying with you on the phone.

Either way, you'll need to make a connection between the phone and PC to enable the photo transfer. And with Windows Phone, that happens exclusively through the Zune PC software. Because Zune is primarily an audio/video solution, I cover this software much more completely in Chapter 6, so please refer to that if you're not familiar with the basics.

Here, you'll interact with Zune solely for the purpose of transferring photos. So you need to get it set up properly first.

Configuring Zune for Photo Transfers

When you connect your Windows Phone to the PC, the Zune PC software should run. If not, you can manually start the Zune application via the Windows Start menu or taskbar. When Zune has detected your phone, it will display a Phone entry in its main menu and, possibly, navigate to the Phone Summary screen shown in Figure 5-10.

FIGURE 5-10: The Zune PC software handles connectivity between your computer and your phone.

Click the Settings link in the top right of the Zune application window to display Zune Settings. Then, navigate to Phone, Pictures & Videos to display options related to the phone's multimedia capabilities. This screen is shown in Figure 5-11.

There are three main options here related to photo transfers.

▶ **Import settings:** By default, Zune will copy all pictures and videos stored on the phone to your PC. These include pictures and videos taken with the device's internal camera as well as pictures you may have saved to the Web. You can optionally choose to automatically delete pictures and videos from the device after the content has been transferred to your PC.

> **NOTE** If you disable the automatic import feature, that doesn't mean you can't transfer photos from the phone to the PC later. You can still do so, using the technique I describe in the next section.

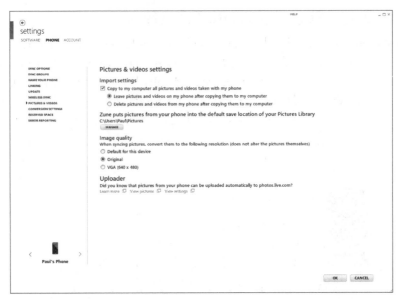

FIGURE 5-11: From this interface, you can configure how Windows Phone handles photo transfers.

▶ **Default save location:** By default, Zune will save transferred pictures and videos from the phone to your Windows 7 Picture Library default save location. (This is C:\Users*username*\Pictures normally.) Unfortunately, you cannot override this setting and instead save transferred photos and videos elsewhere. Instead, Zune simply provides an interface for Windows 7 libraries management, allowing you to change the default save location for pictures on a system-wide basis.

▶ **Image quality:** This option relates to pictures that are synced from the PC to the device, and not the reverse. By default, Zune will sync photos at their original dimensions and quality level. However, you can optionally choose to sync photos in other resolutions instead, which can save on-device storage space. These other options include device default (typically 800 x 480 or 480 x 800) and VGA (640 x 480).

▶ If you do change the image quality setting your original photos will not be resized. Instead, Zune will make copies for syncing purposes and then sync the copies to the phone instead of the original files.

When you're done configuring Zune's photo transfer options, click OK to exit Settings.

Copying Photos to the PC

Photos stored on your Windows Phone can be copied to your PC either automatically or manually. This is determined by the Import Settings option discussed in the previous section.

If you've opted for the default, automatic transfer, Zune will transfer the photos and (camera-shot) videos from your Windows Phone as soon as it's connected. In fact, this often happens so fast you won't even notice it happening.

If you've opted for manual transfer, nothing will happen when you connect the phone to your PC. (Well, nothing photo related anyway.) But you can still transfer photos (and videos) from your phone to the PC. To do so, navigate to Phone - Pictures in the Zune PC software. You'll see a screen similar to that shown in Figure 5-12.

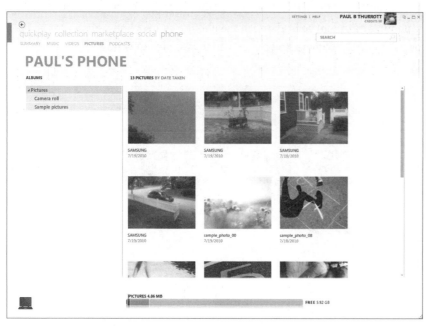

FIGURE 5-12: You can navigate through the pictures library on your phone using the Zune PC software and then transfer any photos you like to the computer.

To manually transfer pictures from the device to the PC, select one or more pictures in the Zune PC software, right-click, and choose Copy to My Collection.

WHERE ARE MY VIDEOS?

You may notice that videos you've taken with the phone's internal camera do not show up in the Camera Roll folder under Phone - Pictures. Don't worry; they are on your PC: You just need to look in Phone - Videos. You can manually transfer these videos in the same way that you transferred pictures.

▶ You can also transfer pictures from other phone based folders in this fashion. For example, pictures you've saved from the Web are stored in a folder called Saved Pictures.

Regardless of how you transfer photos, a number of things happen once the transfer is complete.

First, your photos (and videos, as it turns out) have been copied to a folder structure on your hard drive. This folder structure can be found at C:\Users*username*\Pictures by default. There, you'll find a folder named From *phone name* (where *phone name*, of course, is the name of your phone; on my PC, this folder is named From Paul's Phone). Inside of *that* folder, there will be at least one folder—called Camera Roll—and potentially other folders depending on what's transferred from the phone to the PC.

Every photo (and video) you take with the phone's camera and transfer to the PC will be found inside the Camera Roll folder, which is shown in Figure 5-13.

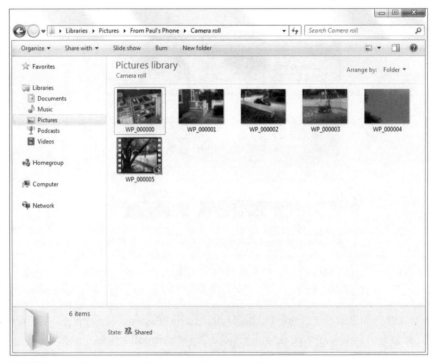

FIGURE 5-13: Pictures and videos you took with the phone's camera are found in the Camera Roll folder.

As you can see, Zune doesn't provide any way to intelligently name your pictures or segregate them into logical subfolders (like "Mark's birthday party" or "Vacation" or whatever), which is lousy. It's just a flat listing of pictures.

Inside of the Zune PC software, something else has happened: The pictures and videos you've imported have been automatically added to the Zune's Pictures and Videos libraries, respectively. (Zune uses the underlying libraries functionality in Windows 7 for determining which folders to monitor for content.) So if you navigate to Collection - Pictures in Zune, you'll see the pictures you just imported, as shown in Figure 5-14.

FIGURE 5-14: Imported pictures and videos show up in Zune's collection views.

USE WINDOWS LIVE PHOTO GALLERY TO IMPROVE YOUR PHONE'S PHOTOS

If you've installed Windows Live Photo Gallery—which is excellent, by the way— you can right-click on individual photos in Zune and choose Edit and Share to edit them in various ways. This includes changing the caption, which will provide a nicer way to reference favorite photos, and performing numerous photo-related cleanups. Windows Live Photo Gallery is part of the free Windows Live Essentials suite and can be downloaded at **get.live.com**.

Syncing PC-Based Photos to the Phone

The Zune PC software also provides a way to transfer photos from your PC to Windows Phone. But this capability is far more sophisticated than the simple transfers you undergo when copying from the phone to the PC. That's because Zune supports sophisticated photo sync capabilities, ensuring that certain parts of your PC-based photo collection are always kept up-to-date on the phone.

Photo sync is configured in the Zune PC Software at Settings - Phone - Sync Options. (Note that the phone needs to be connected to the PC for phone-related options to appear.) This is shown in Figure 5-15.

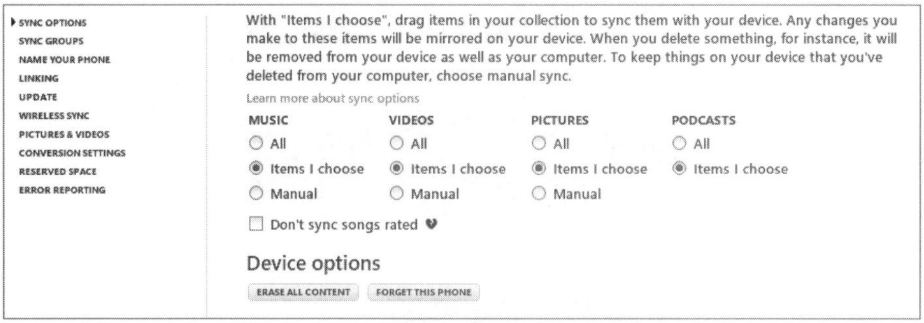

FIGURE 5-15: Sync Options determines how media files are synced between your PC and the phone.

I typically leave this on Items I Choose for all media types, if you're curious.

This interface is discussed in more detail in Chapter 6. But if you consider the Pictures sync options, you can see there are three possible choices: All (sync all of the photos in your Zune Pictures collection), Items I Choose (items you choose for sync will change on the device when they change on the PC), and Manual (for those who wish to micromanage syncing).

After configuring pictures sync the way you want it, you can browse your Zune's Pictures collection and pick some pictures to sync. You can sync content to

FIGURE 5-16: Setting up picture sync with a right-click.

the phone in a number of ways. The most obvious is to drag and drop folders, individual pictures, or a group of pictures from the Zune Picture collection view down into the icon representation of your phone in the lower-left corner of the application. Or, you can right-click one of these items, as shown in Figure 5-16, and choose Sync with *Paul's Phone* (where *Paul's Phone* is, of course, your phone's name).

And that's all there is to it. If you sync a folder, any changes you make to the contents of that folder later—including adding, deleting, or editing existing files—will be reflected on the phone at the next sync.

SHARING PHOTOS AND CUSTOMIZING YOUR PHONE

Once you've begun stockpiling photos on your Windows Phone by capturing them with the internal camera, saving them from the Web, syncing them with your PC, or viewing them in online photo galleries, you may want to take the next logical steps. These include finding your favorite photos, sharing photos with others, and then customizing Windows Phone in various ways with those photos. In this section, I examine all of these possibilities.

Finding Your Favorites

If you've spent any time managing and enjoying digital music over the years, you're probably familiar with the concept of a playlist, which is a way to organize a list of favorite songs so that you can play them back together at any time in the future. With pictures, Windows Phone supports the notion of a collection called the Favorites gallery. This gallery groups specially tagged, or identified, photos and lets you view them together regardless of their individual origins. So it works much like a playlist. It also works like the Favorites list in Internet Explorer (or the bookmarks you'll find in other browsers).

The Favorites gallery can be accessed from the first section in the Pictures hub, and if you just got your phone or haven't worked with this feature yet, it's highly probable that it's empty. (Otherwise, it's possible that your phone maker tagged some bundled photos as favorites.)

Now it's time to add some favorites.

There are two places you can save a favorite. First, in any photo gallery that contains locally saved pictures—Camera Roll, Saved Pictures, or folders synced from your PC—you can tap and hold on an image thumbnail to display a pop-up menu; choose Add to Favorites. Likewise, when you're viewing a photo—and, again, it needs to be a locally saved photo and not a web-based photo—you can perform the same tap and hold action and choose Add to Favorites.

Once you've marked a number of photos this way, navigate to the main section of the Pictures hub and then tap Favorites. Here, you'll see a gallery of your favorite pictures, arranged in the order in which you marked them. You can interact with these photos in the same way that you do with photos in other photo galleries, but there is one important difference: Favorites is not a folder, and marking a photo as a favorite does not remove it from its original location. Instead, Favorites acts like a *virtual folder* in the desktop versions of Windows. That is, it contains *links* (or shortcuts) to the actual photos. It's a *view,* not a container.

Sharing Photos

Managing and enjoying photos on your own is enjoyable enough. But photos are meant to be shared. Fortunately, Windows Phone provides a few different ways to do this.

MANUALLY SHARING PHOTOS

You can manually share an individual (local) photo via any of your connected accounts by tapping and holding on that photo (or, in a gallery, on its thumbnail) and choosing Share. When you do, the Share page will appear, populated with a list of choices that will vary according to which accounts you've configured.

Possibilities here include:

Technically you don't have to specify a contact. You could also manually enter any valid cell phone number and send it to that person as well.

- ▶ **Messaging:** You can share any locally stored photo with any of your contacts using the phone's integrated Messaging (SMS/MMS) utility.

- ▶ **E-mail:** You can e-mail a photo via any configured e-mail account (such as Exchange/Outlook, Yahoo! Mail, Gmail, Hotmail, or whatever). Pictures shared in this way are sent as e-mail attachments.

- ▶ **Upload to Facebook:** Using this option, you can upload a photo to your Facebook account. Note that if you're quick enough, you can tap the blank Comment box to optionally add some comment text to the picture before it's uploaded. (And yes, you do have to be quick: If the connection is good, Windows Phone will upload it before you get a chance!)

- ▶ **Upload to SkyDrive:** This works identically to Facebook sharing, in that you have to be quick if you want to add a comment.

> **NOTE** Photos shared via Facebook and SkyDrive are similar in another way: They're not full-size. Instead, you'll see near-VGA resolution versions of your photos uploaded to those sites. (On both sites, the 5 megapixel photos I uploaded were downsized to 720 x 540.)

TIP You can choose either Facebook or SkyDrive as your Quick Upload site. What this does, ultimately, is save you one click when you want to share a photo with others. So instead of selecting a picture, tapping and holding, choosing Share, and then choosing either Upload to Facebook or Upload to SkyDrive, you can select a picture, tap and hold, and then choose either Upload to Facebook or Upload to SkyDrive, right from that initial pop-up menu. This isn't so much "Quick Upload" as it is "Slightly Quicker Upload."

Photos manually shared via Windows Live SkyDrive are uploaded to a folder called Mobile Photos. You can find this folder online by navigating to `photos.live.com`, then All albums.

AUTOMATICALLY SHARING PHOTOS

Manual photo sharing certainly gets the job done. But sometimes it may be easier to simply configure your phone to automatically share photos. And you can do so, with a number of caveats.

- ▶ First, this type of sharing applies only to photos taken with your phone's internal camera. You can't automatically share other locally stored (or web-based) photos.

- ▶ Second, you can only automatically share photos to one service, Windows Live SkyDrive.

- ▶ Third, you cannot add comments to automatically shared photos unless you manually do so later. (You can do this from the Pictures hub, of course.)

- ▶ And finally, like manual sharing, this feature does not create a full-resolution backup of your photos in the cloud, because of battery life and bandwidth concerns. Instead, you get the same, low-quality, near-VGA version.

If none of these issues turn you off, you can enable automatic photo sharing by visiting the Pictures + Camera settings screen. To find this, navigate to Programs, Settings, Applications, and then Pictures + Camera. You'll see the screen shown in Figure 5-17.

To enable this feature, toggle Auto Upload to SkyDrive to On. When you do, Windows Phone will warn you that this feature will utilize your data plan, which could be a concern if you don't have an unlimited data plan with your wireless carrier.

There's a white box on this screen named Choose an Option. Tap this box to expand a list of choices that includes Friends, Me, Everyone (Public), and Don't Upload. These determine with whom you will be sharing uploaded pictures. They match the default sharing options on Windows Live and I assume they're easy to decipher. Click OK to apply the changes.

> **NOTE** I examine the other options in the Picture + Camera settings screen at the end of this chapter.

Photos automatically shared via Windows Live SkyDrive are uploaded to a folder called Windows Phone Photos. You can find this folder online by navigating to photos .live.com, then All Albums. Note that this folder is different from the location where manually shared photos are located: those photos are in Mobile photos. Why are photos shared in different ways uploaded to different places on SkyDrive? Only Microsoft knows for sure.

Using a Favorite Photo as Wallpaper

You can customize the Windows Phone lock screen with your own picture, providing a nice bit of personalization. And if you choose wisely, you may even smile a little bit every time you turn on the phone.

There are two ways to make this change. You could go through the Lock & Wallpaper interface in Settings. But that's boring. A more likely scenario is that while you're browsing through the photos on your phone, you come across one you'd like to use as wallpaper for the lock screen.

When this happens, tap on the image to load it full screen, tap and hold on the picture, and then choose Use as Wallpaper from the pop-up menu that appears.

You'll be given an opportunity to crop the picture, as seen in Figure 5-18.

To test the new wallpaper, tap the power button to turn off the phone. Then turn the phone on again. In Figure 5-19, you can see a custom wallpaper on the Windows Phone lock screen.

This only works with photos that are stored locally on the phone. If you are browsing an online photo gallery, your only option is Save to Phone.

Changing the Pictures Hub Background

As you've seen, part of the appeal of the Pictures hub is its beautiful background wallpaper, which is used both in the hub and on the Pictures live tile on the phone's Start screen. Good as it may be, the default background wallpaper is going to get a bit boring over time. Fortunately, you can change it anytime you want.

It's easy, once you know the trick. All you need to do is tap and hold on any empty area of the Pictures hub—well, *almost* anywhere—this won't work in the What's New section or on any of the subscreens—and wait for the pop-up menu shown in Figure 5-20 to appear.

FIGURE 5-17: Pictures + Camera settings.

FIGURE 5-18: When you select a new background image, you need to crop it to fit the dimensions of the lock screen.

This menu has two items, Change Background and Change It for Me. If you choose Change Background, you'll be given a Choose Picture screen from which you can navigate around the local picture store to find the picture you want. You'll be given an opportunity to crop the picture, when you're choosing a lock screen wallpaper.

Change It for Me causes Windows Phone to randomly select another picture. As with the first option, the picture will be among those that are locally stored on the phone. Over time, Windows Phone will continue to randomly choose new backgrounds for you, and the gallery that contains that background will be showcased in the middle section of the Pictures hub.

FIGURE 5-19: Changing the lock screen wallpaper is just one of many neat customizations you can make to Windows Phone.

▶ Again, note that you can use only locally stored photos. If you want a web-based picture as the background, you will need to download it to the phone first.

Either way, when you're done making your selection, you return to the Pictures hub, which is newly redecorated (Figure 5-21).

FIGURE 5-20: The secretive way you can change the Picture hub's background image.

FIGURE 5-21: The Pictures hub with a new background image.

CONFIGURING PICTURE HUB OPTIONS

No discussion of Windows Phone's photo capabilities would be complete without a quick look at the Pictures + Camera settings screen, which provides some important configuration options. Remember that this screen is somewhat buried: You must navigate to Programs, Settings, and then Applications to find it. There, you will see the following options:

▶ **Allow the camera button to wake up the phone:** This is the key to Windows Phone's "pocket to picture" capability, so it's set to On by default.

▶ **Include location (GPS) info in pictures you take:** Windows Phone "tags" each photo you take with GPS-based location information, allowing modern photo management solutions, such as Google Picasa/Google Earth, to display maps of the locations where you took pictures. This feature is Off by default.

- ▶ **Auto upload to SkyDrive:** Windows Phone can optionally upload a low-resolution version of every photo you take with the internal camera to Windows Live Sky-Drive, for automatic sharing. Because this can impact battery life and requires a data connection, it's disabled (Off) by default.

- ▶ **Keep location info on uploaded pictures:** If you manually or automatically share photos from Windows Phone, the GPS-based location data will be included with those photos. You may not want that, however, for privacy reasons. If so, set this option to Off. (It's On by default.)

- ▶ **Quick upload account:** You can configure either Windows Live SkyDrive or Facebook as your Quick Upload Account, providing you with a slightly faster way to manually share photos to that account.

SUMMARY

Windows Phone provides a wonderful photo experience that's without peer in the smart phone world. There's an integrated hub called Pictures that aggregates content from your camera, local storage, and various web services, all in one place. It features a What's New section that lets you keep up-to-date with the photos your friends and other contacts are posting, and a variety of galleries from which you can view your own pictures, including those stored in online services.

The bundled camera is excellent, with still picture and video capabilities, and advanced functionality that used to be found only in dedicated, high-end cameras. And thanks to the unique "pocket to picture" feature, you can quickly snap an impromptu photo anytime, even if the phone is off and locked with a password.

Windows Phone integrates with the excellent Zune software so that you can sync photos from your PC to the phone, and copy photos (and videos) from the phone to your PC. And if you want to share photos on the go, Windows Phone offers almost limitless sharing capabilities over messaging, e-mail, Windows Live SkyDrive, and Facebook. You can also automatically upload photos taken with the device's camera to SkyDrive if desired.

And when it comes to customizing your phone, Windows Phone lets you change the lock screen wallpaper, or even the Pictures hub background, to a favorite photo. This lets you truly make the phone your own.

All in all, there's little Windows Phone can't do when it comes to photos. This functionality is one of the best reasons to choose Microsoft's smart phone platform.

Zune to Go: Music + Videos

If you're looking for the ultimate mobile multimedia experience, I've got good news: Windows Phone isn't just a world class smart phone; it's also the best media player on the market. That's because Windows Phone includes stellar, integrated music and video playback functionality, which connects seamlessly to Microsoft's excellent but underappreciated Zune online services. It really is the best of both worlds.

Windows Phone provides a number of useful music and video capabilities. You can manage and play music, audiobooks, podcasts, TV shows, movies, music videos, and even FM radio, all from the device. If you have a Zune Pass subscription, you can stream songs from Microsoft's several-million-strong music collection directly to your device, over the air, all for a low monthly fee. And if you use the Zune PC software, you can manage your digital media collections in Windows and then sync your content to the phone, and even do so wirelessly if you'd prefer.

You can find, buy, and download commercial music, TV shows, movies, and music videos, as well as free podcasts, via the Zune Marketplace. And you can even access parts of this voluminous online store directly from the phone if you prefer. It's your choice.

It doesn't stop there. Thanks to deep extensibility, you're also able to improve Windows Phone's core music and video capabilities with third-party solutions like Pandora, which provides fully customizable, Internet-based radio stations tailored to your particular tastes and available over the air directly to your device. Over time, numerous third-party applications and services will appear, greatly expanding Windows Phone's already-excellent built-in media capabilities.

No matter how you slice it, Windows Phone has you covered when it comes to digital media. And in this chapter, I'll show you how to get up and running and configure Windows Phone to be the best possible media player for you. The first step, however, is to fire up your PC and examine the Zune PC software.

USING THE ZUNE PC SOFTWARE WITH WINDOWS PHONE

One of the interesting design choices that Microsoft made with Windows Phone is that it doesn't really offer much in the way of PC/phone integration. In fact, if you plug a Windows Phone into a Windows-based PC using its USB charge cable, there's precious little you can do from there. Even after downloading drivers, Windows Phone won't show up as an icon in Windows Explorer, and thus it can't be used as a portable hard drive. And you can't download photos from the device using the built-in Windows photo acquisition software as you would with a traditional digital camera (or with competing smart phones).

As it turns out, there's only one thing you can do with your phone when it's attached to a Windows-based PC: You use Microsoft's Zune PC software to synchronize content—typically music, videos, and photo content—between your PC and the device. So for purposes of this discussion, I'll examine the initial PC–Windows Phone linkup via the Zune PC software, and then explain how this PC software can be used to sync digital audio and video content with your device.

CROSSREF In this chapter, I'll focus solely on the ability to sync music and videos between the Zune PC software and your Windows Phone. I cover photo downloading and integration in Chapter 5.

I mentioned in Chapter 1 that you should connect your Windows Live ID to a Zune account for the best Windows Phone experience, so hopefully you've already done that. The next step is to download and install the latest version of the Zune PC software. You can find this software at zune.net.

> **NOTE** Fun fact: The minimum Zune PC software version that works with Windows Phone is version 4.7. That's because Zune was at version 4 when Windows Phone 7 came out, and when you put (Zune) 4 and (Windows Phone) 7 together, you get . . . 4.7. Sort of.

Shown in Figure 6-1, the Zune PC software is pretty straightforward, though if you're familiar with horrible media/sync software like Apple's iTunes, you might be shocked by how pretty and functional this is.

▶ In fact, it's best to install the PC software before you plug your phone into the PC, since the Zune PC software includes the driver software Windows will need to allow the device to sync properly.

FIGURE 6-1: The Zune PC software.

It doesn't make sense to provide a complete overview of the Zune PC software here, but I want to at least hit on the basics, so you can have some understanding of how the software is organized and how it works. The Zune PC software is divided into different views, which are accessed via the main menu of choices along the top left of the application. These include:

► **QuickPlay:** If you're not hugely interested in micromanaging your entire media collection, QuickPlay provides an optional interface for quickly interacting with key parts of that collection, including your favorite items (which can be pinned to this interface, similar to the way Windows Phone live tiles are pinned to the Start screen), new media items, recently accessed media items (called History), and a selection of custom playlists (like electronic, personal radio stations) called Smart DJ. QuickPlay, shown in Figure 6-2, is the default screen displayed when you launch the Zune PC software.

> **TIP** If you disable QuickPlay a few times, Zune will ask if you want to switch to a different default view. You can also manually switch the startup view in Settings, General.

FIGURE 6-2: QuickPlay.

► **Collection:** From here, you can gain access to your entire media collection, including music, videos, pictures, podcasts, channels (themed playlists that are constantly updated and, thus, even more like radio stations, but require a Zune Pass subscription), and mobile (Windows Phone and Zune HD) apps.

Each media type provides different view filtering possibilities. For example, within the Music section, you can switch between artists, genres, albums, songs, and playlists. Videos provides All, TV, Movies, Other, and Personal views. These views are all optimized for the content you're displaying. In Music - Artists, for example, you'll get a three-column view with an artist list, album thumbnails, and a song list, and as you select items, the views all change. But in Music - Albums, the view changes to display large album art thumbnails and a songs list column instead. Some views, such as Music - Playlists, provide only textual columns of information.

ZUNE MAKES IT EASY

The Zune PC software integrates with the libraries feature in Windows 7 to determine which folders it "monitors." So it works with the built-in Music, Pictures, and Videos libraries. It also adds a new library, called Podcasts, to Windows 7. If you add content to any of these locations in Windows, it will automatically show up in Zune and, thus, can be synced with your Windows Phone. This stands in sharp contrast to Apple iTunes, which forces you to manually drag media from the file system into the application. That is, iTunes can't monitor folders throughout your file system automatically, as can Zune.

▶ **Marketplace:** This provides in-application access to Microsoft's online store for Zune and Windows Phone. And while Apple has nothing to fear quite yet—the iTunes Store is still unassailable from a breadth of content perspective—the Zune Marketplace (or Windows Phone Marketplace as it's sometimes called as well) offers a lot of content. This includes music, videos (music videos, TV shows, and movies), podcasts (which are free and come in both audio and video varieties), channels (the aforementioned 21st century radio stations that require a Zune Pass subscription), and mobile apps.

Zune Marketplace, shown in Figure 6-3, can be accessed both from the PC and via your Windows Phone. But there are some advantages to doing so from the PC. First, the onscreen real estate is dramatically more spacious on the PC, and this can lead to a better experience depending on what you're looking for. Second, not all of the Zune Marketplace content is available from your phone. When you're on the go, you can only browse for, and download, music and mobile apps. To get at the rest of the content in the store, you'll need to be on the PC.

▶ **Social:** Because the Zune services are connected to your Windows Live ID, you can connect the two and share your musical preferences with your friends. Those contacts you have in Windows Live that have also connected with Zune will show up in the Zune Social, which is Microsoft's online community for music lovers. From the Social interface in the Zune PC software, you can see your friends' recent music-related activities (that is, which artists, songs, and albums they've listened to most recently and most frequently), view your own musical history and preferences (and, in a cute move, view your badges, which act as the Achievements you'd get on Xbox Live, only this time for music, not games), and exchange messages with friends.

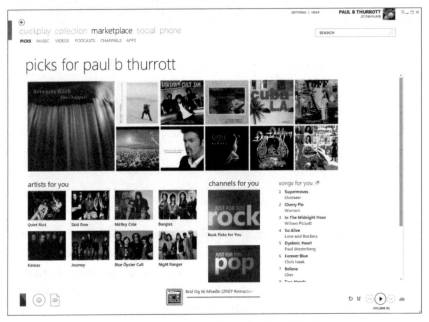

FIGURE 6-3: Zune Marketplace, as accessed from the Zune PC software.

▶ **Device/Phone:** Before there was a Windows Phone, Microsoft created several generations of Zune portable media players, and you can manage those devices—including which content is synced to them—via the Device section. If you have a Windows Phone, this section will be named Phone while that device is plugged in, but it provides similar functionality. Because this is such an important part of the Windows Phone/Zune PC software experience, I'll be examining this interface in more detail in just a bit.

TIP There's a lot more going on with the Zune PC software, of course. If you'd like to learn more, check out my Zune software reviews, overviews, and other articles on the SuperSite for Windows: winsupersite.com/digitalmedia.

Connecting a Windows Phone to Your PC

After the Zune PC software is installed and running, you can connect your Windows Phone to the PC for the first time, using the USB charge/sync cable that came with the device. Windows will search for, and find, the appropriate driver. Once that's complete, it will automatically launch the Zune PC software, which will walk you through a short wizard in which you configure the phone. The first screen of this wizard is shown in Figure 6-4.

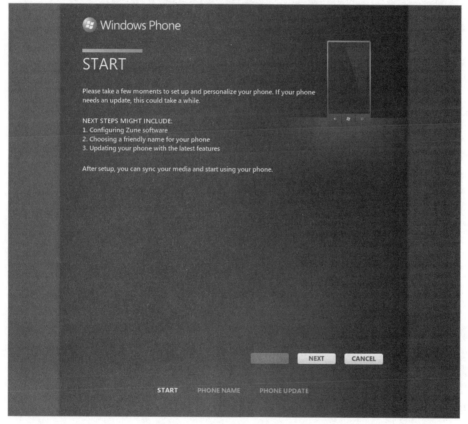

FIGURE 6-4: When you connect a Windows Phone to the PC for the first time, Zune launches so you can configure the device.

Tap Next to continue. In the next screen (Figure 6-5), you can rename your phone to something appropriate (*Paul's phone* or whatever).

▶ You can rename your phone at any time using the Zune PC software. Just navigate to Settings, Phone, Name Your Phone. I describe other phone settings in the Zune PC software in Chapter 16.

FIGURE 6-5: This name will appear wherever your phone is referenced in the Windows Phone ecosystem, including on the Web.

Tap Next again and Zune will check to see if there is a software update for your Windows Phone. You should apply any available updates that are recommended by the software before continuing. Click Next when it's done to finish the initial configuration.

At this point, the Zune software will dump you into the Phone - Summary view as shown in Figure 6-6 and may actually start syncing content to the device. Click the Stop Sync button immediately to prevent this. You're going to want to configure this behavior to your liking first.

Configuring Automatic Media Sync Between Windows Phone and Your PC

Here's how you configure Windows Phone to sync media with your PC. In the Zune PC software, click the Settings link in the upper right corner of the application window. Then, click Phone. This screen, shown in Figure 6-7, provides a menu of settings related to your phone.

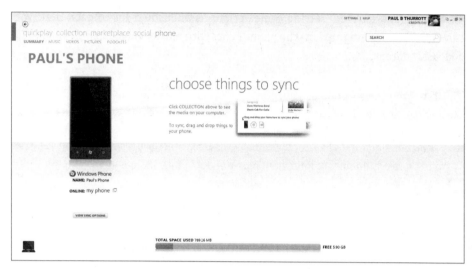

FIGURE 6-6: This screen provides a summary of the content that's moving between the PC and your phone.

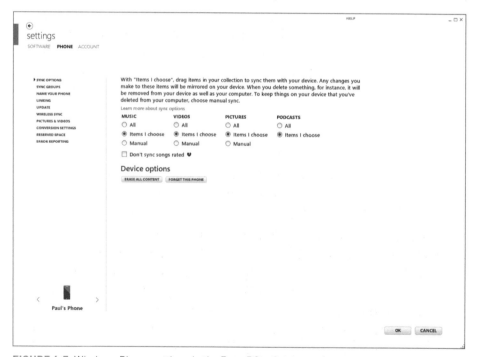

FIGURE 6-7: Windows Phone settings in the Zune PC software.

The top (and selected) setting, Sync Options, is what you're looking for. Here, you can individually configure how the phone syncs with music, videos, pictures, and podcasts content.

> **NOTE** You can also use this interface to "forget" your phone and unlink it from that media collection, or to erase all of the content on the phone. This last bit sounds scary, because it is, but it applies only to the media content on your phone, not other data like contact information. Note, however, that you will want to back up any important information before doing this, including any photos you've taken with the phone's internal camera.

For each media type (except podcasts), you have three options:

▶ **All:** If you select All, the Zune PC software will attempt to sync every single item of the chosen media type with your phone. But unless you have a tiny media library, or a particularly voluminous amount of storage on your phone, you may want to avoid this choice.

▶ **Items I choose:** If you select this option, no content will be automatically copied to the device. However, you can later browse through your collection and then drag and drop media items between the collection and your phone, the latter of which appears as a small dark icon in the lower left corner of the application window. (Don't worry, you'll get a look at this behavior more closely in just a bit.)

This may seem like a good choice, and it often is. But you should be aware of one important detail with this type of sync: If you later choose to delete a synced media item on the PC, or have an item that is automatically deleted over time, like an old podcast, that item will automatically be deleted from the phone the next time you sync.

▶ **Manual:** Aimed at the real Type As in the audience, manual sync gives you ultimate control over what gets on your device, with the caveat that you will literally need to manually manage content synchronization; Zune will do nothing to automate this process for you. (Note that manual sync is not available for podcasts only.)

▶ Fortunately the reverse is not true: If you delete such an item from the phone, it will not be deleted from your collection automatically when you later sync.

If you're looking for some advice, I generally go with "Items I choose" because I like to set up some ground rules for device syncing and then let Zune do the heavy lifting. The key to this is to intelligently create playlists and sync other content that updates over time, and automatically, like podcasts. I'll examine these activities next.

Choosing Media to Sync with the Phone

Even if you have a tiny media library, or a phone with a crazy amount of storage, you shouldn't skip this section. Here, I'll provide some strategies for populating your phone with a reasonable collection of decent media content, regardless of your needs.

USING PLAYLISTS

The number one way to segregate music content you'd like to sync to the device from the wider collection of music you don't want synced is to intelligently create and use playlists. Zune supports two types of playlists, "regular" (or "dumb") playlists, and autoplaylists. Both are created in Collection - Music - Playlists.

▶ **Regular playlists** are just dumb buckets. You can copy content into them (using drag and drop or via Zune's right-click context menu), rearrange the order of the songs (again, using drag and drop), and then sync them with your phone. You create a playlist by clicking New Playlist in the Playlist UI. I assume this is pretty straightforward.

▶ **Autoplaylists**—called smart playlists elsewhere—are much more intelligent, and much more interesting because they are dynamic. That is, the content of an autoplaylist can change over time depending on certain conditions.

Take a look at a few possibilities.

For example, maybe you want to just sync your favorite songs to the phone. Zune uses a three-tier song rating system that utilizes cute little hearts to denote whether you like a song. The three possible choices are Like (a heart), Don't Like (a broken heart), and Not Rated (empty heart). To create an autoplaylist of just those songs you like, click New Autoplaylist to display the Autoplaylist interface shown in Figure 6-8.

Creating this autoplaylist is simple: Give it a name, change the Rating field to "Like," and optionally change the song limit from 100 to another number (or just clear the field to include all eligible songs). When you click OK, your new autoplaylist is created.

You can get more sophisticated, of course. You may not want to mix and match your favorite opera and rock songs, so you can use the Genre field to add or remove songs based on their genre. The possibilities are almost limitless.

FIGURE 6-8: You can create smart playlists, called autoplaylists, in Zune.

BEYOND PLAYLISTS: SMART DJ LISTS AND CHANNELS

Zune also supports two other types of playlists: the aforementioned Smart DJ lists and Channels. Both work like radio stations, in that they semi-randomly create playlists of songs customized to your preferences. But where Smart DJ creates a one-time (though updatable) static playlist, Channels are designed to be dynamic over time. Smart DJ lists can draw content from both your local music collection and, if you have a Zune Pass subscription, via the millions of songs available on Zune Marketplace. Channels, conversely, requires a Zune Pass. Smart DJ lists appear in the Playlists view in Music, whereas Channels get their own view.

To sync any playlist—including Smart DJ lists and Channels—with your phone, right-click it and choose Sync with *Paul's Phone* (where *Paul's Phone* is the name of your phone, of course).

DRAGGING AND DROPPING FAVORITE ARTISTS, ALBUMS, OR GENRES

If playlist creation is too tedious, you can simply drag and drop favorite content from your collection onto a special Windows Phone icon that you'll find in the bottom left of the Zune PC software's application window (Figure 6-9).

This works with individual songs, artists, albums, and even genres. (This works with playlists, too.) You can also right-click on these items to sync them with your phone.

FIGURE 6-9: Drag and drop content from your collection to the phone

CONSIDERING A ZUNE PASS

True music lovers, and those who are still regularly buying music, should consider a Zune Pass subscription. For a low monthly fee—$14.95 a month in the United States at the time of this writing, though the cost is not as bad as it sounds, as I'll soon describe—Zune Pass allows you to stream and download as much music as you want from Microsoft's collection of several million songs in the Zune Marketplace. Zune features like Smart DJ work more effectively when you have a Zune Pass, because they can utilize a much bigger collection of music. And the Channels feature actually requires a Zune Pass.

Zune Pass is particularly valuable for music lovers for another, non-obvious reason. In addition to giving you on-the-fly access to Microsoft's amazing music collection, it also provides subscribers with 10 song credits that can be redeemed each month. These song credits can be redeemed for songs, so instead of purchasing them at $1 each, you get them for free. Point being that if you're buying a lot of music, and would be spending $10 a month on new music anyway—the equivalent of a typical album—the real cost of Zune Pass is just $5 a month. (In the United States, that is; international pricing and availability will vary.)

Zune Pass also works in some surprising places. For example, you can actually access the entire Zune Marketplace collection (social.zune.net/home) via your PC's web browser, log on with your Windows Live ID, and stream full length songs all day long if you'd like, so this is a solution that works great for both Mac users and for those who work in places where they can't install PC software (like the Zune PC software).

The web-based Zune player is shown in Figure 6-10. And for Windows Phone users, Zune Pass provides a way to access the entire Zune Marketplace music collection, over the air, from anywhere you have network (3G or Wi-Fi) connectivity. It's an awesome way to discover new music, even when you're on the go. (I examine this functionality more later in the chapter.)

You can find out more about Zune Pass, and sign up for a free 14-day trial at zune.net/zunepass.

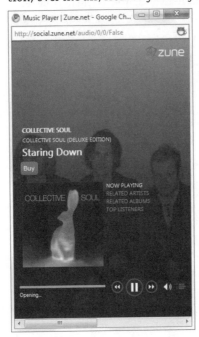

FIGURE 6-10: The Zune web player, in pop-out mode.

SUBSCRIBING TO PODCASTS

Like other modern media player solutions, the Zune platform supports subscribing to, managing, and playing podcasts, and this is an interesting option for those who like to listen to the radio but want content that is tailored specifically to their interests, and isn't location based. Podcasts are audio or video recordings, as you'd find on the radio. Some are spoken word, some are educational, and the quality is all over the map, though as with any other content type, there is some amazing stuff out there.

Unlike radio stations, however, podcasts are distributed over the Internet and are typically downloaded to a PC or device, rather than streamed live in real time.

You can discover podcasts via the Podcasts section of the Zune Marketplace. And if you're looking for a great place to start, might I humbly suggest my own podcast, *Windows Weekly*, which has been produced each week since late 2006. I co-host the show with technology veteran (and all-around nice guy) Leo Laporte, there are both audio and video versions available, and we discuss Microsoft-oriented technologies stories each week including, you guessed it, Windows Phone. You can find out more about the *Windows Weekly* podcast at winsupersite.com/podcast, and subscribe very easily via the Zune PC software.

Syncing a podcast to your Windows Phone is easy: Just navigate to the Podcast interface and drag and drop the podcast (or podcast episode) you want onto your phone. Ta-da!

BEING SELECTIVE WITH VIDEO CONTENT

There are all kinds of ways to get video into your collection and from there onto your device. It's possible to purchase or rent movies, or purchase TV shows or music videos from the Zune Marketplace and sync them from your PC to the phone, for example. With the right software and know-how, you can "rip" DVD movies to your PC and sync those to the phone. (Refer to the Digital Media Core series on winsupersite.com/digitalmedia if this sounds difficult or scary.) Or you can download videos from the Web, or perhaps have some sample videos or even home movies on your PC already. The content is out there.

The problem with video, of course, is that the files are humongous. A typical DVD rip of a Hollywood movie takes up anywhere from 1GB to 2GB of storage space if copied in a high-quality format. Such a file will play on Windows Phone. But when you consider that the typical phones of today have only 8GB to 16GB of storage, it doesn't take a mathematics expert to understand the space concerns. So you're looking at maybe a handful of videos on a typical phone.

For this reason, I recommend manually syncing video content and being very selective about which videos you actually sync to the phone. If you're going on a trip, you may want to watch *Avatar* on your phone's (relatively) tiny screen. But do you really need to carry around a movie like that day to day? Probably not.

ENJOYING MUSIC AND VIDEO CONTENT ON WINDOWS PHONE

If you've spent any time with Windows Phone, you understand that its most compelling user interfaces are those scrolling, panoramic experiences that Microsoft calls *hubs*. There are a number of nice hubs built into Windows Phone, and two of them are specifically related to enjoying digital media content: Pictures, which I discuss in Chapter 5, and Music + Videos, the subject of the remainder of this chapter.

As is so often the case, the Music + Videos hub can vary dramatically depending on how you've configured your device. For example, if you've not synced with any PC-based digital media content, you're going to see a very empty UI, like that shown in Figure 6-11.

But once you've begun using Windows Phone as the ultimate portable digital media player that it is, your Music + Videos hub is going to fill up with content and explode with possibilities. In Figure 6-12, you can see the difference between the empty wasteland of the default view and what a real-world Music + Videos hub can look like.

FIGURE 6-11: The default Music + Videos hub is pretty much empty, with a Zune section and not much else.

FIGURE 6-12: Once you actually start using Music + Videos, the hub explodes with content.

Looking over these figures, you can see that the Music + Videos hub consists of a few basic sections. These include:

▶ **Zune:** This is the device-based Zune software, and it consists of interfaces for browsing through music, videos, and podcast content; an FM radio; and connectivity to the Zune Marketplace.

SYNCING AUDIOBOOKS

If you've configured Windows Phone to work with audiobooks, you'll also see an Audiobooks item. Unfortunately, audiobook sync isn't as seamless as that for music, videos, and other content because you can't do this via the Zune PC software. Instead, you must "sideload" audiobooks onto Windows Phone via third-party PC software from audiobook vendors such as Audible (`audible.com`).

Because the Zune interfaces are so integral to music and video enjoyment on Windows Phone, I will look much more closely at the software in just a moment.

▶ **History:** Albums and artists you've listened to recently will appear in the History section, which can span across two or more screen widths in the hub. Also, the Now Playing panel will appear in this section. (I also examine Now Playing later in the chapter.)

▶ **New:** In the rightmost section, you'll see a collection of media that has most recently been added to the device. This can include music, videos, podcasts, or any other content types supported by Music + Video.

NOTE In case it's not obvious, the design of the Music + Videos hub closely follows the Zune PC software's QuickPlay interface. There are a few differences, of course, the key one being that you cannot "pin" favorite items to Music + Videos (that is, there's no Pinned section in Music + Videos on the device). But you *can* pin artists, albums, genres, and even individual songs to your Windows Phone's Start screen. Now that's customization!

From a presentation standpoint, the Zune section is displayed as a plain text list, but the other two default sections, History and New, utilize graphical thumbnails representing individual artists and albums.

I assume the use of History—which presents the several most recent media items you've enjoyed—and New—which catalogs the most recently added media items—is fairly obvious. So I'm going to jump ahead and examine the various items in the Zune section. I mean, who the heck has ever used Zune before, right?

FOR YOU ZUNE HD USERS . . . I KNOW YOU'RE OUT THERE

If you are one of the few people on earth who used a Zune HD, you know how awesome this device and its software are: The Windows Phone's Zune software is pretty much just a small update over what was included with the Zune HD. But there are two differences you should be aware of.

▶ First, the Zune HD didn't have a dedicated Back button, as does every Windows Phone, so you had to tap the uppermost area of the screen (called the title area in Windows Phone) to navigate back; now, of course, you use the device's physical Back button instead. (And if you do find yourself tapping up in the title area, as I still do from time to time, sorry, it doesn't do a thing.)

▶ Second, some of the items in the various Zune interfaces have been re-ordered for some reason. So if you're used to, say, the Music interface offering Playlists, Songs, Genres, Albums, and Artists, in that order, you may be surprised to discover that Windows Phone uses Artists, Albums, Playlists, Genres, and Songs instead. Why? Only the great mobile gods in the sky can say.

Browsing Music

The Music interface in the Zune section offers access to—you guessed it—all of the music content stored on the device. It provides a simple but elegant front end to this content using a series of pivoting lists, or sections, each of which seems to utilize a unique view style. These lists include:

▶ **Artists:** The Zune Artists list, shown in Figure 6-13, offers alphabetical access to the artists in your synced music.

This list provides the same shortcut ability that's found in the phone's contacts lists: To jump ahead alphabetically, you can scroll, of course, but that gets tedious for long lists. So as a shortcut, you can instead tap one of the highlighted letter boxes. Doing so displays the quick jump grid, which is a grid of letters (Figure 6-14); tap one of those letters to move further down the list. For example, let's say you want to enjoy some music by the artist U2. Sure, you could manually flick your way down to the Us. But instead, just tap "#" or "A" at the top of the list and then "U" in the quick jump grid. Voila! You're there.

FIGURE 6-13: The Artists list.

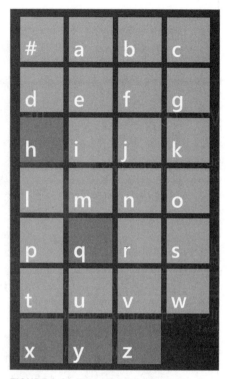

FIGURE 6-14: Thanks to this shortcut, you can quickly navigate through a long list of artists.

From the Artists list, you can do one of two things: If you tap the "Play" icon to the left of an artist's name, Zune will begin playing all of the music you have on the phone made by that artist. (I look at the Now Playing interface later on, however.)

Otherwise, you can tap an artist's name to drill in further. When you do so, Zune switches to a new view featuring that artist, which consists of several pivots: Albums, Songs, and Bio. Furthermore, for most artists, the background of the view will fill in with attractive imagery of that artist. This Artist view is shown in Figure 6-15.

Here, the Albums list consists of all of the albums you have by that artist and, at the bottom, a Marketplace link. If you click this, the albums list will expand to reveal albums by that artist that are available on Zune Marketplace. If you don't have a Zune Pass, you can listen to samples and buy albums and songs. But if you do have a Zune Pass, you can often stream entire albums and songs, over the air.

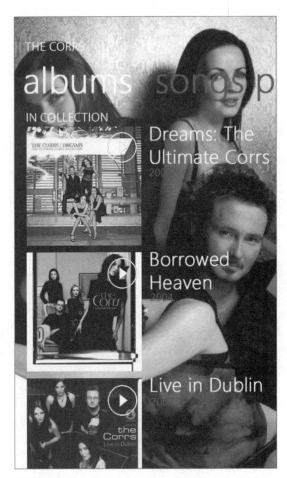

FIGURE 6-15: In Artist view, you can browse through albums and songs, read a bio, and enjoy nice artist imagery.

As before, you can tap the Play icon to play an individual album (it's on the album art this time), or tap an album name to see individual songs (and read a review, as described shortly).

The Songs list lists all of the songs by that artist that are on the device. As with the Albums list, a Marketplace link at the bottom of the list connects to the store online and adds Marketplace-based songs to the list as well. The usual caveats about Zune Pass apply here, too, of course.

The Bio section provides a detailed biography of the band, culled from online music experts. So you can read about a favorite band as you listen to their music.

▶ **Albums:** The Albums list (Figure 6-16) also uses a graphical presentation with album art thumbnails, and it provides the same shortcut, instant play, and drill-down possibilities as the Artists list. When you tap on an album name, you'll navigate to a new screen with Album and Review pivots.

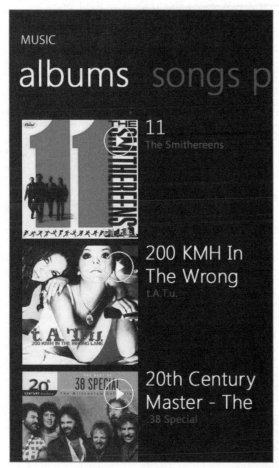

FIGURE 6-16: The Zune Albums list.

On the Album pivot is a Play control and list of the songs you have from that album. The Review tab provides a textual, web-based review of the currently selected album.

> **NOTE** If no review is available, the Review pivot will not appear in this interface.

- ► **Songs:** The Songs list looks somewhat like the Artists list, in that it's mostly text, but there is one important difference: There's no Play icon next to each song. Instead, when you tap a song name, that song simply starts playing, loading the Now Playing interface I'm going to discuss in just a moment. This makes sense because there's no way to drill down further than an individual song.

  The Songs list also provides the shortcut list navigation functionality and a handy "Shuffle All" button at the top to shuffle play the entire list.

- ► **Playlists:** Here, you'll see a list of the playlists (and Smart DJ lists) you've synced to the phone. You can either tap the Play button next to a playlist name to play that playlist, or tap the name itself to browse the songs within.

- ► **Genres:** This works similarly to the Playlists list. You can play an entire genre by tapping the Play button next to a genre, or tap the genre name itself to browse the songs in that genre.

Now Playing: The Music Playback Experience

Music playback is involved enough that it deserves a discussion of its own. There are various ways in which you can trigger playback, but they're generally pretty consis-

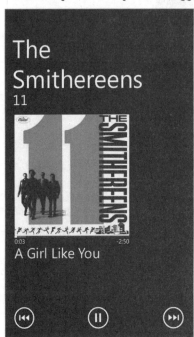

FIGURE 6-17: The Now Playing screen.

tent. In any of the views noted previously, if you tap the Play button next to an artist name, album name, song, playlist, channel, or genre, music will begin playing and you'll switch to the Now Playing view shown in Figure 6-17.

This screen is pretty straightforward, though there are a few gotchas. It provides obvious Previous, Pause/Play, and Forward buttons on the bottom of the screen, for example. But Previous and Forward will only work as expected if there's actually something else in what's called the Now Playing playlist (that is, the list of music that is playing right now). So if you tap the Play button next to an individual song, the Now Playing playlist is a list of one. So tapping Previous or Next will simply cause the same song to restart.

► If you are syncing Channels to the phone, you will see a separate Channels item on the Music pivot.

► If you have an online connection and the content is available on the Zune Marketplace, the Now Playing screen will also display animated artist imagery in the background.

ADDING MORE CONTENT TO THE NOW PLAYING PLAYLIST

To add more content to this Now Playing playlist, simply navigate back into the Zune interface—don't worry, the current song will continue playing—and find something else—an artist, album, song, playlist, genre, whatever—that you'd like to add to the Now Playing playlist. But instead of tapping it, or the Play button next to it, instead you will tap and hold on the item's name. In the pop-up menu that appears, choose Add to Now Playing.

LOOKING CLOSER AT NOW PLAYING OPTIONS

But wait, there's more to the Now Playing screen. Considering the content that's available onscreen, you'll see an artist name, an album title, some album art (or at least space for that album art), the song progress, and the name of the song. Many of those elements are actually interactive.

If you tap the artist name or album title, for example, Windows Phone will navigate to the artist page for the currently playing artist, allowing you to browse through the albums, songs, and bio for that artist.

If you tap the album art, three new controls will (temporarily) appear.

▶ The first is **Repeat**, which you can tap to toggle between on and off.

▶ The second, **Like**, determines your rating for the current song; you can tap this repeatedly to toggle it between the three possible states. (Changes are synced back to the PC.)

▶ The third control is **Shuffle**, which can be toggled between on and off; when on, the Now Playing list plays in a random order.

If you tap the song name, you will navigate to a plain text rendition of the Now Playing list. You can tap an individual song to jump immediately to that song if you'd like.

NOW PLAYING PERSISTENCE

The most interesting thing about music playback is that it's persistent. That is, you don't have to stick around in Music + Videos to listen to music. Instead, you can simply hop in, start some music playing, and then go off and do other things through the Windows Phone interface—browse the Internet, answer e-mail, whatever—and the music will simply keep playing.

Of course, you can still control the playback in different ways. And if you get a phone call while listening to music, the music playback will fade away and pause. When the call is complete, the music will start back up again.

▶ Oddly, you cannot clear the Now Playing playlist, or remove or rename individual songs. Instead, you simply start another selection—artist, album, or song—playing. That resets the Now Playing playlist to include only the newly selected song(s).

So say you've got a playlist going and you're reading e-mail. But for whatever reason, you want to control the music playback in some way. To do so, tap one of the volume buttons on your Windows Phone and the small volume control screen overlay shown in Figure 6-18 will appear, no matter where you are, including on the lock screen.

FIGURE 6-18: The playback overlay lets you control music playback no matter what you're doing.

From this simple interface, you can do a number of things. You can pause the currently playing song, switch to previous songs with the Previous button, or fast forward to upcoming songs in the playlist with the Next button. Using the hardware volume controls, you can lower and raise the volume. (Lower it to zero and it mutes.) You can also toggle the phone's ringer between normal and vibrate, though that doesn't affect music playback.

If you happen to navigate back to Music + Video while music is playing, the hub will actually come up in the History section (instead of Zune), where you'll see the large Now Playing button shown in Figure 6-19. If you tap this button, the full-screen Now Playing screen will appear.

Watching Video

The Zune Videos interface provides a simple front end to the video content you've synced from the PC and access to the even simpler Windows Phone media player. The interface is divided along the same pivots as is the Zune PC software's Videos collection, with separate sections for All, TV, Music (that is, music videos), Movies, Other, and Personal.

There aren't a lot of options here. You can scroll through the lists to find the video you want. If you tap the video, it will begin playing, full screen or nearly so, as shown in Figure 6-20. And you can tap and hold on individual items to pin them to the Start screen or delete them from the device. That's about it.

▶ Some, but not all, of these sections will not appear if there is no content of that type on the device.

FIGURE 6-19: This Now Playing button is read-only, but if you tap it, you'll be transported to the Now Playing screen.

FIGURE 6-20: Videos play full screen and offer no real playback options.

During playback, which occurs via the Windows Phone media player, you can tap the screen to bring up three controls, Rewind, Pause/Play, and Forward. You can tap and hold on Rewind and Forward to "scrub" backward and forward, respectively, through the currently playing video.

> **NOTE**   Unlike with music, video playback isn't persistent. If you're watching a video and tap Back or Start, or otherwise leave the playback screen, video playback still stops. The next time you watch a previously viewed video, you'll be given the option to resume from where you left off.

Enjoying Podcasts

The Zune Podcasts interface (Figure 6-21) is likewise simple, and divided into just two sections, one for audio podcasts and one for video podcasts. In either case, you can drill down into individual podcast episodes, play an entire podcast (where episodes play according to episode number), or play an individual podcast episode.

FIGURE 6-21: Zune Podcasts.

There are a couple of nuances with podcasts, however. Most professionally created podcasts provide some sort of descriptive text for each episode, and this text can be read by tapping on an episode name. Also, podcasts support a toggle called "Played/Not Played," which allows you to keep track of which episodes you've listened to (or watched), and which you have not. When you start listening to (or watching) a podcast episode, it's marked as played. If you'd like to change that, you can tap More and then Mark as Not Played (or Mark as Played) from the podcast episode's details page.

> **NOTE**   Audio podcasts, like music, are persistent, and will continue playing if you exit Music + Videos or even turn off the phone. Video podcasts, of course, are not persistent.

Listening to the Radio

The Zune Radio experience is pretty straightforward but comes with a few interesting twists. When you select Radio from the Zune section, you're presented with the simple radio interface shown in Figure 6-22.

This interface has just a few elements to consider. In the center of the screen is the virtual radio dial. To scan for in-range stations, just flick left or right in the center of the screen and the radio will seek the next available station. When it finds one, it will stop.

When you're tuned into a station, you will see information about the station name and, if the station provides RDS or RT+ signals, the currently playing song and artist name. You can press the Add button (which looks like a "+" sign and a star) in the top left of the screen to add the current station to your list of favorites. Additionally, a Pause button appears in the lower center of the screen; press this button to pause FM radio playback. Tap it again to resume playback.

There's also a Favorites button in the lower left of the screen. Tap this to bring up the list of saved favorite stations.

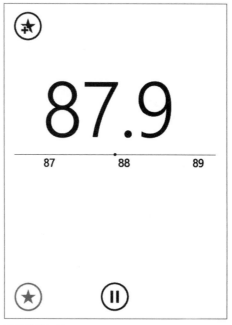

FIGURE 6-22: The Zune Radio experience.

That's right: The Zune Radio works like your television's DVR, allowing you to pause live radio and resume at a later time. Well, not too much later. But there's certainly enough buffer time to handle the stray phone call or whatever.

BUYING SONGS YOU HEAR ON THE RADIO

One of the coolest hidden features in the Zune software is that you can actually buy songs you hear on the radio. The key to this is that RDS and RT+ signal data I mentioned earlier; in order to purchase a song that is currently playing, the station must also be sending such a signal. (Furthermore, the song must be available on Zune Marketplace.) You'll know it's supported because a shopping cart button will appear in the lower right of the screen. To purchase the currently playing song, press this button and an "Added to current" notification will appear. To actually complete the purchase, visit the Zune Marketplace, as described in the next section. Your pending purchases will be available via the Cart item in the menu.

NOTE Radio broadcasts, like music and podcasts, are persistent, and will continue playing if you exit Music + Videos or turn off the phone.

While other media content plays through the device's speakers normally, and through a headset when one is plugged in, the radio can be manually switched between either speaker type. To do so, tap and hold in the center of the screen until a pop-up menu appears. Then, tap Radio Mode: Headset (or Radio Mode: Speakers) to switch the output.

Buying Content in the Marketplace

The Zune Marketplace is Microsoft's online store for digital music (purchase), music videos (purchase), TV shows (purchase and rent), movies (purchase and rent), and podcasts (free, and in audio and video forms). While the Zune Marketplace browsing experience is generally better on the PC using the Zune PC software, Microsoft does provide a basic interface to the Zune Marketplace on Windows Phone devices as well. This section quickly takes a look at both.

ZUNE MARKETPLACE ON THE PC

On the PC, the Zune Marketplace is accessed via the excellent Zune PC software. As you can see in Figure 6-23, this software provides a graphically rich way to discover new music, TV shows, movies, and other content.

FIGURE 6-23: Zune Marketplace offers some rich interfaces, like this artist landing page.

For the most part, purchasing content in Zune Marketplace on the PC is straight-forward. There are, however, a few things you should know about.

▶ **Microsoft Points.** Inexplicably, Microsoft doesn't typically price items in the Zune Marketplace using dollars or local currency (as they do on the device). Instead, the company forces you to use a micropayment system called Microsoft Points that has its own exchange rate. You can pre-purchase Microsoft Points in bundles of various amounts (where 400 Microsoft Points is $4.99 in the United States, 800 Microsoft Points is $9.99, 1600 Microsoft Points is $19.99, and 4000 Microsoft Points is $49.99). Or, if you don't have enough in your account to cover a purchase, you can buy them on the fly during your purchase.

> **NOTE** Microsoft Points are also used to make purchases in the Xbox Live Marketplace, Microsoft's online store for gamers. You can pre-purchase Points on the Web by visiting **xbox.com/en-US/live/microsoftpoints.htm**.

▶ **So what's the price? And can I buy or rent?** And speaking of issues with buy-ing content, Zune Marketplace often doesn't advertise the price of an item up front. This is particularly problematic with movies. Some movies are available for rent only. Some can be purchased or rented. And some movies can be pur-chased in High-Definition (HD) or standard definition (SD) formats. You won't know until you really dive in. And even then, you won't know what the price is until you click on the Buy or Rent button.

Incidentally, if you do choose the HD option on a purchased movie, you'll be provided with both HD and SD versions of the film. The SD version will be synced to your Windows Phone (if you ever choose to do such a thing), whereas the HD version will play on your PC (or, as you'll soon discover, to your HDTV with an Xbox 360).

▶ **Rental silliness.** When you attempt to rent a movie, you're presented with the bizarre screen shown in Figure 6-24, though your own experience might admittedly be less confusing if you have fewer compatible devices.

So what's going on here? Unlike with Apple's iTunes Store, when you rent a movie from Zune Marketplace, you must choose—at the time of rental—which device you will use to watch the movie. (Compatible devices include your PC, a Zune HD device, or a Windows Phone.) You cannot later change your mind, either: If you choose Windows Phone, you can't watch it on your PC. Why? I don't know. I just know that those are the rules.

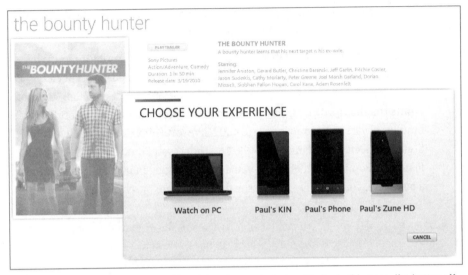

FIGURE 6-24: Zune Marketplace makes it hard to rent movies. Maybe in this case, I'm better off just skipping it.

ZUNE MARKETPLACE ON WINDOWS PHONE

Compared to its PC-based sibling, the version of Zune Marketplace that's available on Windows Phone is significantly detuned. In fact, I don't like it very much at all except for one significant improvement over its PC-based brethren.

The first issue is content. You can only browse music content from the device-based version of the Zune Marketplace, and not music videos, TV shows, movies, or podcasts. That seriously limits the usefulness of this service on the go, requiring Windows Phone users to spend quality time with their PCs if they want to find new content online.

Second, the interface feels a lot less expansive than the Marketplace experience on the PC. And it's not just onscreen real estate: The selection of available music content is just limited. On the PC, you can quickly browse channels, playlists, the top 100 songs, music videos, numerous genres, new releases, recommendations, top songs, top albums, and top playlists, all from a single, rich screen.

On Windows Phone, things are more cluttered and confined. The Zune Marketplace interface, shown in Figure 6-25, has separate sections, or columns, for the artist of the week, featured artists (in text list form), new album releases (with thumbnails), top albums (text), and genres. And that's it.

If you want to really drill down into Zune Marketplace on Windows Phone, you're going to need to search. And as you may have guessed by now, that means you just need to tap the phone's Search button to bring up the simple Marketplace Search interface shown in Figure 6-26.

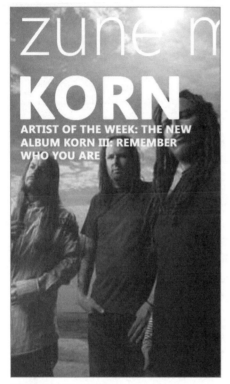

FIGURE 6-25: Zune Marketplace on Windows Phone.

FIGURE 6-26: Tap the phone's Search button and you can search Zune Marketplace for your favorite music.

Fortunately, the results lists are reasonably rich. But in its current v1 form, Zune Marketplace on Windows Phone isn't a great way to discover new music, unless you happen to enjoy the very small handful of artists that Microsoft features each week.

NOTE As noted previously, there *is* one very good thing about phone-based access to the Marketplace. Songs on the Windows Phone version of the Zune Marketplace are listed only in dollars (or your actual currency), rather than in Microsoft Points. Maybe they've seen the light.

> **NOTE** You may recall that different views in the Zune software on Windows Phone provide a Marketplace link at the bottom so that you can browse similar content in Microsoft's online store. Well, the search results lists and other views in Zune Marketplace take the opposite approach and provide a Collection link at the bottom so you can see similar items in your own collection. Cute!

WHY ZUNE IS DIFFERENT

Since introducing the Zune platform in 2006, Microsoft has always sought to differentiate itself from the competition—read: Apple, with its iPod players at first, and then, over time, iPhone as well—in various ways, all while copying key parts of their strategy as well. The results have been interesting, with some technical successes to Zune's credit. To date, however, Apple's i-ecosystem has outperformed Zune to an almost ludicrous degree in the marketplace.

For starters, Zune has always been about community, a place for music lovers to share their preferences with others, electronically, over the air, and on the Web. (The very first Zune players featured a way to wirelessly send, or "squirt," music to other Zune players, but this feature was dropped because there were so few Zune users, and thus no one to share with.)

In 2007, Microsoft debuted Zune 2, which started the Zune's now traditional excellence in PC software, and the Zune Social was born, extending the previous social features dramatically. Zune 3 added Channels (combining the best features of podcasts and playlists), Wi-Fi syncing and on-device store access, and more. And then with the Zune 4 platform, Microsoft introduced multi-touch on the Zune HD player and the beginnings of Xbox Live integration.

Today, the Zune platform is mature and achingly powerful, and as has always been the case, it offers some important advantages over the competition, especially Apple. In this section, I'll take a look at a few of the cooler advantages.

Over-the-Air Zune Pass

If you're a music lover, Zune Pass is a no-brainer, especially if you were going to purchase at least one CD's worth of music a month anyway. But some of the advantages of Zune Pass aren't particularly obvious, and that's especially true of Windows Phone.

Windows Phone is different from previous compatible devices (that is, Zune Media players) because it has a pervasive 3G wireless connection and can thus be connected to the Internet at almost any time. So anyone with a Windows Phone can browse and search the Zune Marketplace's music collection, over the air, and listen to 30-second samples of songs.

If you have a Zune Pass, it gets even better. When you browse and search the Marketplace, you can listen to entire songs, not just 30-second samples. In fact, you can also add Marketplace-based songs to the device's Now Playing list and build a streaming playlist as you move around, out in the world. To do so, just find a song in the Marketplace, tap and hold, and select Add to Now Playing from the pop-up menu that appears. Want to download the song to your device for offline listening? Choose Download instead.

Try that with an iPhone.

Wi-Fi Media Sync

While you must initially sync media between your Windows Phone and the PC via a USB cable, you can perform subsequent syncing, automatically, and wirelessly, via your home's Wi-Fi network. So anytime your phone connects to your home Wi-Fi network in the future, it will automatically and wirelessly stay up to date with the latest music, videos, podcasts, and other content that you wish to sync.

To configure this feature, connect your phone to the PC and sync normally. Then, in the Zune PC software, choose Settings, Phone, and then Wireless Sync. Then, just step through a short wizard that determines which Wi-Fi network will be used for automatic Wi-Fi media sync. It's that simple.

Again, try that with an iPhone.

> **NOTE** Here's how Wi-Fi sync works. If you, say, return home from a day out, the phone will automatically connect to your home wireless network (or whichever network you configured for Wi-Fi sync.) But it won't sync unless you plug it into electrical power. Ten minutes after you do *that*, Windows Phone will silently sync with the PC, over the air.

Always Available Video Purchases

When you purchase movie or TV content from the Zune Marketplace, Microsoft makes that content available to you from any Zune-compatible device in the future. These include the PC (via the Zune PC software), the Xbox 360 (which includes built-in Zune software solutions for videos and music), and portable devices like the Zune HD and Windows Phone. And these videos are available for either download or streaming. So you could conceivably purchase a movie on your PC, walk into the living room, fire up the Xbox 360, and then stream that movie, from Zune Marketplace, directly to your HDTV. And yes, if the movie is available in HD, it will stream in 1080p HD quality. In fact, this is an impressive feature, and one that Apple has yet to match.

You can see previously purchased video content that is available for streaming (or download) in the Zune PC software via the Purchased section of the Videos collection. As you can see in Figure 6-27, previously purchased content has a little Wi-Fi badge, indicating you can stream or download that selection.

FIGURE 6-27: Previously purchased content follows you from device to device so you can stream (or download) it later at any time.

NOTE While you can install the Zune PC software on any number of PCs, and log on with your Windows Live ID on each, only three of them can be configured to download previously purchased content, or download Zune Pass music. However, the other PCs can still *stream* previously purchased content and music from Zune Marketplace, including from the Web.

Likewise, you can have only three devices (Zunes and/or Windows Phone) connected with your Windows Live ID at a time.

If you want to change which PCs and devices are linked to your account, navigate to Settings, Account, Computers and Devices in the Zune PC software. Note that you can remove only one PC and one device from your account each month.

Zune Promiscuity

One of the best things about the Zune PC software is that it doesn't lock you into connecting your device to just a single PC, as does Apple's rigid iTunes software. Yes, you will typically configure a single PC to be linked with your Windows Phone for media sync purposes. But if you have multiple PCs, you can connect your Windows Phone to those PCs, as a guest, and copy content back and forth.

Read that one twice, because I know it's hard to believe. But it's true: You can use your Windows Phone as a conduit between two or more PCs, copying content back and forth between all of them, as long as you've logged on with your Windows Live ID on each.

Again: Try *that* with an iPhone. Actually, don't bother. It won't work.

THROWING APPLE A LITTLE LOVE

It's worth mentioning that the Apple i-ecosystem—including the iPhone, iPod, iPad, iTunes and iTunes Store, and so on—still has some important advantages over Zune as well. First and perhaps most important is content: While the Zune Marketplace is reasonably well-stocked, the iTunes Store makes the Microsoft offering look like a corner farm stand on a slow weekday by comparison, offering a wealth of music, movie, TV show, application, podcast, iTunes U (e-learning), audio- and e-book offerings, and more. Apple's products are also far more well-supported from a hardware accessory standpoint, with an army of compatible cables, docks, cases, headsets, power and sync adapters, speakers, and other devices, most of which are specifically designed only to work with Apple products.

So what's a poor Windows Phone user to do? Well, it's not all bad. We have access to a great collection of digital media via Zune Marketplace and of course a growing collection of Windows Phone–specific apps as well. We're free to purchase songs from Apple's iTunes Store (but not other content) and use that with our devices as well, since that content isn't digitally protected in any way (and is of high quality). And I think it's important to remember that Windows Phone has many other usability advantages beyond the Zune capabilities as well. Arguably, that's why we're here in the first place, right?

MORE MUSIC: PANDORA AND OTHER SERVICES

Before moving on, it's worth noting that the Zune software and services built into Windows Phone are, in many ways, just the beginning. In fact, Microsoft fully expects other companies to come along and build their own digital media applications and services right into Music + Videos. And when they do, these competing solutions will be able to offer the same level of integration that Zune does today.

What does this mean? Well, under the hood, the Zune software on Windows Phone is using standard Windows Phone media playback transports, codecs, and players to get the job done. So when you play a song or a video from Zune, or whatever, it's not a Zune player that appears, it's the Windows Phone player. And that player software is available to others as well. It's not just there for Zune.

This integration carries over to many of the bits described in this chapter. Third parties will be able to take advantage of the overlay player that appears on top of other Windows Phone experiences, allowing music playback (really, audio playback) to persist outside of Music + Videos. They'll also be able to hook into Zune Marketplace, providing users with a way to purchase songs they hear through other services.

The canonical example of this type of integration is the Pandora music service (pandora.com). Pandora is an online radio station, basically, available in free and paid versions, that builds dynamic playlists, called stations, which are based on your favorite artists or genre.

Users can access Pandora over the Web, of course, but the company behind this service has also built dedicated mobile clients for a number of smart phone platforms like the iPhone, Android, Windows Mobile, and more. And by the time you read this, hopefully, a version will be made available for Windows Phone as well.

Of course, Pandora is only one of what will likely be dozens of third-party music and video applications and services that will ship for Windows Phone in the year ahead. And unlike on other mobile platforms, the incredible hooks that Microsoft has built into Windows Phone generally, and Music + Videos specifically, will provide these services with the ability to create incredible, integrated experiences that just feel like part of Windows Phone.

> **NOTE** Another important distinction that will aid third-party media players is that they won't have to reinvent the wheel. All of the media playback available in Windows Phone occurs through a built-in system media player. Even the Zune interface uses this player, and not its own proprietary player. What's interesting about the system media player is that it is compatible with a number of digital rights management (DRM) systems, like WMDRM and PlayReady, only the first of which is Zune compatible. So services that use these technologies—Real Rhapsody, Amazon On Demand, and others—could very easily port their products to Windows Phone.

SUMMARY

Out of the box, Windows Phone offers a superior digital media experience that is unrivaled on other smart phone platforms. Thanks to the deep integration in the Music + Videos hub, the excellent Zune media capabilities, unique Windows Phone–only features such as over-the-air Zune Pass, Wi-Fi media sync, and more, and coming integration with a collection of third-party applications and services, Windows Phone is the obvious choice for music and video lovers.

Of course, the Microsoft platform does fall short in a few areas, key among them the vastness of the content that's available in Apple's iTunes Store. This is a gap Microsoft can hope to close over time, I suppose, though I don't expect that to realistically happen any time soon.

No matter. The rich media experiences in Windows Phone are, to my mind at least, a bigger advantage. This is one place where the innate advantages of Windows Phone really put Microsoft's smart phone platform over the top. It's a digital media revolution.

CHAPTER 7

Having Fun: Windows Phone and Games

From the earliest days of the video game industry, gamers have longed to take their games on the go. In the early 1980s, we were thrilled about hand-held Mattel football games that featured LED lights and noise-generated blips and beeps. In the late 1980s, Nintendo arrived with the first GameBoy, which featured a black and white screen. Subsequent generations of portable game machines culminated in today's popular Nintendo DS and Sony PSP units, while mobile warriors can be found playing Solitaire or Minesweeper on their PC-based laptops more often than crunching numbers in Excel.

In the smart phone world, Apple's creation of the App Store unleashed a new wave of mobile gaming based on the iPhone's touchscreen interface. While popular, iPhone gaming is also limited, both by the relatively paltry hardware that Apple provides and by a lack of cross-platform development capabilities. If developers want to port an iPhone game to a different smart phone, they're on their own: Apple specifically doesn't allow developers to create cross-platform games that run on the iPhone.

The result is a bifurcated market where only the very best and most well-funded titles are ever ported between the various mobile platforms. Fortunately, Microsoft has a solution, and it's one that will be attractive to mobile game and application developers alike, even before the software giant's hardware partners have sold a single Windows Phone. The strategy is simple: First, give Windows Phone the hardware prowess to become a killer gaming machine. And then, allow developers to write games that work not just on Windows Phone but also on Microsoft's best-selling Windows and Xbox 360 platforms as well. It's what we call a win-win.

WINDOWS PHONE: GREAT MOBILE GAMING PLATFORM

Looking over the minimum hardware specifications for Windows Phone, a suddenly obvious thought emerges: This thing looks like a killer mobile gaming device. And that's not a happy coincidence. When Microsoft decided that it would rein in the hardware diversification that doomed its previous mobile platform, Windows Mobile, it also decided to shoot for the moon. So Windows Phone devices all include some pretty serious hardware.

Here's what I'm talking about:

- A 1 GHz or faster microprocessor
- A DirectX 9-capable graphics processing unit, or GPU, for hardware-accelerated 3-D graphics
- At least 256MB of RAM and 8GB or more of Flash storage
- A capacitive touch-based display with four or more contact points and support for only two possible resolutions, 800 x 480 (WVGA, which will be far more common) and 480 x 320 (HWVGA)
- An accelerometer

Each of these components reads like the description of a dedicated gaming device. And every single one of these components is inside of your phone.

From a hardware perspective, then, Windows Phone is a great gaming platform. It provides the features developers want, but also a consistent target for developers since the hardware support is universal across devices. With Windows Mobile, there were so many processor architectures, so many CPU clock speeds, so many screen resolutions, and other differences, that making even a simple game run properly across devices was almost impossible. On Windows Phone, it's not just possible, it's easy, and since the basic hardware requirements are so high-end, developers won't need to cater to the lowest common denominator.

FIGURE 7-1: Some Windows Phones will include a hardware keyboard, but game developers can't count on that. Here are some of the hardware keyboard types Microsoft supports.

It gets better. Developers will be able to more easily port existing PC and Xbox 360 games to Windows Phone. They'll be able to write games that work on all three systems. And they'll even be able to write certain classes of games where gamers can compete against each other from different platforms. In the beginning, this interaction will occur only between Windows Phone and Windows-based PCs. But it will be extended to the Xbox 360 over time.

▶ Missing of course, is a hardware keyboard, which could prove useful for games. Some Windows Phone devices will ship with hardware keyboards like the one shown in Figure 7-1. But since developers can't count on that hardware, most games will simply assume it's not present.

THE CROSS-PLATFORM GAMING FUTURE

Don't misunderstand what this means: Windows Phone–based gamers won't be fragging PC-based gamers in *Call of Duty XXIV* anytime soon. While it is theoretically possible for developers to create games in which Windows Phone gamers and Windows PC–based gamers can compete together in real time, this won't be common, at least not in the near future. Instead, the first generation of these cross-platform games will be turn-based games, such as *Battleship*, *Checkers*, or *Backgammon*. In such a game, a Windows Phone–based player could make a move from this device. And then, later on, a Windows-based competitor could make her own move, on the PC.

Another possible—but, again, unlikely—scenario involves splitting play between two of the possible platforms. Perhaps you're competing in the single player campaign of a shooter on your Windows Phone while commuting home from work. (Obviously, not while driving.) When you arrive at home, you settle down in front of your PC, boot up the PC-based version of the same game, and pick up where you left off on the phone.

Finally, Microsoft (and, presumably, third parties) have also created Windows Phone games (and other experiences) that complement bigger, console-based games. For example, a *Halo Waypoint* app on Windows Phone will provide *Halo* fans with all of the up-the-minute *Halo* information they want, even though they can't (yet?) play an actual Halo game on the phone. And fans of the *Crackdown* series of Xbox 360 games will probably enjoy *Crackdown 2: Project Sunburst*, a Windows Phone–specific game that is a companion, of sorts, to the console titles. It doesn't look or play like the *Crackdown* games on the 360, but it takes advantage of unique phone features—like Bing Maps—to let gamers keep active in one of their favorite game environments.

Getting excited yet?

The key to this gaming interaction between Windows Phone, Windows, and the Xbox 360 is an evolving software stack that is present in Windows Phone, on Windows PCs, and on the Xbox 360 console. It includes three key pieces:

▶ **Silverlight:** Essentially an application framework and runtime environment based on Microsoft's .NET managed code libraries, Silverlight is also the basis for the Windows Phone OS. So when developers create Windows Phone applications, they do so in Silverlight. And many games, especially casual games, will be written within this environment as well. Some portability exists between Windows Phone apps and the Silverlight environment Microsoft has created for Windows and the Web.

▶ **XNA:** The most advanced and capable Windows Phone games will be written with the XNA technologies, which include a framework and runtime environment, also based on .NET but optimized for 2-D and 3-D gaming, and an integrated development tool called XNA Game Studio. XNA games can target Windows Phone, Windows, and Xbox 360 (as well as the Zune HD), and developers can target Windows Phone, Windows, and Zune HD for free. XNA makes things easier on developers by providing a single development environment. So they can easily reuse code, even entire game engines, between the platforms, or even port the same games between the supported platforms.

▶ **Xbox Live:** Microsoft's amazing online game service for the Xbox 360 provides a wide range of functionality for gamers, including (but not limited to) multiplayer gaming with matchmaking, in-game achievements with gamer points, friends lists, in-game and extra-game communications capabilities, leaderboards, and much more. It works with certain Windows-based games through the awkwardly named Games for Windows - LIVE, and now it works with Windows Phone as well.

Looking at games on Windows Phone, there are basically two types of games; those that are part of Xbox Live and those that are not. And while it may be convenient to think of Xbox Live titles as being more professional, that's a bit of a stretch. I think of it more like this: Anyone can write a game for Windows Phone, and those games can be as sophisticated (or not) as the developer wishes. But those games that wish to take advantage of features like achievements and leaderboards will need to be part of Xbox Live. And to become part of Microsoft's curated, tightly controlled online service, there are some hoops to jump through. Generally speaking, the world's biggest developers will be using Xbox Live features while individual developers will not. But that's just a generality.

Xbox Live is so important to the Windows Phone game experience that I'm going to take a side trip now to show you what's going on with this exciting online service. Then I'll have you to take a look at which parts of Xbox Live are available on Windows Phone, and jump from there into the Games hub, which is the central location for all of your gaming activities on the phone.

UNDERSTANDING XBOX LIVE

Xbox Live—or "Xbox LIVE" as Microsoft likes to write it—began in 2002 as a feature of the original (pre-360) Xbox console. Back in the early days, it was essentially a vehicle for *Halo* and *Halo 2* multiplayer gaming, and indeed many of the core features we now associate with Xbox Live came out of Microsoft's experiences with those early Halo games.

The modern Xbox Live service came to life in 2005 with the launch of the Xbox 360. (And if you're familiar with Games for Windows - LIVE, you know that this service essentially delivers an almost complete Xbox Live experience on Microsoft's dominant PC platform as well.) At this time, Microsoft greatly enhanced Xbox Live, offering the core capabilities and experiences that Xbox 360 gamers still enjoy today.

Microsoft also offers two types of Xbox Live accounts, a free Silver account type and a paid Gold account type. Xbox Live Gold members pay about $50 a year for the privilege, and they represent a little over half the subscriber base. (And with almost 30 million people using Xbox Live every day, that's some serious money changing hands each year.)

Of course, Xbox Live Gold subscribers must get something for their troubles. Microsoft rewards its paying customers with some unique features, most of which fall into two neat categories: Multiplayer online games (the Xbox 360's traditional hard-core audience) and forward-leaning multimedia and social networking features (one potential future for the Xbox 360).

On the gameplay side, Xbox Live Gold subscribers get online multiplayer gaming, party and party chat functionality, and video chat capabilities. But they also get access, on the Xbox 360 console, to Netflix movie streaming (which requires a Netflix subscription), Sky Player (UK only), Facebook and Twitter access, Last.FM Internet music streaming, Zune music and video access, and more.

When you sign up with Xbox Live, you must create an Xbox Live account. What this really means is that you're creating a Windows Live ID, because Xbox Live—like Windows Live, Zune, and other Microsoft services—simply uses the same underlying identification service. So at the time of sign-up, you can use your own e-mail account, no matter where it's from, and Xbox Live will turn that e-mail address into a Windows Live ID. Or, if you already have a Windows Live ID, through Hotmail, MSN, or wherever, you can simply use your existing account. I discussed the need to properly manage a Windows Live ID in Chapter 1, so for purposes of this discussion, I will assume that you've done so and are using this same account for gaming purposes.

NOTE You can only have one "primary" Windows Live ID on Windows Phone, and this account will be used for contacts and calendar sync, feeds (in the People hub and in the Pictures hub), marketplace access (Zune, Apps, and Games), and, yes, for Xbox Live access via the Games hub, as I describe in this chapter.

Xbox Live Accounts

Each Xbox Live account consists of the following general features:

▶ **Gamertag:** This is your identity, or name, on Xbox Live, and it maps to the name you've established for your Windows Live ID. If you're not happy with this name, you can change it, but Microsoft charges $10 in order to prevent kids from constantly changing their names.

NOTE I have three Windows Live IDs that are associated with Xbox Live Gamertags. My most frequently used account is simply Paul Thurrott and this particular name is tied to my original Hotmail account. But I also have a Paul B Thurrott gamertag, associated with my primary Windows Live account, and now a WinPhone Paul gamertag that I created for testing purposes while writing this book. Don't do this to yourself: Create and maintain a single Windows Live ID and gamertag, and nurture it forward through the years.

▶ **Gamer Zone:** This item describes what type of gamer you are and can be set to Recreation, Pro, Family, or Underground.

▶ **Gamer Picture:** This is a small, usually simple picture that represents you online (Figure 7-2). Xbox Live Silver gamers have one Gamer Picture, which is shown to all users, while Xbox Live Gold gamers can have two, one for friends and one for the general populace. If you have a video camera add-on for the Xbox 360 console, you can use that to take a still photo of yourself as a gamer picture, but only for friends to see.

▶ **Motto:** This is a 21-character textual representation of who you are and what you stand for. I've used such bon mots as "The end is listless" and "Pwned."

▶ **Avatar:** Beginning in 2009, Microsoft added another graphical representation of your Xbox Live account, this one in the form of a cartoon-like character called an Avatar. Based largely on the Nintendo Wii's similar "Mii" characters, an avatar can be designed to look (somewhat) like you. A typical avatar is shown in Figure 7-3.

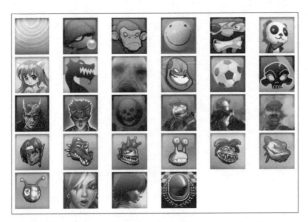

FIGURE 7-2: Gamer Pictures are like low-resolution icons and are usually pretty generic.

FIGURE 7-3: Avatars are far more animated than gamer pictures and can be more representative of what you really look like.

▶ **Name:** Your real name or, alternatively, a nickname.

▶ **Bio:** A text box with up to 499 characters.

▶ **Location:** Really just a text field with up to 40 characters of explanation.

▶ **Privacy Settings:** You have fine-grained control over various privacy settings, including those related to voice and text, camera, profile, online status, video status, friends list, game history, member content, Xbox marketing, and partner marketing.

▶ **Profile:** Your Xbox Live profile consists of the Gamertag, Gamer Zone, Gamer Picture, Motto, Avatar, Name, Bio, Location, and privacy settings information described previously.

▶ **Rep:** This is your reputation score, on a scale from one to five. Every Xbox Live member starts at three and your rep can go up or down from there based on your experience (the more you play, the higher the rep) and whether any other gamers complain about you online (the more you misbehave, the more people complain, and the more your rep declines).

▶ **Gamerscore:** Each Xbox Live game can assign Gamer Points to individual achievements, as I'll soon discuss. These points are applied to your Gamerscore, which starts at zero. The higher your Gamerscore, the more experienced you are, generally speaking, though many hard-core gamers only play in multiplayer matches that don't provide multiplayer achievements and thus might have deceptively low Gamerscores. Likewise, those with higher Gamerscores could be "Achievement point whores," as we call them, or even cheaters.

▶ **Gamercard:** Your Xbox Live Gamercard (Figure 7-4) combines your Gamertag, Gamer Picture, Rep, Gamerscore, and Gamer Zone into a single, easily viewable overview of your Xbox Live account, or gamer persona.

TIP If you are a particularly active Xbox Live member, you may want to share your online accomplishments with the world. One way you can do this is to embed a graphical representation of your Gamercard in a web page or blog. Microsoft explains how to do so at **xbox.com/myxbox/embedgamercard.htm**.

▶ **Messages:** Using an email-like system, Xbox Live members can message each other using text, audio, and video chat. These messages aren't ever broadcast via normal e-mail systems (via the e-mail associated with your Windows Live ID), but you can view and respond to them on the Xbox 360 and, for text messages, via the Zune PC software as well.

▶ You can optionally enable Windows Live Messenger integration as well, allowing you to chat in real time with friends on the PC.

▶ **Friends list:** As with Facebook and other social networking services, you can "friend" other people online, send and receive friend requests, see what your friends are doing online in real time, send messages to friends, and more. The Xbox Live Friends list is sorted by online status, so that online friends are listed first.

▶ **Players list:** Xbox Live also tracks the players you've most recently played against so you can find them again later and request a rematch, send feedback (positive or negative), or send a friend request.

▶ **Games list:** Xbox Live also tracks the games you've most recently played, as well as the achievements you've most recently earned, including all of the achievements earned in each played game. Friends can examine your account to see which games you've played, and which achievements you've earned, and compare them to their own results.

If there's a problem with Xbox Live accounts—and there is—it's that much of the profile and Gamercard-type information can only be edited, at this time, from an Xbox 360 console. So even though you can log on to xboxlive.com from any web browser, you can only view your Xbox Live account information, not edit much of it. What this mean to you is simple: If you're new to Xbox Live, maybe joined because of Windows Phone, and don't even have an Xbox 360 console, your account is going to look pretty weak.

▶ Microsoft tells me that on-phone Xbox Live account editing will be possible, probably by the time you read this.

FIGURE 7-4: An Xbox Live Gamercard.

Consider Figure 7-5. Here, you can see a newly created Xbox Live account with a blank avatar, no friends, and so on. There's not a lot you can do to make this thing look any better unless you get an Xbox 360. Hopefully that will change over time.

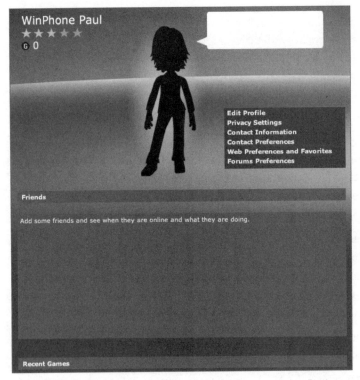

FIGURE 7-5: That's one bleak looking account you've got there, Paul.

A more experienced Xbox Live account is shown in Figure 7-6.

Games and Achievements

One of the best reasons to join Xbox Live, and this is as true on Windows Phone as it was previously on the Xbox 360 console (and, to a lesser extent, on Windows PCs, with Games for Windows - LIVE), is the games. Sure, Xbox Live offers some multimedia and social networking functionality on the console, but the real reason for this service is to get people together so they can compete against each other online.

These online competitions take two general forms. That is, you can compete implicitly with your friends and others by trying to rack up higher overall Gamerscores, by completing single player games, and single player achievements, before others do, and so on. You can also compete explicitly with others via online multiplayer games. On the

Xbox 360, the most common of these games are online shooters, such as those in the *Call of Duty*, *Gears of War*, and *Halo* series. But there are many other wildly popular online game types on Xbox Live as well.

FIGURE 7-6: This account has been around since before the Xbox 360.

If you are at all competitive, you'll be immediately drawn to Xbox Live's achievements system. On the Xbox 360 console, each game is generally given up to 1000 achievement points to dole out, typically via any number of individual achievements. When you do trigger an achievement—perhaps by completing an in-game level or other task, the console pops up the ever-popular Achievement Unlocked message (Figure 7-7), which provides the name of the achievement. You can tap a button on the Xbox 360 console to learn more, including how many achievement points you've earned and the description of the achievement. You can also view your overall Gamerscore to see how the achievement points affected things.

On the Xbox 360, different types of games can award different total achievement points. Most retail games provide up to 1000 achievement points, as noted previously.

FIGURE 7-7: The single greatest notification you can get on the Xbox 360.

(This is true for retail Games for Windows - LIVE games as well.) Xbox Live Arcade titles, which are downloaded to the console from the Xbox Live Marketplace and are generally smaller and less complicated than full retail titles, can provide up to 200 achievement points. Additionally, each game type can assign additional achievement points via downloadable (usually paid) content, like level add-ons. So a retail game can add up to 250 more achievement points, per quarter, via add-ons. And an Xbox Live Arcade game can add up to 50 more achievements points, but can do so only once.

Xbox Live games also support a feature called leaderboards, which are ranked lists that are relevant to the individual game. In a shooter like *Call of Duty*, for example, there are leaderboard lists for most overall points, most overall victories, most victories per game type, and so on.

XBOX LIVE ON WINDOWS PHONE: NOT THE FULL MEAL DEAL

Xbox Live is a pretty stunning service. And Windows Phone is the first smart phone—indeed the first mobile device of any kind—powerful enough to accommodate such a service. But Microsoft is only providing access to a select set of Xbox Live features on the phone, and not the complete set you get on the Xbox 360.

There are many reasons for this, including the fact that many non-gaming Xbox Live features on the Xbox 360 are already present in other ways on Windows Phone. Part of it is pragmatic: While it's possible that Microsoft will increase the number of Xbox Live features that are available on Windows Phone over time, you have to start somewhere, and Windows Phone certainly provides a decent subset of the gaming-oriented Xbox Live features found on the console (and on Windows).

The following Xbox Live features are available on Windows Phone:

▶ **Gamertag**, including your profile information: Name, Gamerscore, and Gamer Picture. As you know, your phone connects to you via your Windows Live ID, which links to your Gamertag.

On an Xbox 360, you can have up to four profiles logged on at one time for split-screen multiplayer game purposes. For what I assume are obvious reasons, Windows Phone supports just one profile.

▶ **Avatar:** You (and Windows Phone games) can access the avatar that is associated with your account, though it's a static still image, not an animated 3-D object as it is on the Xbox 360.

> **NOTE** Microsoft says it intends to enable support for the animated, 3-D version of the avatar on Windows Phone in the future.

▶ **Friends list:** For game invites and game comparisons.

▶ **Achievements:** Windows Phone games can provide up to 200 achievement points per game title, spread out over 5 to 20 awards per game. Each achievement has an associated award name, description, and a picture. Note that these are real achievements in that they will show up on the Xbox 360 and on Windows alongside your console- and PC-based achievements.

▶ **Leaderboards:** Like their console-based brethren, Xbox Live games on Windows Phone can support in-game leaderboards, so you can compete with friends, compare scores, and so on. For games that run on both Windows Phone and other supported platforms, the Windows Phone leaderboard is a separate entity (that is, it is specific to the phone version of the game).

▶ **Trial mode:** Unique to Windows Phone, Xbox Live games can offer a trial mode where the user downloads the entire full game for free, but certain features—like levels—are locked by the developer. From within the game, the user can choose to unlock the full version of the game, and pay for it, without leaving the game.

> **NOTE** As I indicated, trial mode is unique to Xbox Live games. More important, perhaps, a game must offer trial mode in order to utilize Xbox Live on Windows Phone.

▶ **Game invites:** These are actually handled through the Mail application on the phone, but they're viewed, and responded to, from within the Games hub, described shortly. You can choose recipients for invites via the same People hub-based contact picker that is used throughout Windows Phone.

USING THE GAMES HUB

On Windows Phone, the Games hub is the center for all of your on-device gaming activities and the place you will visit to play games, examine your Xbox Live profile and achievements, view and send game invites, buy and try new games, learn more about new games and gaming-related events, and more. Shown in Figure 7-8, the Games hub is representative of the panoramic experiences in Windows Phone, offering a sweeping, multiscreen interface that pans from left to right.

FIGURE 7-8: The Games hub.

There are four basic sections, or columns, in the Games hub: Collection, Spotlight, Xbox Live, and Requests. I will examine each of these now, but as a reminder, you can play two different types of games on Windows Phone: Xbox Live games and non-Xbox Live games. Both types of games are accessed through the Games hub, but they're presented a bit differently in the Collections view, and are advertised a bit differently in the Games Marketplace.

Collection

When you first access the Games hub, you're presented with the Collection view, shown in Figure 7-9.

From this interface, you can browse through all of the games you've downloaded and installed on the phone and, toward the bottom of the list, also a select few games that Microsoft is promoting. Games are ordered with the most recently played titles first, and if you have both Xbox Live and non-Live games, they will simply be intermingled here.

▶ *Much of the content in the Games hub relies on web-based information. So if it's out of date, or you just want to check if there are newer updates, simply tap and hold anywhere in the Games hub. Then choose Refresh from the pop-up menu that appears.*

That said, Xbox Live games are prominently differentiated with an Xbox Live banner as shown in Figure 7-10. (These games offer additional capabilities over other, non-Live games, as I discuss elsewhere in the chapter.)

FIGURE 7-9: The Collection view.

FIGURE 7-10: Xbox Live games are obviously differentiated from non-Live titles.

Under an Other Games segment in this section, Microsoft advertises current game promotions in the Games Marketplace. You can also tap the Get More Games link to visit the Games Marketplace and browse from there. (The Games Marketplace experience is described later in this chapter.)

To start a game, simply tap its thumbnail.

Spotlight

In the Spotlight view, Microsoft provides a feed-like list of news items related to Xbox Live. These include tips about games, advertisements for new games, and other related information (Figure 7-11).

When you tap on an individual item in the Spotlight view, Internet Explorer launches so you can find out more (Figure 7-12).

Spotlight can also be used to notify you about software updates for the games you've already purchased. These updates will also be noted when you visit the Windows Phone Marketplace.

FIGURE 7-11: Spotlight view.

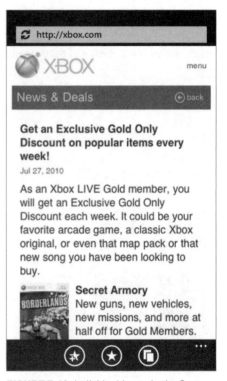

FIGURE 7-12: Individual items in the Spot-light feed are viewed online, via IE.

Xbox Live

In this section, you'll find some basic information from your Xbox Live account, including your avatar, Gamertag, Name, Gamerscore, and the last achievement you acquired. Because Xbox Live is cross-platform, that achievement could come from any of the supported platforms, Xbox 360, Windows, or Windows Phone. The Xbox Live section is shown in Figure 7-13.

Many of the items on this screen are links to web-based content. You can tap your avatar, Gamertag/*name*/Gamerscore, or most recent achievement to find out more.

Remember that Windows Phone supports only a subset of the overall Xbox Live features or, as Microsoft describes it, the Xbox Live features that make sense on the phone. (These functional differences were described earlier in the chapter.)

One of the obvious differences is the avatar: On the Xbox 360 console, your avatar is quite animated, and if you leave him alone onscreen, he'll bound around in amusing ways. On Windows Phone, for now at least, the avatar is decidedly less animated. In fact, he's a static PNG image.

NOTE You can find my avatar's static image at `avatar.xboxlive.com/avatar/Paul%20B%20Thurrott/avatar-body.png`. To find yours, simply replace my Gamertag (`Paul%20B%20Thurrott`) with your own, using the %20 characters to replace any space that may be in your own Gamertag.

Requests

Game requests utilize the same onscreen overlay as incoming phone calls, messages, and voicemails, and they can interrupt you when you're doing something else on the phone, giving you the opportunity to drop what you're doing and pick up a game. If you choose to ignore such notifications, or are simply away from the phone when they arrive, these pending game invitations and other request-related notifications are delivered into the Game hub. You can view them from the Requests section (Figure 7-14).

FIGURE 7-13: Your avatar and other gamer info in the Xbox Live view.

FIGURE 7-14: Requests.

There are three possible request types you can find here:

▶ **Invitation:** When someone asks you to join them in a game online, an invitation is generated.

▶ **Your Turn:** Windows Phone provides support for asynchronous, turn-based games such as Backgammon, Scrabble, and so on. In such games, the two players take turns in isolation and then alert each other that it's their turn through this interface. This is a neat idea, and it makes even very casual game experiences a social experience you can have, over time, with other people.

▶ **Nudge:** If someone hasn't gotten a response from you in a while, they can send a nudge, which is like a gentle reminder that they're still waiting on you.

FIGURE 7-15: The Games live tile will display a badge when you have new requests.

▶ Note that the Games hub live tile can be branded with a number badge, indicating the number of missed notifications. So if you have two pending requests, you'll see a number two in the live tile badge, as shown in Figure 7-15.

PLAYING A GAME

To play a game at any time, tap its thumbnail in the collection view.

Games are, of course, unique experiences. Some will work only in the portrait view that is standard for most productivity games while others—likely most games, over time—will run only in landscape view. A typical 3-D action game is shown in Figure 7-16.

Most games will rely on the device's touch screen to provide a virtual control scheme, and these controls will vary from game to game. If the game offers a way to invite other gamers into the game, or send similar requests, that functionality, too, must be implemented by the game maker and so will vary from title to title as well.

While playing a game, you can be interrupted by notifications for phone calls, voicemails, and text messages, using the standard slide-down notification overlay, or toast, that's used elsewhere in the system. So this works in a manner with which you are likely already familiar.

The most eagerly anticipated interruption, of course, is the achievement, which can be provided in Xbox Live–compatible games. Achievement notifications work just like other Windows Phone notifications, using a toast overlay like that shown in Figure 7-17. You can tap this overlay to pause the game and learn more about the achievement.

FIGURE 7-16: If the Xbox 360 is any guide, 3-D shooters will be common on Windows Phone.

FIGURE 7-17: An in-game achievement.

FINDING MORE GAMES IN THE MARKETPLACE

If you're interested in browsing through the selection of available games for download—free, trial, and paid titles are available—you need to access the Windows Phone Marketplace. This is available on the phone, and via the Zune PC software. I describe the Zune PC software experience in Chapter 16, so I want to take a look at the on-device experience here.

The third Marketplace entry point on the phone is in the Zune area of the Music + Videos hub. But that link provides access only to music content, not apps or games.

On Windows Phone, there are two main entry points for the Marketplace if you're looking for games. You can use the dedicated Marketplace application in All Programs. Or you can side load the Marketplace's App experience through the Games hub. Just tap the Get More Games link at the bottom of the Collection view.

The Games area on the Marketplace (Figure 7-18) is an ever-evolving collection of game titles, divided into common areas such as Featured, Top, New, Free, and so on, as well as a list of game genres and all games. Remember, too, that you can search from within the marketplace at any time by tapping the phone's Search button.

As with other apps on the Marketplace, each game will be presented on its own page with various tidbits of information, including the name, developer, price, description, screenshots, rating, reviews, and links to related games (Figure 7-19). You can share the game—via e-mail or messaging—buy it, and, if available, try it. You can even leave your own rating and review if you'd like.

FIGURE 7-18: The Games marketplace.

FIGURE 7-19: A specific game page.

SUMMARY

Thanks to its stellar minimum hardware specifications, which include a powerful CPU, GPU, and an advanced display, Windows Phone has the chops to compete with the top mobile gaming platforms out there. But this hardware would be wasted if there wasn't software to take advantage of it, and here Windows Phone has an even bigger lead over the competition, with impressive tools and technologies for developers and a cross-platform strategy that the iPhone and Android can never match.

Put this together with the online game–related services backing Windows Phone—Xbox Live and the Windows Phone Marketplace—and you can see that Microsoft's new mobile offering is going to make a serious dent in the gaming world. This deep integration with Microsoft's proven and popular services means that gamers can enjoy the achievements, friend lists, game requests, and other popular Xbox Live features while on the go. And with a coming generation of games, they'll even be able to play turn-based games with players on Windows PCs and Xbox 360 consoles.

There are many excellent reasons to choose Windows Phone over the competition. But mobile gaming is clearly among the best.

CHAPTER 8

Browsing the Web

If Apple's iPhone has established anything, it's that mobile users will no longer tolerate second-rate web browsers in smart phones. And that means delivering the "full" Web in addition to the mobile Web, and doing so in a way that works well given the limits of the smart phone form factor.

It seems simple enough, but it wasn't always that way. And with the recent proliferation of devices with rich mobile web browsers, web site owners have responded by targeting these devices with a new class of web application specifically tailored to the small screens. In many ways, the mobile web application market is almost as dynamic as that for native mobile applications. And unlike those applications, web apps don't have to be rewritten for each smart phone OS, so they're easier to deploy and maintain.

Microsoft's solution for this market, as it is on the PC desktop, is called Internet Explorer. Loosely based on a version of the Windows web browser that shipped a few years back, Internet Explorer for Windows Phone offers all the basic web browsing features you expect, plus some deep integration with other Windows Phone–only functionality.

A (SHORT) HISTORY OF THE MOBILE WEB

Mobile web browsers—those web browsers designed specifically for mobile, non-PC devices—have existed for virtually as long as their traditional, PC-based brethren. But until very recently, they were notably horrible, offering a vastly different browsing experience than what we expected and received on the PC.

Microsoft was a pioneer in the market for mobile browsers and thus must shoulder much of the blame for this situation. Because of the limitations of its early Windows CE incarnations, mobile versions of Internet Explorer on CE, Pocket PC, and Windows Mobile were designed primarily to access specially designed mobile web sites instead of the "full" Web. Unfortunately, the small market for these devices led to only a small selection of mobile-aware web sites. So users of such systems were forced to navigate the full Web using a little portal with rudimentary display capabilities. The results were unsatisfactory at best.

Over the years, Microsoft and other browser makers did update their mobile products on a fairly reasonable schedule. But mobile browsers always lagged behind the desktop products, technologically, in some cases by years. And because web site owners did little to customize their sites for the tiny PDAs and smart phones of the day, the gap between the full Web and the mobile Web only grew bigger.

There was some innovation, of course. Various third-party browser makers, notably Opera, tried to provide mobile users with a more desktop-like user experience. But these products were often fairly expensive at a time when desktop browsers were free. And few customers seemed interested in paying for such software.

And then the iPhone happened. When Apple announced the iPhone in 2007, it promised (among other things) to provide users with a full-featured mobile web browser called Safari that was based on its desktop Safari browser for both Mac OS X and Windows. And this wouldn't be a terribly scaled down version of Safari, either: Instead, the iPhone version of the browser would render web pages almost exactly like the desktop version.

▶ Safari for iPhone doesn't support Adobe Flash or Sun Java, two popular but unreliable and performance adverse web technologies; the jury is still out on whether this was brilliant or misguided.

Though Safari was somewhat flawed at first, it was dramatically better than any other mobile browser to date. (In fact, in many ways it's still the one to beat.) But where Safari really succeeded was in two key areas.

▶ First, its popularity forced web site makers to finally start designing their sites to work properly on small, highly mobile devices like smart phones.

▶ Second, because Safari for iPhone used the same basic rendering engine as the desktop Safari, it was the first to actually render the full Web correctly on a smart phone. This opened up a whole new world to mobile users.

This latter bit was aided by some Safari features we now take for granted on smart phones. You could double-tap on web site areas (such as paragraphs, text columns, or pictures) to automatically zoom to that place onscreen. It supported pinch zoom gestures and flick-based scrolling. It supported both portrait and landscape viewing modes, so you could turn the phone in space to view the current web page in a different orientation. All of these functions now work similarly—heck, just about identically—on Windows Phone (and on virtually all other modern mobile browsers).

The version of Internet Explorer found in Windows Phone is a small improvement over the previous generation Internet Explorer Mobile products, which appeared in Windows Mobile 6.5 and the Zune HD. So if you're familiar with those browsers, or with Safari on iPhone, you'll find Internet Explorer for Windows Phone to be at least passingly similar.

DIFFERENCES IN MOBILE IE VERSIONS

There are differences, of course. Speaking broadly, Internet Explorer for Windows Phone is more full-featured than IE for Zune, with features such as Find On Page, picture saving and sharing, and others that weren't available on Microsoft's portable media player.

Oddly, IE for Windows Mobile 6.5 has a number of useful features that were dropped for Windows Phone, including methods for switching between mobile and desktop rendering modes on the fly, text sizing, copy and paste, and so on. That's because Internet Explorer, like much of Windows Phone, has been vastly simplified by design. IE does provide some basic sharing functionality, as you'll see, but it's not very good for recording or storing data for later use elsewhere, with a few exceptions.

The key to Internet Explorer for Windows Phone, I think, is that it provides an iPhone-like browsing experience with all of the multi-touch functionality people expect from modern mobile web browsers. As you'll see in a bit, it does fall short in a few key areas. But this browser displays the "full" Web quite well, and thanks to its advanced text rendering and some other modern technologies, it looks good while doing so.

USING INTERNET EXPLORER ON WINDOWS PHONE

If you're familiar with other mobile browsers, such as Safari on iPhone or the Google Android Browser, you'll be right at home in Internet Explorer for Windows Phone. Shown in Figure 8-1, this browser looks and works much like the competition, offering up standard UI components such as an Address Bar and an Application Bar stocked with a few useful, browsing-related features.

FIGURE 8-1: Internet Explorer on Windows Phone.

> **TIP** Internet Explorer is found on the default Windows Phone Start screen. If you don't see it, however, you can find it in More Programs by tapping the right arrow in the upper right of the Start screen. To add Internet Explorer to the Start screen, press and hold on the Internet Explorer item in More Programs. In the pop-up that appears, select Pin to Start.

Navigating on the Mobile Web

Page navigation in Internet Explorer works much as it does in PC-based web browsers, albeit with full support for multi-touch and finger swipe gestures. You can perform the following basic navigational actions:

- ▶ **Page scrolling and zoom:** Within a web page, scrolling and zooming works like it does elsewhere in Windows Phone. You can flick the screen up or down to scroll through a page, and you can pinch and double-tap to zoom (and un-zoom).

- ▶ **Manual navigation:** You can tap the Address Bar to enter a web page URL manually using a pop-up virtual keyboard (Figure 8-2). When you tap return, the web page will start loading.

  As you type in the Address Bar, a pop-down list will appear with suggested web sites. These sites will be suggested based on what you're typing. So if you start typing **www.goo**, Internet Explorer will suggest sites like *google.com*.

> **NOTE** When you load (or reload) a web page in Internet Explorer, the browser displays a very subtle page loading animation. You can see this if you look closely at the Address Bar: A tiny progress bar will move across the top; it is colored to match the accent color of your Windows Phone theme (so it's blue by default).

You can also perform limited editing to an existing URL in the Address Bar. This can be handy if you want to just change some of the URL but not delete the whole thing and start over. To edit the URL, tap the Address Bar once. This selects the entire URL, as shown in Figure 8-3, providing a handy way to type over it and start over from scratch.

If you don't want to start over, tap the Address Bar again. This places a thin vertical cursor at the place you tapped. (Roughly speaking; your big gorilla fingers don't exactly offer laser-like precision.) This can be seen—barely—in Figure 8-4.

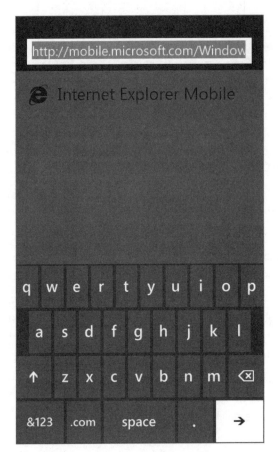

FIGURE 8-2: Like desktop browsers, Internet Explorer provides an Address Bar for manually navigating to specific web pages.

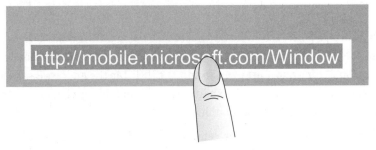

FIGURE 8-3: Tap a URL once to select all of it.

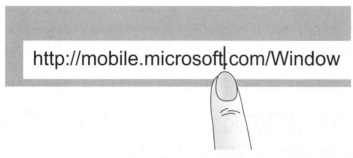

FIGURE 8-4: Tap again to display a cursor.

To move the cursor to a new location, press and hold in the Address Bar. As you do so, you'll notice a new I-beam cursor appears above the Address Bar (Figure 8-5), so you can see its position more clearly as you move left and right through the Address Bar. It's located above the Address Bar because your finger is blocking this control as you press down. So move your finger down on the screen, and the i-beam cursor will move into the Address Bar so you can position it precisely.

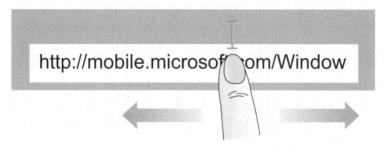

FIGURE 8-5: As you move the cursor, a green selection I-beam cursor appears.

When this I-beam cursor is visible, you can drag the cursor around the Address Bar with your finger and place it where you want. Let go of the screen, and the I-beam cursor appears to fade into the main cursor. You can then use the onscreen keyboard to add text, or delete text, at the cursor's current location.

> **WARNING** What you can't do, alas, is select just *parts* of the text, as you can in desktop OSes like Windows, and in other mobile systems like the iPhone or Android. (As a result, you also cannot cut, copy, or paste text from within the Address Bar, or from anywhere else in IE for that matter.) This limitation is a maturity issue: As a brand-new mobile platform, Windows Phone hits the high points, but it sometimes falls flat on some expected functionality.

▶ **Landscape mode:** Like some other Windows Phone applications, Internet Explorer works in both the default portrait display mode and when rotated into landscape mode. You may prefer this landscape view because it provides more horizontal space and can render some full-sized web sites in a more legible fashion, as shown in Figure 8-6.

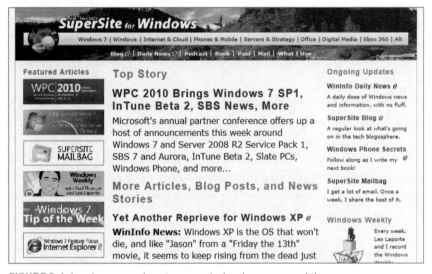

FIGURE 8-6: Landscape mode puts more pixels where you need them.

> **WARNING** The problem with landscape mode, however, is that you lose the onscreen controls, including the Address Bar and Application Bar. So in a sense, it emulates the full-screen mode in desktop versions of IE. But it also hides functionality that you may want. You'll have to switch back to Portrait mode to access these features.

▶ **Refresh and Stop:** You can refresh the current web page by tapping the Refresh button in the Address Bar. While the page is loading, the Refresh button turns into a Stop button that you can alternatively tap to prevent a page from loading.

▶ **Back:** To navigate back to the previously visited web site—and really, you're going to love this one—you actually tap the hardware Back button on the Windows Phone. That's right, there's no Back button in IE; you use the phone's button instead.

▶ Notice anything missing? That's right. Internet Explorer has no concept of a homepage. The very first time you run the browser, it will simply display an empty page. Subsequently it will launch and display the last page you viewed.

▶ **Forward:** To navigate forward to a web site you previously visited but then "backed" away from, you need to access the Forward command, which is hidden in the More menu. (On desktop browsers, the Forward button is prominently displayed on the main toolbar next to the Back button.) The Forward item is grayed out if this functionality is not currently available, but it's still visible in the menu.

SECURE SURFING

As you're browsing around the Web, you may notice a small lock icon that appears in the Address Bar. This indicates that the current web page is a *secure* web site that is certified by an Internet trust organization. This works similarly to desktop browsers, and while it's remotely possible that a malicious web site could somehow spoof the browser into believing the site is safe, for the most part you can trust such sites.

▶ **Save passwords:** Like PC-based web browsers, Internet Explorer can automatically save passwords for sites that require you to log on. In fact, this is the default behavior. (You can visit IE Settings to change this.)

WARNING One temporary limitation of Internet Explorer for Windows Phone is that it does not ship with support for Adobe Flash, a popular if somewhat controversial web application environment that is particularly common on online game and video sites. Adobe says it will create a version of Flash for Windows Phone, and by the time you read this, maybe it has.

Searching the Web

One of the most common activities people do on the Web is search for information using a search engine like Google or Bing. With Windows Phone, you have two options here. You can use the integrated Bing search feature, which is tied to the Search hardware button on the front of your phone. Or you can manually visit a search engine web site in Internet Explorer—like google.com—and search from there. There's no search engine built into IE per se—Bing is built into Windows Phone, instead—and there's no way to change the "default" search engine in the browser, because there isn't one.

CROSSREF If you're interested in discovering how web search—and other types of search—work with Windows Phone, please check out Chapter 9, which covers the integrated Bing functionality.

Finding Text on the Current Page

After searching via a search engine of some kind, there's oftentimes a second step that many don't consider, or least forget about. That is, once you get a list of search results and navigate to one of the pages it recommends, you're confronted with a long article with lots of text. And in order to find what you're looking for within that page, you have to search yet again.

There are other reasons why you might want to search for information within a web page, but no matter: The end result is the same, and this activity is probably even more common on the mobile Web because the small size of the displays makes it more ponderous to scroll through long articles of text.

Fortunately, Internet Explorer provides a handy way to search for text on the currently displayed web page. And as with the desktop versions of Internet Explorer, this feature is called Find On Page.

To enable Find On Page, tap the More button and then tap Find On Page from the pop-up menu that appears. The Find On Page interface, shown in Figure 8-7, is simple enough, with a text box and virtual keyboard. To find text on the page, just type the text for which you want to search.

Find On Page does not find text as you type. But once you've tapped Return, the text box and virtual keyboard disappear, and Find On Page provides some new commands. The first text that matches your search criteria is highlighted in green, as shown in Figure 8-8 (though this screen shot isn't in color), and you can navigate between matching text using a pair of Previous and Next buttons at the bottom of the screen.

To navigate to the next matching text, tap Next. You'll notice as you go that the current item is highlighted in green while other entries are highlighted in yellow. Obviously, you can tap Previous to navigate backward through the list of found items.

To exit Find On Page, tap the Back button.

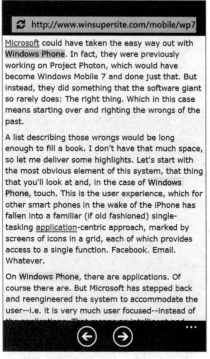

FIGURE 8-7: With Find On Page, you can find text in the current web page.

FIGURE 8-8: Find On Page highlights found terms and lets you navigate between each instance.

Working with Favorites

Like other web browsers, Internet Explorer supports the notion of bookmarks, which are locally stored shortcuts to web page addresses, or URLs (Uniform Resource Locators). But Microsoft doesn't use the term bookmarks for some reason. Instead, it calls these shortcuts *Favorites*.

Regardless of the name, I assume you're familiar with the concept. And on Windows Phone, Internet Explorer provides two prominent Application Bar buttons related to Favorites. This suggests to me, at least, that Microsoft believes Favorites to be as important in the mobile space as they are on the PC desktop.

ADDING A FAVORITE SITE

The first of these buttons, Add, is the leftmost button on IE's Application Bar. Tapping this button will display the Add Favorite screen, shown in Figure 8-9, which lets you add the currently-viewed web page to your Favorites list.

Simply rename the Favorite (if required) and tap OK to save it.

VIEWING FAVORITES (AND HISTORY TOO)

To access lists of stored favorite web sites and recently visited sites, tap the Favorites Application Bar button, which is the second (star-shaped) button from the left. IE then displays the awkwardly named Favorites Center, which can be seen in Figure 8-10.

FIGURE 8-9: You can add frequently used web pages to your Favorites list.

FIGURE 8-10: IE's Favorites Center.

NOTE I know you're dying to learn why this is called Favorites Center and not just Favorites. There are two reasons. First, it is modeled after the Favorites Center in the desktop version of IE. And second, like those desktop-based versions, Favorites Center doesn't just store your Favorites. It's also the place you go, illogically, to view your web browser history.

From the Favorites list, or section, you can tap any item to navigate to that web site.

TIP You can pivot over to the History list to access previously-visited web pages; just scroll through the list and tap the one you want. You can also delete your entire browsing histo ry—but not individual items—by tapping the Delete (trashcan) button, which is shown in Figure 8-11. IE will ask you to confirm this decision.

There's actually another way to delete your browser history by navigating to Internet Explorer Settings. I take a look at this interface later in the chapter.

MANAGING FAVORITES

To edit or delete an individual Favorite, tap and hold on its name. After a few seconds, a context menu will appear, as shown in Figure 8-12. From this menu, you can edit the item—change the name and/or URL—or delete it.

WARNING Note that Internet Explorer will not ask you to confirm your decision when you tap delete, so be careful with this.

FIGURE 8-11: You can view (and delete) your list of recently accessed web pages from the History list.

FIGURE 8-12: And they said right-click wasn't possible with a finger press.

> **TIP** Because the Windows Phone screen isn't that spacious, you may want to delete some of the preset Favorites that Microsoft and, possibly, your phone maker or wireless carrier have spuriously added to this list. Do you really need quick access to the MSN web site? Probably not.

Pinning Web Sites to the Start Screen

It's possible to pin shortcuts to many items, not just applications, to the Windows Phone Start screen. Among these items are individual web pages, as it turns out. And using a simple interface in Internet Explorer, you can easily access the sites you use the most from the convenience of your device's Start screen.

> **NOTE** Note that these pinned shortcuts bear no relation to the browser's stored list of Favorites. Web sites pinned to the Start screen are not automatically placed in the Favorites list, nor are favorite web pages automatically pinned to your Start screen. These two things are completely separate.

To pin a web page to the Start screen, navigate to that page using Internet Explorer. Then, tap the More Application Bar button and tap Pin to Start, as shown in Figure 8-13.

IE will close and the Start screen will appear, with a new live tile representing the web page you just saved at the bottom of the screen (Figure 8-14). The tile utilizes a thumbnail representation of the underlying web page, with no descriptive text.

From here, you can perform a few actions to this live tile. First, press and hold on the live tile. As you do so, the Start screen enters edit mode. In this mode, the other live tiles on the screen appear to shrink a bit, and a new Unpin badge appears in the upper right of the live tile, as shown in Figure 8-15.

To delete, or unpin, the live tile, tap the Unpin badge. The live icon is immediately removed, with no warning, and the Start screen exits edit mode.

To reposition the live tile, simply drag it to whatever location you prefer. The other live tiles will reposition themselves when necessary to accommodate the new arrangement.

> **TIP** You can select other live tiles while in edit mode, and you may need to do this to move the tiles around as you prefer. As you select a live tile, it becomes full-sized and adopts the Unpin badge.

It would be nice if you could edit the live tile in some way either by providing descriptive text or by selecting a different icon or graphical representation for the underlying web page. Unfortunately it's not possible to do either.

FIGURE 8-13: From the More menu, you pin the current web page to the Start screen.

FIGURE 8-14: A frequently accessed web page is added to the Start screen.

FIGURE 8-15: In edit mode, the selected live tile adopts an Unpin badge.

To exit edit mode, tap an empty area on the Start screen or tap the Back button.

Once a web site is pinned on the Start screen, you can tap that live tile at any time to navigate immediately to that page using Internet Explorer. That is, the tile works like any other live tile, but instead of just launching IE, it also navigates to the proper page.

Sharing Web Sites

In addition to saving Favorites and pinning frequently accessed web sites to your Start screen, you can also share useful web sites with others. To do so, navigate to the page you'd like to share and then tap the More button on the Internet Explorer Application Bar and then Share Page. When you do so, the Share page appears, as shown in Figure 8-16.

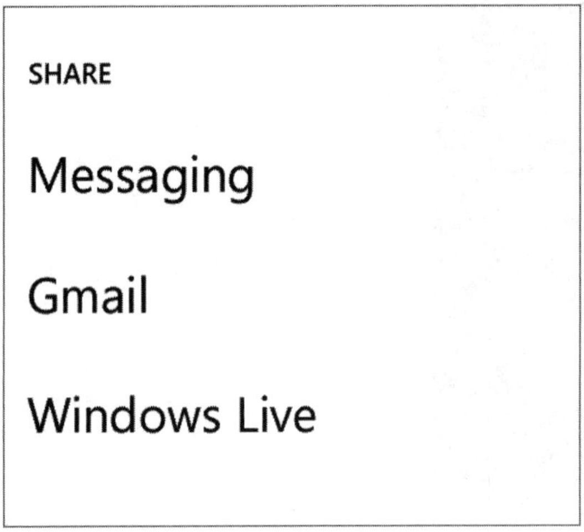

SHARE

Messaging

Gmail

Windows Live

FIGURE 8-16: IE makes it easy to share useful web pages with others.

> **TIP** Note that the list of sharing possibilities you will see here depends on which services and accounts you've configured for use with Windows Phone. You will always see a Messaging option—for sharing over SMS, or text messaging—but the other options, Windows Live, Outlook, and so on will appear only when you've set up the appropriate accounts.

Tap the account with which you'd like to share the page.

If you select Messaging, the Messaging application opens with the To field selected and the virtual keyboard visible, as shown in Figure 8-17. The name of the web page and a clickable URL are provided in a prepared text message. From here, you can start typing the name of a contact, and Windows Phone will auto-fill names from your address book as you type. (Alternatively, you can tap the Choose a Contact button, which looks like a + sign, to manually choose a contact from a list.)

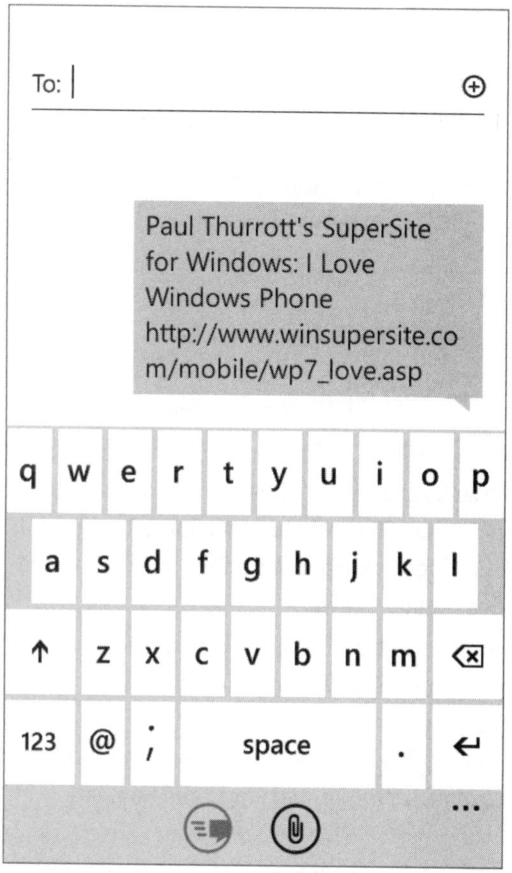

To: | ⊕

Paul Thurrott's SuperSite
for Windows: I Love
Windows Phone
http://www.winsupersite.co
m/mobile/wp7_love.asp

| q | w | e | r | t | y | u | i | o | p |

| a | s | d | f | g | h | j | k | l |

↑ z x c v b n m ⌫

123 @ ; space . ↵

FIGURE 8-17: Sharing a web page with Messaging.

Tap the Send button to send the text message and share the useful web page.

If you select an email-type account such as Windows Live, Gmail, or Exchange, Windows Phone will open a new e-mail message with the To line highlighted so you can add a contact name or address. The subject line is automatically filled out with the name of the web site. And the body includes a URL to the web site so that the recipient can visit the site for themselves. You can, of course, edit the e-mail as you see fit.

▶ *You can also type a phone number into the To field if you'd like.*

If you tap the Back button, you will exit the e-mail interface and the message will not be saved (or sent).

Working with Tabs

As a power mobile user, you're going to want to work with multiple web pages at the same time. On desktop-based web browsers, you typically do so with multiple browser windows and multiple tabs within those windows. Browser tabs allow a single web browser window to contain multiple web pages, and instead of switching between windows, you switch between these pages inside of the single window. A typical example of web browser tabs can be seen in Figure 8-18.

FIGURE 8-18: Browser tabs in the desktop version of Internet Explorer.

The version of Internet Explorer in Windows Phone is powerful, but it must work within the constrained screen size dictated by the device's form factor. It must also work within the confines of the Windows Phone OS. So this browser doesn't support multiple windows, because Windows Phone doesn't support free-floating windows as do desktop versions of Windows. But it does support tabs.

Windows Phone's IE handles tabs a bit differently, however. That is, Internet Explorer doesn't provide a row of tabs at the top of the display, allowing you to select an individual web page at a glance and tap it to select. The reasons for this are pragmatic: Such a row would occupy too much valuable onscreen real estate, and if the user added more tabs, it would be hard to identify individual pages and navigate through those tabs.

To get around the form factor limitations, Internet Explorer instead provides a Tabs button in the Application Bar. (It's the third button over from the left.)

> **TIP** If you have two or more tabs open, the Tabs button provides an in-place count of the number of open tabs. So if there are two browser tabs open, there will be a small number 2 on the button. If you have three tabs open, the number will be 3, and so on. (No number appears if only one tab is open.)

When you tap this button, the Tabs display appears, as seen in Figure 8-19.

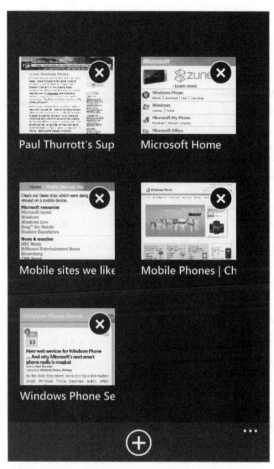

FIGURE 8-19: The Tabs interface makes it easy to navigate between open browser pages.

This interface provides a grid of icons, each representing open browser tabs. Each icon provides two ways for you to identify the underlying web page, including a thumbnail representation of the page and the page's title, in text, below the icon. (Or, at least part of it. Longer web page names get cut off.)

To add a new browser tab, tap the Add (+) Application Bar button at the bottom of the screen. IE will open a new browser tab and an empty page will appear in the browser. From here, you can navigate to a new page by typing an address manually in the Address Bar or by selecting a Favorite.

To display a different tab, simply tap the appropriate icon in the Tabs display. IE will switch to that tab immediately.

> ▶ You can open up to six different browser tabs at a time, no more. When six tabs are open, the Add button in the Tabs display will be grayed out.

To delete a tab, tap the Close badge (X) in the upper-right corner of the appropriate icon. IE will close that tab without warning—so be careful when tapping—and rearrange the remaining icons accordingly.

> **TIP** If you enter the Tabs display by mistake, you can also use the Back button to simply return to the page you were viewing.

Copying and Sharing Pictures from the Web

While Windows Phone doesn't really offer much in the way of text selection and copy and paste, it does provide a way to save and share pictures you find on the Web. Both of these operations are started in the same way: Once you've found a picture you like, simply press and hold on that picture. As you can see in Figure 8-20, a pop-up menu will appear with two choices, Save Picture and Share.

▶ **Save Picture:** This choice lets you save the selected picture to the Windows Phone. Pictures saved in this fashion are stored in a folder called Saved Pictures, which can be found in the Pictures hub (covered in Chapter 5). Navigate to Pictures, All, and then Saved Pictures to find your saved pictures, as shown in Figure 8-21.

▶ **Share:** This option brings up the familiar Share interface discussed earlier in the chapter, allowing you to share the picture via (MMS) Messaging, e-mail, or another configured account. No surprises here.

Downloading and Viewing Files

Windows Phone offers only limited support for downloading and saving files to your device. And it's important to understand that this capability exists only between the phone and the cloud (Web). There's no way to copy a file from your device directly to a PC, for example, or to copy files in the reverse direction, from the PC to the phone. So you'll always need to use the Web as an intermediary for most file types.

The big exception, of course, is photos. As noted previously in this chapter, you can save web-based files to the phone through Internet Explorer. You can then copy them to your PC using the Zune PC software, and I explain this process in Chapter 6.

FIGURE 8-20: Getting pictures off the Web is actually pretty straightforward.

FIGURE 8-21: Pictures saved from the Web are stored on the device and made available through the Pictures hub as you'd expect.

But what about other file types? Here are some common file types, and how they interact with (or, don't interact with) Windows Phone when they're accessed on the Web via Internet Explorer.

▶ **Office documents:** When clicked, Word documents, Excel spreadsheets, and PowerPoint presentations are opened in the appropriate Office Mobile application. They are not, however, automatically saved to the device. So if you want a local copy of the document, you'll need to choose More and then Save As from within the application. You can find out more about the Office Mobile apps and how Windows Phone interacts with online documents in Chapter 12.

▶ **PDF:** Windows Phone cannot view or download files in Adobe's popular PDF format. It's possible that Adobe will deliver a version of its Reader app for Windows Phone or otherwise supply this compatibility. But out of the box, you'll see a message like that in Figure 8-22 if you attempt to open a PDF file.

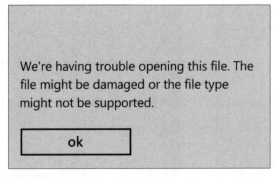

FIGURE 8-22: Unfortunately, Windows Phone cannot view PDF files (yet).

▶ **Text:** If you click a text file link in Internet Explorer, it will display directly in the browser. You cannot download these files to the phone.

▶ **Audio/video:** If you tap on a Windows Media Video (WMV), Windows Media Audio (WMA), MP3, or other supported audio or video file type, it will load and then play. You can find out more about Windows Phone's support for audio and video formats in Chapter 6.

▶ **ZIP:** Amazingly, Windows Phone can natively open ZIP files and provide access to their contents. So if a ZIP file contains file types with which Windows Phone is compatible, the device will act accordingly. For example, you could download Office documents and view and edit them later in the appropriate Office Mobile application. Windows Phone ZIP support is shown in Figure 8-23.

▶ **EXE:** Windows Phone doesn't know how to handle an EXE (executable) file. These files are typically found in desktop versions of Windows and can be used to transmit viruses and other malware. This will never be an issue on Windows Phone.

CONFIGURING INTERNET EXPLORER

Like most Windows Phone apps, Internet Explorer offers a Settings interface where you can configure various browser features. You can access this interface in two ways. First, you can display the More menu in the application itself and then tap Settings. Or, you can navigate to Settings, Applications, and then Internet Explorer in the Windows Phone UI. Either way, you'll arrive at the screen shown in Figure 8-24.

FIGURE 8-23: Windows Phone can open standard ZIP files.

FIGURE 8-24: From here, you can configure a number of features related to Internet Explorer.

The following options are available:

► **Allow cookies on my phone:** Checked (and thus enabled) by default, this option allows web sites to store bits of information about you locally so that your experience on the web site is more refined. One typical use for this functionality involves saving session information so you don't need to manually log on every time you revisit the same site.

> **NOTE** More sophisticated browsers—including all desktop browsers, but also Apple's iPhone—draw a distinction between cookies that originate on the web sites you visit and those that originate on other web sites. Why is this important? You may be okay with the *New York Times* knowing about what you do on their web site, but you may not be okay with advertisers on that site saving information about your browsing habits; that latter case is what cookies that originate on other web sites covers. It'd be nice to have a choice.

▶ **Let Bing suggest sites as I type:** By default, Internet Explorer will suggest web sites as you type in the Address Bar. This option can be disabled if you find that behavior annoying or unhelpful.

▶ **Website preference:** Internet Explorer can work in two basic display modes, Mobile (the default) and Desktop. In Mobile mode, IE will automatically load the mobile version of a site you visit, when available. But if you select Desktop, you can bypass the mobile version and access the "full" version. This can be desirable with certain web sites, such as when the mobile version doesn't provide access to content you want to view.

▶ **Delete history:** This button can delete all temporary files, browsing history, cookies, and saved passwords from the phone.

▶ **Privacy statement:** Click this, and IE will navigate to the current version of Microsoft's privacy statement on the Web.

▶ What this option doesn't provide is a way to individually delete just the temporary files, the browsing history, the cookies, or the saved passwords. It's all or nothing.

MISSING FEATURES

There are a number of common web features Internet Explorer doesn't support. Thanks to the built-in Bing search functionality—discussed in Chapter 9—there's no notion of a search engine in the browser, and thus you cannot switch search engines. There are no visible anti-fraud controls, no way to disable technologies such as ActiveX or JavaScript, no support for RSS feeds, and no pop-up blocking controls.

SUMMARY

Like other modern smart phone platforms, Windows Phone offers a way to experience the Web on the go via a web browser that can access both mobile and full-featured web sites. While it's not as powerful as Apple's Safari, Internet Explorer does at least hit the high points, with a decent rendering engine, tabs, Favorites, Find On Page, and other basic functionality.

Internet Explorer is also an excellent Windows Phone citizen, with multi-touch, gesture, and landscape viewing support; deep integration with the Bing service; its ability to easily share web resources across multiple services; and even photo and document viewing and saving capabilities. You can even pin individual web pages to your Home screen, providing a way to access them quickly and easily every time you turn on your device.

Ultimately, Internet Explorer is just one way in which you'll access web-based services. And as you'll discover in the next chapter, some of Windows Phone's most integrated web experiences actually come via more dedicated applications, such as Bing.

CHAPTER 9

Searching on the Go with Bing

IN THIS CHAPTER

▶ Understanding and using Bing and Windows Phone search

▶ Searching the Web

▶ Searching for news and images

▶ Using Bing maps, finding local resources, and getting directions

▶ Shopping online

▶ Getting instant answers

One of the nice things about a smart phone like Windows Phone is that you'll always have it with you when you're out and about. And since Windows Phone is always connected, thanks to its 3G networking and Wi-Fi capabilities, and aware of its own location, because of the integrated GPS hardware, that means you can use it to find things nearby. This is useful in a number of situations, such as when you want to find a good local restaurant or movie times for the local theater.

Microsoft considers search so central and so important to Windows Phone that every one of these devices must have a Search button right on the front. And while this Search button works in a variety of situations and in different applications throughout Windows Phone, it is also always connected to the Bing app and, via networking connectivity, to the Bing online search service. Bing, of course, is Microsoft's search platform, and its inclusion on Windows Phone is both useful and welcome.

Indeed, in a world where the term *search* has become somewhat synonymous with *Google*, you may be surprised to discover how superior Bing can be, and how well it works when integrated as deeply as it is in Windows Phone. Bing is there when you want to search for local resources, and perform traditional Web, news, and image searches. But it's also there when you want to search your phone's contacts list, your call history, or even your OneNote notes. It's not just an app on the phone. It's a deeply integrated experience. And in this chapter, you're going to find out all about it.

BING: A DIFFERENT WAY TO SEARCH

On other smart phones, search is handled differently depending on where you are in the user interface. For example, Apple's iPhone supplies on-device searching via a dedicated search screen that can be found to the left of the default home screen. This utility can be used to search data repositories on the phone, such as the contacts list, iPod content, e-mail, or calendar items. If you want to search the Web, however, you must first start the Safari web browser and then access its search box. If you need to search for a destination or travel route, you must first start Maps. None of these search experiences work similarly, and each is located in a different place. You, as the user, are oddly required to know which app to use in which situation.

With Windows Phone, Microsoft provides a different way to search. It's called Bing, after the software giant's web-based search engine, and it's not just different, it's also *better*. And that's true for a number of reasons.

▶ **Bing is always available.** Thanks to a dedicated hardware Search button found on the front of all Windows Phones, you always know where to go.

▶ **Bing is consistent.** The Bing search experience works similarly—often identically—no matter where you are in the user interface. You don't have to learn different interfaces in different applications. (That said, there are some differences from app to app, as I will note later in this chapter.)

▶ **Bing is integrated.** You can tap that Search button no matter where you are, and you'll be searching within the context of the task you're trying to accomplish. And well-written third-party applications—that is, those not written by Microsoft—can utilize Bing for their own search functions.

▶ **Bing is connected.** Thanks to its hooks to the Bing online service, you can change the focus of a search at any time. That means that you can redirect a news search about Apple (the company) to a local search, so you can find the local Apple Store. (And, I presume, boycott it.) Or buy apples locally. Or get a recipe for apple pie. The possibilities are endless.

One (Search) Button to Rule Them All

As noted earlier, every Windows Phone has a dedicated Search button as shown in Figure 9-1. And, generally speaking, each time you tap this button, which is found on the bottom right of the front of your device, the Bing search experience will load.

Search button

FIGURE 9-1: Every Windows Phone has a Search button.

What's interesting is that the Windows Phone Search button works a bit differently depending on where you are in the UI when you tap the button. In the vast majority of Windows Phone experiences, tapping this button simply launches Bing. This is true of such applications and hubs as Messaging, Calendar, Internet Explorer, Xbox Live, Pictures, Music + Video, Office, and Me.

But in other experiences, the behavior is a bit different. If you are using the Phone application, or the People hub, and tap the Search button, an integrated search experience opens on top of the application, allowing you to search the underlying contacts database.

Tap the Search button in Mail, and an integrated search experience appears on top of the app, letting you search through the various mailboxes associated with the currently used account.

Maps and Marketplace work similarly, with the Windows Phone integrated search experience opening on top of the app.

Microsoft Office works a bit uniquely. In most cases, tapping Search will launch the Bing app. But Excel, OneNote, and Word also provide in-app Find functionality so you can find text within spreadsheets, notes, and word processing documents, respectively.

In cases where an application provides an in-app search or find experience, you can learn more about that behavior in the appropriate chapter in this book.

Understanding the Bing Interface

The first time you launch the Bing application, you'll see the prompt shown in Figure 9-2.

It's very important, in this case, that you tap the Allow button. The reason being that Bing can really only do its thing when it knows where you are. Under the hood, Bing is accessing your phone's GPS through Windows Phone's location services to determine your location, since many of the results it provides refer to local resources.

When you get past this prompt, and when you launch Bing in the future, you'll arrive at a screen similar to that in Figure 9-3. As you can see, Bing provides a very pretty and picturesque background image, and it changes every single day.

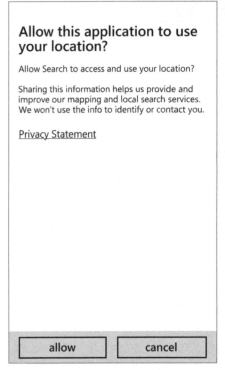

FIGURE 9-2: Bing wants to know where you are. To work properly, it *needs* to know where you are.

FIGURE 9-3: The Bing app prominently features the Bing image of the day.

NOTE The image you see in Bing on Windows Phone is the same image you'll see on the Web if you browse to `bing.com`. These beautiful pictures have proven to be so popular with users that Microsoft has released several Bing wallpaper themes for desktop versions of Windows, and many sites have cropped up to archive the images. One of the best can be found at `istartedsomething.com/bingimages`.

Of course, the Bing app is more than just pretty pictures. You'll find the following onscreen objects in the app as well:

▶ **Search bar:** At the top of the Bing app is a prominent search bar. Bing will try to ascertain the context of your search automatically and display results according to the appropriate category (Web, Local, or News).

> **TIP** As you type a search query in the Bing search bar, suggested searches will auto-complete, as shown in Figure 9-4. This can save a lot of time, especially when Bing autodetects what you're typing.

FIGURE 9-4: Bing provides search suggestions as you type.

▶ **Voice search:** Because every Windows Phone comes with a microphone—it *is* a phone after all—Bing allows you to alternatively search by voice instead of by typing text. Just tap the Voice search icon, which resembles a microphone and can be found to the right of the search box. Voice search looks and works like the phone-wide voice command functionality in Windows Phone, as shown in Figure 9-5.

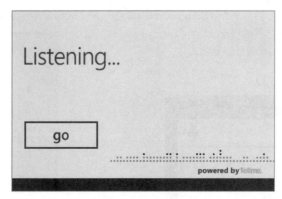

FIGURE 9-5: Search by speaking into your phone . . . What a concept.

▶ **Image callouts:** If you look closely at the Bing picture of the day, you will see small, square callout boxes here and there onscreen. (They appear a few seconds after the Bing app loads.) These boxes provide more information about the underlying image. To find out more, tap one of the boxes and you'll see an informational pop-up appear, as shown in Figure 9-6.

NOTE Each of these pop-ups is also secretly a link. So you can tap the callout text to find out even more detailed information about the underlying picture on the Web. The callouts act as a set of clues about the picture, and if you're still not sure about what you're looking at, or the inspiration behind the picture, click the callout text to find out more.

▶ **Picture origin:** There's also a secret area on the screen which you can tap to find out the origin for today's Bing picture of the day. To see this information, just tap the lower right corner of the screen. Bing will provide a pop-up that shows the title of the picture and to which photo archive it belongs.

FIGURE 9-6: Give Microsoft credit for providing Bing with both beauty and brains.

BING ON OTHER SMART PHONES

Bing apps for other mobile systems—including iPhone, Android, and even Microsoft's previous mobile OS, Windows Mobile—include a number of other UI features, including a home button, back and forward buttons, and a grid of manual search types. For Windows Phone, however, Microsoft has elected to follow its own design mantra and simplify things quite a bit. So what you see in Windows Phone is far more streamlined. Don't worry; it's also full-featured.

USING BING

In fact, this is the only way to launch Bing. It doesn't appear in the More Programs list, like other applications.

You launch the Bing application by tapping the Search button on the front of your Windows Phone.

Bing is a full-featured search service, of course, and it tries to autodetect the type of search you'll need and provide the appropriate result type filter. Most searches performed directly from the Bing application fall into one of three categories: Web, Local, and News. So these are the category filters you'll see in the search results.

BING TRIES TO UNDERSTAND WHAT YOU'RE SEARCHING FOR

What's interesting here is that Bing will examine what you're searching for and attempt to provide the correct default view. So if you search for *Bastille Day* on Bastille Day (July 14), it will return news results as the default view. But if you search for something like *Windows Phone Secrets*, it will return Web results as the default view. It's not always what you want. But it's easy enough to switch the view, as you'll soon see.

As with other Windows Phone interfaces, Bing utilizes a pivot-based columnized interface for its search results. In this case, Bing search results can be pivoted through, or are organized into, three columns, or *sections*. They could be sorted in different orders, depending on what you search for, but you will see these three sections.

▶   The first, Web, provides a list of relevant web-based search results.

▶   The second section, which you can reach by flicking to the left, is Local. This provides local businesses and other resources.

▶   Flick again, and you'll find a section of News search results.

This three-column search results interface is shown in Figure 9-7.

The next sections examine the different types of searches you can perform.

Searching the Web

Bing provides standard web searching functionality and works much like rival web search engines from Google and Yahoo. To search the Web, tap Home and then Search. The Bing search experience opens. From here, tap the search box and begin typing your query. As you'll see, Bing will provide suggested search queries as you type. You can select one as you go or just tap Enter when you're ready to search.

If you search for an item that can't possibly be misconstrued as a local resource or news items (for example, *puerco pibil*, the fantastic pulled pork dish popularized by the movie *Once Upon a Time in Mexico*), Bing will open its search results screen with the Web section already displayed onscreen, as shown in Figure 9-8. If not, you can flick left or right to make sure the Web results are displayed.

Navigating through the results screen is straightforward, and you can use your well-developed scrolling skills to make quick work of the list. When you find an interesting result, simply tap it with your finger to see more. This causes the web page in question to open, not in Bing, but in Internet Explorer (Figure 9-9).

From here, you can perform several actions. If the page is what you were looking for or is otherwise valuable, you may choose to save it for later use. In such a case, you can simply tap the Add button in the Internet Explorer toolbar. This will display the Add Favorite interface shown in Figure 9-10, allowing you to optionally rename the favorite and edit the URL if desired.

FIGURE 9-7: Bing's search results are filtered into categories that you can pivot between.

FIGURE 9-8: Bing tries to provide the correct view depending on the search term you've entered.

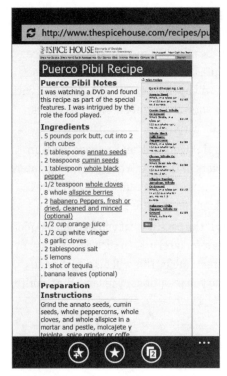

FIGURE 9-9: Bing opens Internet Explorer when you click on web links in the search results list.

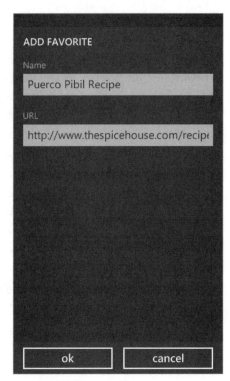

FIGURE 9-10: Using Internet Explorer, you can save favorite search results as Favorites.

If you'd like to share this link with someone else via e-mail, messaging, or through a social networking service such as Facebook, tap the More button and then Share Page. This launches the standard Windows Phone Share interface, which is described elsewhere in this book (including Chapter 8, in which we discuss IE).

If you simply want to return to the list of search results in Bing, tap the phone's Back button.

If you instead want to return to the main Bing screen, tap the phone's Search button.

Reading and Searching for News

Increasingly, PC and mobile web users are turning to search engines for news. So Bing, like Google, offers a news service that isn't curated by human editors but is instead populated entirely by algorithms. (Michael Crichton would have had a field day with this one.)

> **NOTE** You can view Microsoft's take on this service at **bing.com/news**. It's shown in Figure 9-11.

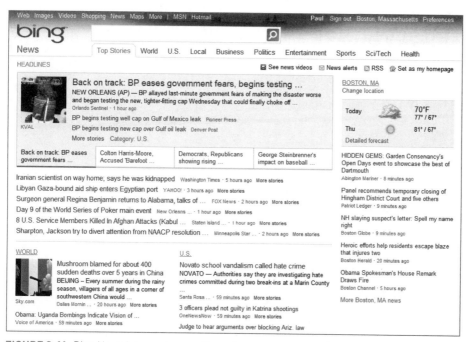

FIGURE 9-11: Bing News lets you browse through current news stories.

The Bing app on Windows Phone does not let you browse this site in the same way. Instead, it provides a way to search for news items. This can be handy for those times where you've heard that something happened—like a volcano eruption or sports event—and you want to find out more.

> **TIP** If you are interested in accessing the Bing News browsing experience on Windows Phone, visit **bing.com/news** with Internet Explorer on the device. It will load the traditional web version of Bing News. You can save this as a Favorite and, optionally, pin it to your Start screen.

To search Bing for news, launch the Bing app and then type in an appropriate query. When the search results page appears, pivot over to the News section if necessary. Bing news search results are shown in Figure 9-12. From here, you can scroll through the list of available stories and tap on any you find interesting.

Whitey bulger

news web loca

Interpol unveils global appeal to track down Whitey Bulger,

P ARIS - International police agency Interpol
yesterday launched an unusual appeal to the
global public to report sightings of 26 leading
Boston Herald - 1 week ago

Pick wisely Deval Patrick, voters watching

B e careful, Deval. There's another DeVille
waiting just ahead. I speak of the possible fiasco
that threatens your next appointment to the
Boston Herald - 1 minute ago

Former 'Most wanted' briefly stopped in KC

Kansas City police today detained a reported
gang leader who made it to the FBI's Ten Most
Wanted Fugitives list in 2007 and was released
Kansas City Star - 1 day ago

FIGURE 9-12: Bing's news service takes nice advantage
of the Windows Phone UI.

Finding Things Locally

One of the best uses of a smart phone, in my opinion, is finding local resources while
you're on the go. These resources can include numerous things, such as restaurants,
movies, shopping and related services, transportation, hotels, hospitals, pharmacies,
sightseeing, sporting events, and virtually anything else you can imagine. If it can
happen where you are—or nearby—your Windows Phone is your greatest ally. And the
service you'll use is Bing Local.

As with other search types, you can perform local searches via the Bing app's
search box. If the search results don't display the Local section by default, just pivot
over to that view.

FINDING LOCAL STORES VERSUS SHOPPING ONLINE

Don't confuse the *shopping and related services* I just mentioned as meaning *online shopping*. Here's the distinction: If you want to find a physical retail store near you, use Bing Local. If what you want to do is buy something on the Web, you should still use Bing, because Bing can help you find the best prices. But to do so, you'll go through the Bing Shopping interface. This is described later in the chapter.

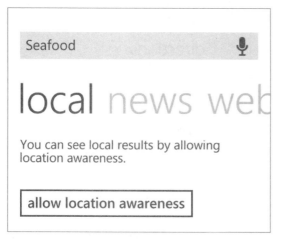

FIGURE 9-13: Privacy freak? No local search for you!

▶ *If you didn't allow Bing to access your location information, it won't provide local search results. Instead, you'll see the screen shown in Figure 9-13. Of course, from here, you can tap Allow Location Awareness to enable this functionality.*

So how does this work in the real world? Say you're in the city and want to find a nearby seafood restaurant. Launch Bing, then tap on the search box and type **seafood**, and then tap Enter. From here, Bing search results will display a map of the local areas and a list of relevant local restaurants, as shown in Figure 9-14.

NOTE Be careful, as some of the results are ads. You can tell the difference by looking at the small flag next to each entry. Search results will have a number in the flag (1, 2, and so on), whereas ads will have a letter (A). Tapping an ad will also launch Internet Explorer, whereas local search results, as you'll see, behave completely differently.

When you select a local search result, Bing transforms into a new mode where you can discover more about this establishment (Figure 9-15).

FIGURE 9-14: Local results are often accompanied by a map.

FIGURE 9-15: Bing provides a lot more information about local businesses.

In this mode—which resembles Bing's shopping mode—you can pivot between the following sections, or columns:

▶ **About:** This section lists pertinent information about the business, including its address, average rating (based on user reviews), directions (which triggers the Maps experience, described in the next section), phone number, and web site. Each of these entries is a live link, so you can tap them to navigate to a different experience. For example, when you tap a phone number, Windows Phone begins dialing that number, as shown in Figure 9-16.

▶ **Reviews:** In the Reviews section, you'll find user reviews gathered from reputable web sites (Figure 9-17). As with any product comparison, these reviews should be scanned and evaluated for the occasional crank review, which can skew the rating.

▶ **Nearby:** On the Nearby section shown in Figure 9-18, Bing displays other businesses nearby.

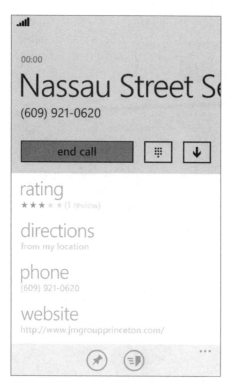

FIGURE 9-16: Bing's information screens aren't just for looks: Each item can be tapped to trigger another action.

FIGURE 9-17: Bing gathers reviews from around the Web so you can get an accurate picture of a place.

Remember that on all of these sections, everything can be tapped to see more. If you tap a review on the Reviews section, for example, Internet Explorer will load the web page from which the review comes. And on the Nearby section, you can tap the map to see a better view of the places nearby—shown in Figure 9-19—or tap a listed location to drill down even further. It's all interactive.

Of course, sometimes you are looking for something very specific. Maybe you have a gift certificate to a particular restaurant or want to find a certain retail store. In these cases, it's often faster to simply search for the exact place name using Bing. So tap the search box and enter the name of the establishment or location you're looking for.

Using Bing Maps

Hopefully, that beautiful Bing map from the previous section has you thinking about maps. And as it turns out, Windows Phone does indeed ship with a wonderful Maps interface, powered by Bing. There are two ways you can access this interface. First, you can simply search for a location in the Bing app. When you do so, a map thumbnail will appear at the top of the search results, as shown in Figure 9-20. When you tap this thumbnail, Bing switches into its Maps mode.

As with Bing, the first time you enter the Maps interface, Windows Phone will prompt you about whether you'd like to provide this application with access to your location information. Obviously you will need to allow this in order to use Maps.

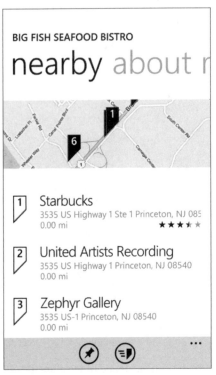

FIGURE 9-18: Did you want to grab a coffee or see a movie after dinner?

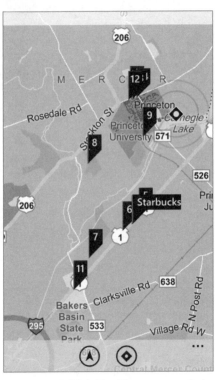

FIGURE 9-19: With Bing Maps, you can find out how to get there from here.

Second, you can simply run Bing Maps as a standalone app. It's available from the All Programs list, but if you think you're going to be using it often enough, you can of course pin Maps to the Start screen.

Either way, Bing Maps works as you'd expect, all while supplying what I think is the most attractive mobile maps interface yet provided on a smart phone.

> **TIP** Maps navigation works like other Windows Phone apps. You can scroll around by flicking the screen and zoom in and out by pinching the screen.

FIGURE 9-20: Bing provides Map thumbnails for locations so you enter Bing Maps.

Like other map solutions, Bing Maps works in one of two ways. You can use it to locate yourself and find out where you are. Or you can use it to provide directions to another location.

TIP Actually, there is a third possibility: You can also use Maps to look at another location. Say you want to navigate Paris, France, but you're stuck in the United States at the moment. Using the Bing search experience, you can search for *Paris, France*, and the top item in the search results list will be a map thumbnail. Tap that to explore the City of Light. Or, from within Maps, tap the device's Search button to bring up a search box. Enter Paris, France and then tap Enter. Away you go.

Before you examine these two modes in greater detail, first take a look at the different options you can enable in Maps, as these can greatly change the look of the interface. To see the available options, tap the More item in the Application Bar and you'll see the list with various options, as shown in Figure 9-21.

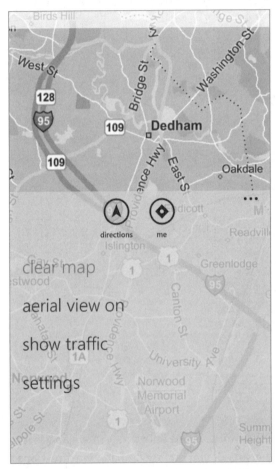

FIGURE 9-21: You can enable different options in Maps to change the look of the application.

These options can include:

▶ **Aerial view:** By default, Maps displays using a flat, graphical view style. But if you enable aerial view—by tapping the Aerial View On option—Maps changes to a satellite-style display. In Figure 9-22, you can see the default view style (left) and aerial view (right) side-by-side.

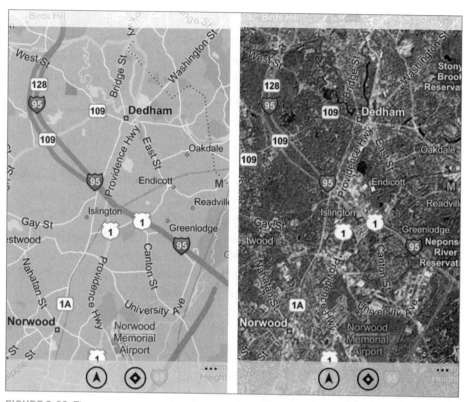

FIGURE 9-22: The same map, shown with aerial view off (left) and on (right).

▶ **Traffic:** When you tap Show Traffic, Maps will display green, yellow, or red lines on top of major surface roads to indicate the quality of the traffic. On this scale green is no/little traffic, yellow is some traffic, and red is heavy traffic. Plan accordingly.

Okay, now it's time to take a look at the two Maps modes.

THE MAPS APP AND POWER MANAGEMENT

While Windows Phone is generally pretty aggressive about power management, you'll notice that the phone automatically stays powered on longer when you're in Maps than it does in other situations. That's because the device assumes you need access to your location information when you use Maps. And in many cases, such as in a car, the device is likely to be connected to power anyway.

FINDING WHERE YOU ARE

To locate your current location in Bing Maps, tap the Me toolbar button. This is the rightmost of the two buttons and resembles a diamond. When you do so, Maps performs a nifty little animation where you appear to fly up out of the current view and then zoom into your current location. When it finds the exact place, a yellow circle appears on the map and appears to radiate, as shown in Figure 9-23.

GETTING DIRECTIONS

To get directions to a specific location, tap the Directions button. (Cutely, it resembles the Federation insignia from *Star Trek*. Or if you're not a total nerd, an arrow.) When you do, Maps enters Directions mode (Figure 9-24).

There are a number of interesting things going on here. First, the Start field is automatically set to My Location because Maps assumes you want to find directions from your current location to some other location. Second, the End field is selected, so you can type in your destination and find an appropriate route.

FIGURE 9-23: You can run, but you can't hide . . . from Maps.

FIGURE 9-24: Maps provides a handy Directions mode for finding your way out of here.

You aren't stuck with My Location as a starting point, however. To change that, tap the Start field. This will automatically select My Location, allowing you to type over it. You can type in a place name, or even a ZIP code. (You can do the same for the End field as well.)

To the left of the End field is a small arrow. If you tap this, the locations in the Start and End fields will reverse. This is of course useful if you use Maps to navigate to a location and then want to use it later to find your way back.

When you are ready to plot the route, tap the Enter key on the virtual keyboard. Maps will think a bit and then switch into a new view in which the route is displayed in list form, with each step in the route. This is shown in Figure 9-25.

You can scroll through this list as you would any Windows Phone interface, and as you tap individual steps in the directions, the map and list will advance to keep up.

Note, too, that there are Walk and Drive icons at the top of this screen. For longer distances, Maps will assume you want driving directions, but you can tap the Walk icon to change to walking instructions.

USING MAPS ELSEWHERE IN WINDOWS PHONE

In addition to launching Maps manually via More Programs, or surreptitiously through Bing, you can also trigger this application in other places throughout Windows Phone. Indeed, anywhere an address appears, it's possible that you can tap on that address, launching Maps, which will then navigate to that address.

The most obvious example of this behavior is the People hub, which lists your contacts from various online services. I discussed this important interface in Chapter 4, but if you're viewing a contact card that has any address information, you can tap that address and view it right in Maps. When you do, Maps displays the address in a little flag as seen in Figure 9-26.

Always interactive, Bing Maps lets you tap the flag to find out more about the location and find nearby businesses. It's like it can't help being helpful.

Searching for Images

If you're familiar with Bing on the (PC-based) Web, you know that Microsoft's search service is notably good at finding and displaying images, thanks to its unique layout. Bing has found particular success with amateur celebrity watchers as a result, and while I can't claim to be part of that crowd, I certainly understand why they'd be drawn to Bing. The PC-based image search functionality is shown in Figure 9-27.

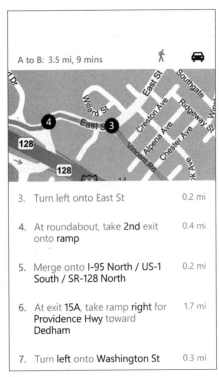

FIGURE 9-25: With Maps, you *can* get there from here.

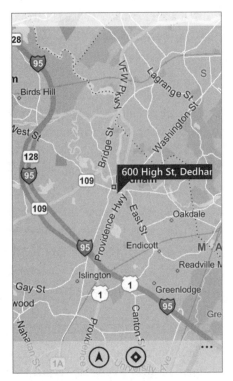

FIGURE 9-26: Locate your contacts on the map.

FIGURE 9-27: Bing's image search on the PC.

NOTE Bing's image search is so good, in fact, that Google simply copied it in a 2010 update to its own image search functionality, Google Images.

On Windows Phone, Bing search doesn't try to emulate the PC experience. Instead, it doesn't offer image search at all, which is kind of odd when you consider that Microsoft's Bing apps for other mobile platforms do offer this functionality.

So what gives? How does one search for images with Bing on Windows Phone?

Oddly and incredibly, you use the regular Bing web site, via Internet Explorer. In fact, you can navigate directly to images.bing.com to view the same exact interface you get in the PC, but squished down to accommodate the smart phone's small screen, as shown in Figure 9-28.

FIGURE 9-28: Look familiar? To search for images on the Web using Windows Phone, you must use the Bing web site.

If you're dead-set against using the "full" web on your phone, there's an alternative. Microsoft offers a stripped down mobile version of the Bing web site at m.bing.com. If you navigate there in Internet Explorer on Windows Phone, you should see something like the screen shown in Figure 9-29.

From here, you can search for a topic related to pictures you might like (such as the aforementioned *Paris, France*). When you do, the mobile Bing site segregates its search results into categories such as web, images, news, and local. Just tap the images link to display the mobile version of Bing images, as shown in Figure 9-30. It's not nearly as pretty as the full version—heck, it's not pretty at all—but it does get the job done.

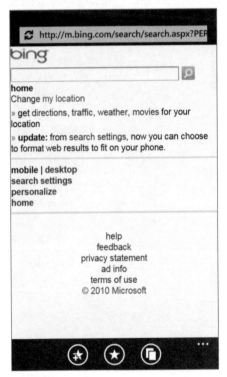

FIGURE 9-29: Bing's mobile site.

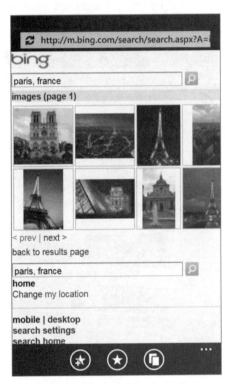

FIGURE 9-30: Bing's mobile site for images.

CROSSREF I'm not going to waste too much time documenting these sites, other than to remind you that the Web is an excellent place to find wallpaper and other images for your phone. I discuss doing this in Chapter 5, during the discussion about the Pictures hub.

Shopping Online

While I'm discussing great Bing functionality that didn't make its way to Windows Phone, shopping comes immediately to mind. On the PC Web, Bing's Shopping experience (bing.com/shopping) is unmatched and is in fact one of the best reasons to use the service. It works much like local search, but with categories related to product types such as Baby & Nursery, Beauty & Fragrance, Books & Magazines, Cameras, Clothing & Shoes, Computing, and so on. Inside of each of these categories, too, are sub-categories. So if you navigate into, say, computing, you'll see items such as Computers, Input Devices, Mobile Devices, Printers, and more. (These sub-categories are often further broken down into additional sub-categories, so keep digging.) The Bing Shopping experience can be seen in Figure 9-31.

Where Bing Shopping really starts to get interesting is in its search results. Rather than a rote text listing like many other search types, Bing Shopping provides a more visual results list that includes product images, as in Figure 9-32. It's not as visual as image search, but that's by design: In Bing Shopping, you can see the product and other information, including ratings, without navigating to sub-pages.

FIGURE 9-31: Bing Shopping . . . again, on the PC.

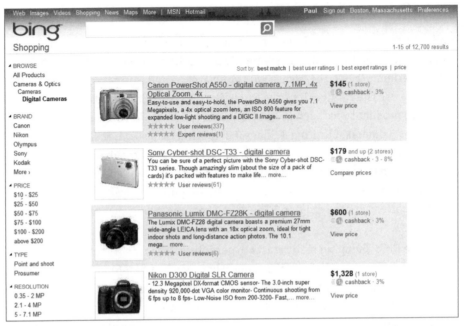

FIGURE 9-32: Bing Shopping's results lists are visual, so you can see the products in question.

Bing Shopping also provides an interesting number of filters, which are provided in the left-hand task pane on the web site. You can sort by brand, price point, type, or other categories, each of which varies from product type to product type.

When you drill down into an individual item, you'll also discover a wealth of information about each product, including ratings and reviews, places to buy sorted by price, scorecards, product images, specifications, and more. This can be seen in Figure 9-33.

And when you're ready to buy, just tap Where to Buy and then the Go to Store link next to the chosen store. You'll be transported to the product page on the correct site so you can purchase it online.

So, that's all very good and everything, but what does this have to do with Windows Phone? Not much. As with image searching, you can indeed visit the full Bing web site and perform shopping searches via Windows Phone. So everything described earlier works in the same way—albeit via a smaller screen—on Windows Phone, but only if you perform these searches through Internet Explorer.

What's missing this time around is a mobile web shopping experience. Unlike with image searches, there's no way to use the mobile version of Bing to go shopping. You have to use the full version.

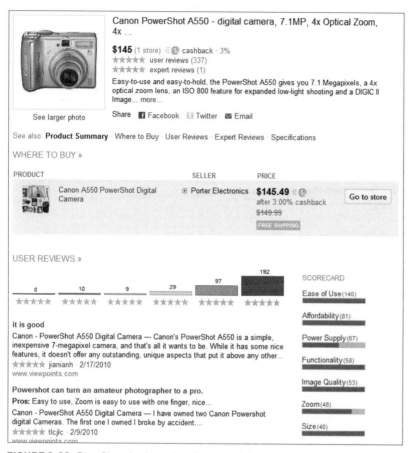

FIGURE 9-33: Bing Shopping's product lists are rich with information, so you can make an educated choice.

Getting the Weather Forecast . . . and More

While there are plenty of things you can search for with Bing, one of the neatest (if not obvious) ways to use this service is to get what Microsoft calls *instant answers*. The most obvious of these is the weather forecast.

To find the weather for your current location, open the Bing app and type **weather** in the search box. Bing will think for a bit and then display a nifty weather forecast at the top of the web search results, as shown in Figure 9-34.

FIGURE 9-34: Bing provides some instant answers, including the weather forecast.

And yes, you can discover the weather elsewhere too. Simply type **weather** and then the name of a location (or a zip code) in the Bing search box. The display will be identical, except that the location will change.

> **TIP** If you want a more immediate way to get this forecast, you can check out the many available weather applications in the Windows Phone Marketplace. Or, you can simply tap the weather display in the Bing search results to load the MSN Weather site (in Internet Explorer) with the same forecast displayed. Then, tap More, then Pin to Start to pin the weather forecast to your Start screen.

> **NOTE** Bing supports many instant answer types on its full web site, but only some of these are available from the Bing application on Windows Phone.
>
> Instant answers that are supported in the Bing app include finance (stock prices), flight status, music, and weather. Those that are not supported include area codes, conversions, dictionary, encyclopedia, flight deals, health, holidays, hotels, local listings, math, movies, news, shopping, sports, and tracking packages.

CONFIGURING BING

Bing offers only a handful of configurable options, but it's still worth quickly investigating its Settings interface. (Note that it's called Search, not Bing.) These options include:

- ▶ **Use my location.** By default, Bing is configured to automatically search using your current location. This can be very convenient, obviously, for such things as movie, local, and even news searches. But sometimes you want to search for things in a different place. Perhaps you're researching for an upcoming trip or a night out in a different city. In such cases, you can configure Bing to use a manual location, and then specify what that location is. Subsequent searches will then be applied to that location, and not your current location.

- ▶ **Get suggestions from Bing as I type.** Enabled by default, this option allows Bing to monitor your search query as you type and then make suggestions as appropriate. If you disable this option, Bing will not make search suggestions.

Additionally, there is a Delete History button that deletes all previously typed search terms from your phone. Tapping this button will trigger a confirmation notification.

SUMMARY

Bing is something of an enigma on Windows Phone. On the one hand, the application is actually missing a few features that are found in the Bing apps on other mobile platforms, including those made by Microsoft's competitors. But Microsoft makes up for this by deeply integrating Bing into the Windows Phone experience. On Windows Phone, Bing isn't just an app. It's an interconnected part of the entire phone.

Thanks to the inclusion of a dedicated Search button on every Windows Phone, Bing is instantly available, literally at the tap of a finger, no matter where you are or what you're doing, in the phone. It provides the key functionality you'd expect on the go, including quick access to web, local, and news searches. And it provides instant answers, voice search capabilities, and deep map integration with turn by turn navigation and direction capabilities.

In the few areas where Bing falls short, the web version of the service picks up the pieces. You can search for images and shopping advice via Bing on the Web, in Internet Explorer, and with some search types there's even a version of the site customized for the small screens on mobile devices like smart phones. All in all, if you want to find something, Bing can make it happen.

CHAPTER 10

Managing E-mail on the Go

When you consider the ever-growing list of features that make a smart phone seem smart in the first place, e-mail support has to be near the top of the list. Indeed, e-mail is curiously well suited to life on the go, especially for those who receive a lot of the stuff. And Windows Phone, in particular, offers a great solution for mobile e-mail.

The Windows Phone Mail application offers everything you need to manage e-mail, including a highly optimized user interface and support for multiple e-mail account types and multiple accounts of the same or different types. It utilizes common e-mail features such as flagged and urgent messages, attachments, CC and BCC support, and the reading of textual and graphical e-mails. It also works in either portrait or horizontal display modes, so you can manage mail the way you want to.

What's interesting about Mail is that Windows Phone handles multiple e-mail accounts quite a bit differently than it does multiple contact or calendar accounts. You'll see why this is so, and how you can work around this odd limitation, as I explore Windows Phone's Mail application in this chapter.

PUSH IT: A LOOK AT MOBILE E-MAIL

Mobile communications has existed for almost as long as there have been mobile devices, though of course the advent of pervasive wireless network connectivity finally made this scenario both interesting and viable and, eventually, indispensable. Early PDAs offered simple communication solutions, including mobile e-mail, but they required PC connectivity or, in rare cases, a mobile modem in order to send and receive messages over the air.

The first big breakthrough in mobile e-mail came courtesy of Research In Motion (RIM), which started not with PDAs but rather with pagers, tiny mobile devices that utilized communications networks to send simple messages to customers. These pagers gradually morphed into the Blackberry line of smart phones, which adopted e-mail, web browsing, text messaging, contacts management, and other functionality, just as PDAs also morphed into smart phones by adding telephony capabilities.

RIM's early experience in the wireless world gave it an interesting advantage in certain areas, and the company was the first to offer what's now called "push" support for e-mail, as well as contacts and calendars. Previous to push, mobile devices would occasionally poll servers wirelessly for new data and then sync whatever changes had occurred. But push technologies perform the same feat in a far more efficient manner: Instead of requiring clients to blindly ask for changes on a schedule, push-based services simply "push" changes down to the clients, and they do so only whenever a change occurs. The result is that devices get better overall battery life since they're not constantly sending out wireless feelers.

The Blackberry push technologies were so successful that the rest of the industry simply copied RIM and added similar functionality to their own products. Microsoft added push support to Exchange Server and its Windows Mobile product line in 2007, as did Apple, tentatively, with the first iPhone. (Over the intervening years, Apple broadened the iPhone's support of push.)

Today, no modern smart phone platform would be complete without push support, not just for e-mail, but also for contacts and calendar. And while Windows Phone does support pre-push technologies, it is optimized for push-based e-mail support specifically. So in cases where an e-mail account could be configured in different ways, it's always best to go with the push option if you're given a choice.

> **NOTE** Windows Phone supports push e-mail through a technology called Exchange ActiveSync (EAS), which works with Exchange accounts (of course) as well as Gmail and some other e-mail services. Check with your e-mail provider to see if they offer EAS support, as many do, and more are coming on board all the time.

UNDERSTANDING ACCOUNTS AND E-MAIL

Back in Chapter 1, I explained why creating and properly configuring a Windows Live ID is key to the Windows Phone experience. When you log on to your phone with this ID, you're creating an account on the phone. And this Windows Live–based account is considered your *primary* account because it interacts with a variety of web-based services that are central to Windows Phone and, perhaps more important, unique to this ID. Web services that can only be connected to your primary account include your Messenger social feed (which populates the What's New lists in the People and Pictures hubs), Xbox Live account, Marketplace account (for Zune-based content as well as apps and games), Zune Pass subscription, OneNote note-syncing, Windows Live photo posting, Find My Phone (described in Chapter 16), and more.

This primary account is also used for contacts sync with the People hub, calendar sync with the Calendar app, and, if you enable it explicitly, e-mail as well. These services are available via a number of account types, not just your primary account. So depending on the type(s) of accounts you've configured, you may have an interesting mix of services providing e-mail, contacts, and calendar data to your phone.

E-mail is, perhaps, the most basic of these services because it is the most common among the different account types. In fact, when you examine these account types, you'll see that all of them offer e-mail except Facebook. Some of them, in fact, offer *only* e-mail.

And when you combine that fact with another interesting Windows Phone tidbit—that you can have multiple accounts of the same type configured on one phone—you can see that it's possible that you could have an awful lot of e-mail happening on that little device. So it's a good idea to get it right.

Before continuing, I want to take a quick look at the account types you can configure in the Email & Accounts settings interface for e-mail. These include:

- **Windows Live:** This account type can be configured as your primary account (e-mail, contacts, calendar, photos, feeds, and more) or as a secondary, "normal" account with e-mail, contacts, and/or calendar sync. You must have at least one Windows Live account, which functions as your primary account. But you can configure multiple other Windows Live accounts as well.

- **Outlook:** Designed for Exchange-type servers, this account type works with e-mail, contacts, and/or calendar data. But it's not just for Exchange. In fact, the Outlook account type will work with any account that uses EAS on the back end. And that's a surprising number of services, including Gmail/Google Calendar, Microsoft's Hotmail, and many others.

- **Yahoo! Mail:** This account type is for e-mail only and uses the IMAP prototype to synchronize the view on your phone with your server-based e-mail. IMAP is superior to the older POP3-style email accounts that were common a decade ago, but unlike EAS, it works only with email.

- **Google:** Microsoft explicitly supports Google's Gmail (for e-mail and contacts) and Google Calendar because the services are so popular, but it's not much harder to configure this account type using the Outlook option. Behind the scenes, the accounts are configured the same way, using EAS.

- **Other Account or Advanced Setup:** If the e-mail account you're using doesn't fall neatly into one of the above categories, you can use one of these options to configure the account on Windows Phone. Both work similarly, are designed explicitly for e-mail only (no contacts or calendar), and will work with virtually any e-mail account there is, regardless of the required access protocol (POP3, IMAP, or whatever).

Okay, so here's a recap. You must have a primary (Windows Live–based) account, and you may have any number of other accounts, including multiple accounts of the same type. Depending on the type, these accounts will provide access to different services, including e-mail, contacts, and calendar. Got it?

Good, but here's the wrinkle. With contacts and calendar services, Windows Phone provides a single, integrated experience that lets you view the content from multiple services in a single place. With contacts, that place is the People hub. With calendars, it's the Calendar app. In both cases, you can view and interact with multiple accounts' worth of data, all in one place.

That is not how e-mail works. In fact, Windows Phone handles e-mail in a way that is completely the opposite of how it handles contacts and calendars. More important, maybe, the way Windows Phone handles e-mail is also in opposition to the Windows Phone mantra of integrated experiences. Put more simply, there is no such thing as a unified inbox on Windows Phone, a feature that is common to other smart phones such as the iPhone or those based on Google Android. Instead, Windows Phone creates a different Mail application for each configured e-mail account.

That may sound counterproductive. And certainly, there is room for debate on this one. But there's no debating that Windows Phone does work this way. So rather than complain, let's just figure out a workable solution. And believe it or not, I actually have that solution (discussed in the sidebar that follows). It's not perfect. But depending on your situation, it could make a big difference.

CONFIGURING WINDOWS PHONE TO USE ONLY ONE E-MAIL ACCOUNT BUT GET ALL OF YOUR E-MAIL FROM MULTIPLE ACCOUNTS

Okay, suppose you have multiple e-mail accounts, as I do. And suppose you, like me, would prefer not to configure your phone with multiple e-mail accounts, each of which would require a dedicated e-mail interface of its own.

The way to get around this is to determine which of these accounts is the most important to you. And then use that as a "master" account of sorts, where that one account polls your other accounts for e-mail up on the server. How you do this varies from service to service, but in my experience, both Google's Gmail and Microsoft's Hotmail services work quite well. Plus, they're both free and offer unlimited storage.

You can configure your master e-mail account for this functionality using its web interface. In Gmail (**gmail.com**), you can find this interface in Settings, Accounts and Filters. There's a Check E-mail Using POP3 section where you can configure connected accounts.

In Hotmail (**hotmail.com**), this interface can be found in Options, More Options, Send and Receive Mail from Other E-mail Accounts.

If your master e-mail account doesn't support the polling of other accounts, you could instead forward e-mail from each account to the master account. This, too, varies from account to account. But in Gmail, you can find the controls at Settings, Forwarding and POP/IMAP. In Hotmail, this interface can be found in Options, More Options, Send and Receive Mail from Other E-Mail Accounts.

(continues)

(continued)

I mentioned that this approach isn't perfect because, well, it isn't. If you aggregate all of your e-mail accounts via a single master account on the Web and then configure Windows Phone to access only that master e-mail account, the phone will have no idea "where" mail is coming from and no way to reply using a particular account. If this isn't an issue for you, then go for it. If it is, you'll have to put up with Microsoft's non-unified inbox approach in Windows Phone. Or, optionally, you could see whether the mobile web interface for that "master" e-mail account works well enough in the phone's browser, Internet Explorer. You could always access your mail from there instead (though in doing so, you'd lose out on the notification integration that the Mail app provides).

Of course, you may actually want to access all of your e-mail accounts separately. If that's the case, just use Windows Phone as Microsoft intended. For each e-mail account you create, Windows Phone will create a new e-mail application in the All Programs list. And you are free, of course, to pin as many of them as you'd like to the Windows Phone Start screen too. In the course of writing this book, I've had several e-mail accounts configured simultaneously on the phone, and it works fine.

Regardless, for the rest of this chapter, I'm going to approach e-mail as if it were a single entity. And that's because regardless of how you access your e-mail—either through a single, consolidated account, or via multiple e-mail accounts, each with its own app—you can only access one e-mail app at a time.

NOTE If you're using only one e-mail account on your phone, and it's the one from your primary Windows Live ID, you'll need to make sure that e-mail access is enabled, because it often isn't by default. (Contacts and calendar access, oddly, *is* automatically configured.) To do this, visit the Email & Accounts settings interface, tap Windows Live, and then make sure the Email check box, under Content to Sync, is checked. In fact, it's worth making sure that this account is otherwise configured optimally. Check out the section, "Configuring Mail and E-mail Accounts," later in the chapter for more information.

USING MAIL

If you enjoy the rich graphical user interfaces in hubs such as Pictures or Music + Video, the Windows Phone Mail application (Figure 10-1) might come as a bit of a shock. By default, it presents a stark interface, with black text on a bright white background that Microsoft claims is ideal for the primary e-mail activity of reading. (This does little to explain why Calendar, also text-based, uses white text on a black background by default. Moving on . . .)

Try to get over your initial impression of this application because it's actually a highly efficient and capable e-mail solution. In fact, I'd be surprised if it didn't win you over after only a few minutes. If you've spent any time at all with mobile e-mail solutions on other platforms, you'll understand why immediately.

The key to this success is Windows Phone's pivot-based, single screen application user interface, which is used to nice effect in Mail. Rather than bore you to tears with an interface based around folders—remember, Windows Phone works the way *you* think rather than force you to understand how *it* works—Mail instead presents commonly needed e-mail *views* such as all e-mail, unread e-mail, flagged e-mail, urgent e-mail.

> **NOTE** That said, Mail does of course have to work within the confines of the folder-based storage system used by your e-mail solution. So these views are showing the contents of your Inbox filtered in different ways. To see other folders, tap the Folders button in the Application Bar.

Mail starts up in the All (for "all e-mail") view. But you can easily swipe the screen horizontally to pivot, or navigate, through the other views. The Unread view, shown in Figure 10-2, for example, displays only those e-mails that are currently unread.

The Flagged view displays those messages that are said to be *flagged*, a Microsoft invention that is used heavily throughout the software giant's many e-mail applications, servers, and services. In the Microsoft world, a flagged message is one that requires follow-up. So you can "set" a flag on an e-mail, and "clear" a flag, which is like removing the flag. But good worker drones will "complete" a flagged message, meaning that they followed up as required. This doesn't, but should, release a Scooby Treat. Maybe in the next version.

In Figure 10-3, you can see messages that are flagged (need follow-up) and completed (have been followed up on).

▶ Interested in changing Mail's appearance? You can't. For some reason, there are no configuration options for this feature.

FIGURE 10-1: Mail.

FIGURE 10-2: The Unread view displays only those messages that have not been marked as read.

NOTE If you use Gmail, you may be interested to know that Google's scaled-down version of a flagged e-mail is a "starred" e-mail: You can assign a star to individual e-mails in the Gmail web-based interface to special messages or as a visual reminder that you need to follow up on that e-mail later. Unfortunately, starred messages do not show up as flagged messages in Mail for some reason.

In the Urgent view, you see those messages that have been specified by the sender as having an urgent priority rating. By default, e-mails are sent with a normal priority rating, and while it's even possible to specify low priority in some e-mail solutions, including Mail on Windows Phone, that's rarely used. How is this different from a flagged message, you ask? Primarily in two ways. First, it's a de facto industry standard in the sense that virtually every e-mail solution supports creating and understanding urgent mails. And second, as noted previously, this rating is applied by the sender, not by the receiver, as is the case with flagged e-mails.

The Urgent view is shown in Figure 10-4. As you can see, urgent e-mails are marked with an exclamation point badge, indicating (at least to the sender) that it's important.

FIGURE 10-3: Flagged and completed mails.

FIGURE 10-4: Urgent e-mails are important, at least to the person that sent them.

Looking at the All view again, you can see a conglomeration of the other views. There will be messages with flags, messages marked as urgent, and unread and read messages. Each of these is denoted in a different way. For example, unread messages appear slightly different than read messages: Their subject line is bolded and colored with your theme's highlight color, as shown in Figure 10-5.

FIGURE 10-5: An unread e-mail (top) and a read e-mail (bottom) appear visually different.

Additionally, some e-mails you receive will include attachments, which are one or more external files that are attached to the message, by the sender, before being sent. Typical attachments include Office documents, ZIP files, pictures, and more. In Mail, messages that include attachments feature a paperclip badge, as shown in Figure 10-6.

FIGURE 10-6: Messages with attachments feature a prominent paperclip badge.

You navigate through any of the e-mail views as expected, by swiping your finger across the screen vertically. You can also perform certain actions on one or more e-mail messages, send your own e-mails, and more. I examine these possibilities next.

Triaging E-mail

I'm not sure how ugly your e-mail is, of course, but I receive hundreds of e-mail messages every day, and I can't—and don't want to—read every single one of them. The reasons for this are pragmatic, and should apply to your own e-mail as well. Much of the mail I get is unwanted, such as mailing lists that I inadvertently signed up for online, or advertisements. I still get the occasional spam e-mail, too: The Nigerian banker scammers have apparently moved on to different countries but are still in fine form, from what I can tell.

A step up from that are the e-mails I do want to get but don't always require a lot of attention: Google and Bing news alerts about technology companies fall into this category. And then there's real work e-mail, and in my case, lots of reader mail. These e-mails may require research and thought, and in many cases deserve responses.

Whatever kinds of e-mail you get, one strategy for dealing with the volume, especially at the start of each day, is to triage your e-mail, or go through the list and apply actions to blocks of e-mail in bulk. And this is a task that good mobile e-mail solutions, including Windows Phone's Mail, excel at.

To triage your e-mail in Windows Phone, launch the Mail app. It will appear in the All view, as always.

First, just delete the unwanted mail. To do so efficiently, tap the Select button in the Application Bar; it resembles a list of checked items and is the third of the four available buttons. This changes the view a bit, adding a selection box next to each e-mail message header, as shown in Figure 10-7.

▶ There's another, less obvious way to enter this selection mode: Just tap to the left of any e-mail message header.

INBOX - WINDOWS LIVE
all unread flag

Netflix Shipping   3:25p
For Tuesday: Alvin and the Chipmu
To make sure you get your Netflix er

Amtrak Guest Rew.   3:22p
Paul, exclusive bonus points on Ac
Paul, don't let the summer go by wit

Bernard, David   3:05p
RE: keynote speaker needed
Please, sir, may I have an abstract. :)

Stephanie Thurrott   3:02p
To-do list for the home swap
Here's the list we made last year. Ma

Aer Lingus Vacatio   3:02p

FIGURE 10-7: With selection boxes displayed, you can apply actions to multiple e-mails.

Now, scroll down the list and locate any messages you can safely delete. Tap the selection box next to each of the messages (Figure 10-8). When you're done, you can apply a number of actions to those messages as a group, but of course in this first pass the goal is to permanently delete the unwanted mail. So tap the Delete button in the Application Bar. Poof! All those messages are gone.

Hopefully, this has dramatically pruned your list of unread e-mail. In my case, the next thing I do is read and then file those messages I want to save but don't need to act on. I wouldn't typically do this in bulk as before, but that's certainly possible: Just tap the Move button instead of Delete when you're ready, and then select a folder to which to move those messages in the pop-up folder list that appears. (This list will vary from e-mail account to e-mail account, since each e-mail account and service uses a slightly different folder management structure, and of course, you may have created your own folders as well.)

INBOX - WINDOWS LIVE

all unread flag

☑ Netflix Shipping   3:25p
For Tuesday: Alvin and the Chipmu
To make sure you get your Netflix el

☑ Amtrak Guest Rew   3:22p
Paul, exclusive bonus points on Ac
Paul, don't let the summer go by wit

FIGURE 10-8: Once you've selected multiple messages, you can then delete them (or perform other actions), all at once.

Actions you can apply to multiple messages include:

▶ **Delete:** This permanently deletes the selected message(s) as noted previously.

▶ **Move:** This permanently moves the selected message(s) from the inbox to whatever folder you specify.

▶ **Mark as read:** This makes it appear as if the selected message(s) are read (even if they were never read).

▶ **Mark as unread:** This makes it appear as if the selected message(s) are unread (even if they were actually read).

▶ **Set flag:** This marks the selected message(s) as flagged.

▶ **Complete:** This marks the selected flagged message(s) as completed.

▶ **Clear flag:** This marks the selected flagged or completed message(s) as cleared (or "unflagged," or like any other e-mail message).

Your morning e-mail triage may vary slightly from what I just described, but I've found that it makes a big difference to do this before settling in and really spending time with the messages that matter. Once you do this, you're ready to read and, when necessary, reply to such messages.

NOTE Mail is one of those applications that works in both portrait and landscape display modes. So if you prefer the horizontal space, flip the phone 90 degrees in either direction and you'll see something like the display in Figure 10-9. Note that the Application Bar always stays fixed to the side of the screen that borders on the device's Back, Start, and Search buttons. But these buttons visually rotate in space so they're always correctly oriented, which is a nice touch.

FIGURE 10-9: Mail in landscape display mode.

Reading an E-mail

To read an individual e-mail message, simply tap the message header. (This works in any of the main Mail views.) Mail will then display this message, full screen, as shown in Figure 10-10.

NOTE The individual message views also work in landscape display mode, as you can see in Figure 10-11. You may find that certain e-mail messages are easier to read in this orientation.

You can scroll through messages as you do other Windows Phone screens, and if the message is an awkward fit for the confined real estate on your phone (Figure 10-12), you may find you have to really scroll around to see all of it.

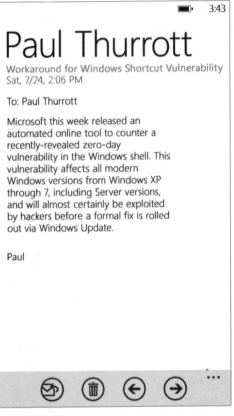

FIGURE 10-10: An e-mail message.

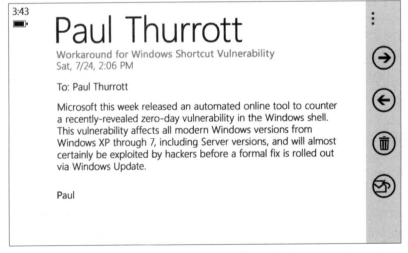

FIGURE 10-11: An e-mail message in landscape display mode.

There are other strategies for dealing with mis-sized e-mail messages. For example, Mail supports the pinch and double-tap zoom features in Windows Phone, so you can try to resize the e-mail using your fingers, often to great effect. However, you may find that such e-mail messages, while being properly laid out on the screen, are now unreadable because the fonts are so small. An example of this is shown in Figure 10-13.

FIGURE 10-12: Some e-mail messages just aren't designed for the mobile world.

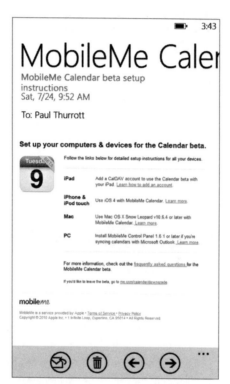

FIGURE 10-13: Even when they're "fixed" they might not look so good.

When you receive an e-mail from one of your contacts that has a configured picture, you're in for a nice visual treat: A picture of that contact will appear at the top of the e-mail, as shown in Figure 10-14.

If you receive an e-mail with external pictures—that is, pictures that are not attached to the e-mail but are rather linked to from web sites—those pictures will not be displayed by default, as shown in Figure 10-15. This is primarily out of privacy concerns: Junk mail senders can send e-mail messages that track whether external pictures were viewed; this can verify to them that they are sending mail to a valid address, thus unleashing a torrent of new spam mail.

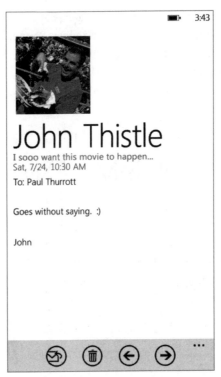

FIGURE 10-14: Messages from your contacts are often adorned with a contact card picture.

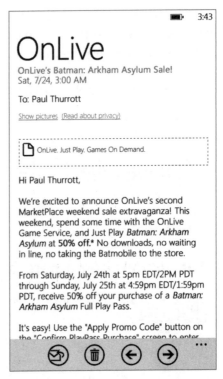

FIGURE 10-15: External pictures are blocked from e-mails by default.

NOTE On the PC desktop, such pictures are not displayed for security reasons as well, since e-mail messages can also be linked to deliberately malformed picture files that actually include dangerous malware. This is much less of a concern on the comparatively closed Windows Phone environment, at least right now.

You can, of course, enable the display of external pictures in e-mails. But you must do this on an e-mail–by–e-mail basis. To do so, tap the Show Pictures link at the top of the e-mail message. When you do, the message will load the pictures and redisplay as shown in Figure 10-16.

E-mails sent with attachments will feature an attachment badge under the header information (Figure 10-17).

You can tap this badge—or the attachment text right next to it—to download the attachment. (Microsoft doesn't automatically download them, to prevent mis-taps and preserve bandwidth.) Once you do this, the attachment badge changes to a new badge that visually represents the attached file. (This could be a mini Word icon for Word documents, a ZIP file icon for compressed files, a picture icon for image files, and so on.) Now, you can open the attachment: To do so, just tap the attachment icon or text.

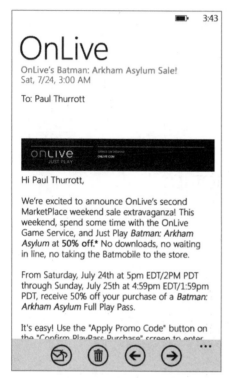

FIGURE 10-16: The same e-mail, now with pictures loaded.

FIGURE 10-17: Attachments must be down-loaded before they can be opened.

How Mail responds will depend largely on the type of file you're opening. Some common attachment types include:

- ▶ **Office documents:** Word documents, Excel spreadsheets, and PowerPoint presentations will open in the appropriate Office Mobile application. From there, you can view the document or save the document to the phone for later use.

- ▶ **Text files:** When sent via e-mail attachment, text files open in Word Mobile.

- ▶ **Picture files:** Common image file types will open in Windows Phone's internal image viewer. You can tap and hold on these images to save the picture to the phone or set it as wallpaper for the lock screen.

- ▶ **Music and video files:** Common multimedia file types will open in Windows Phone's system media player and begin playback.

▶ Some common file formats, such as Adobe PDF, are not natively supported by Windows Phone. But it's possible that your phone maker or wireless carrier will add this support, or that a downloadable add-on will become available.

▶ **ZIP files:** Windows Phone natively supports the ZIP compressed file archive format. When you open such a file from within Mail, you will see the contents of the ZIP file in a full-screen display like that shown in Figure 10-18. From here, you can open individual files inside the ZIP file as you would normally.

FIGURE 10-18: Windows Phone natively supports ZIP files.

Aside from simply viewing an e-mail, you can also perform a number of other actions at this point:

▶ **Respond:** In traditional, PC- or web-based e-mail solutions, you will typically see separate Reply, Reply to All, and Forward buttons, allowing you to respond in different ways to the current message. Windows Phone, of course, is working with dramatically less onscreen real estate than is the PC. So these three options have been condensed into a single Application Bar button, Respond. This is such a common and important action that it's covered separately, in the next section.

▶ **Delete:** Tap the Delete button in the Application Bar to delete the current message.

▶ **Read the previous or next e-mail:** Tap the Newer (left arrow) Application Bar button to display the next newest e-mail message. Or, tap the Older (right arrow) button to navigate to the next oldest e-mail message.

▶ **Toggle flag:** This option, available via the More list, lets you toggle the current message's state between flagged, completed, and cleared.

▶ **Mark as unread:** When you display a message in Mail, it is automatically marked as read on the server. But you can use this option to mark the message as unread.

▶ **Move:** This option lets you move the current message from its current location to another folder in your e-mail solution's storage structure.

Responding to E-mail

If you want to reply to an e-mail message or forward it to another party, you can tap the Respond button on the Application Bar. When you do so, you will see two or three options, depending on the original message.

These options include:

▶ **Reply:** This option generates a reply e-mail that will go only to that person who sent the original e-mail.

▶ **Reply All:** This option generates a reply e-mail that goes to the person who sent the original e-mail as well as any other recipients of the e-mail. (That is, other people who were included in the To: or CC: lines in the original message. I explain CC in the next section if you're not familiar with this term.) You will only see the Reply All option if the original message was sent to two or more recipients.

NOTE Most e-mail solutions use the term Reply to All instead of Reply All.

▶ **Forward:** Here, you are literally forwarding the current e-mail to one or more third parties. It works like a reply (or reply all) except that the person who receives your message wasn't necessarily included in the original conversation.

Aside from the recipient(s), Reply, Reply All, and Forward all work similarly. You can add and remove recipients from the To: line (again, see the next section), edit the Subject, and add your own bit to the message body, which appears above your optional signature and, below that, the original message. You can optionally add an attachment as well. A typical email reply can be seen in Figure 10-19.

When you Reply or Reply All, the Subject line is changed from *text* to *RE: text*. When you Forward a message, the Subject line is changed to *FW: text*.

Composing E-mail

Reading, triaging, and responding to e-mail is all well and good. But sometimes you need to start your own new e-mail. Not surprisingly, this is simple to do in the Windows Phone Mail app.

From any main Mail view, just tap the New ("+") button. This will trigger a new mail message, which should resemble Figure 10-20.

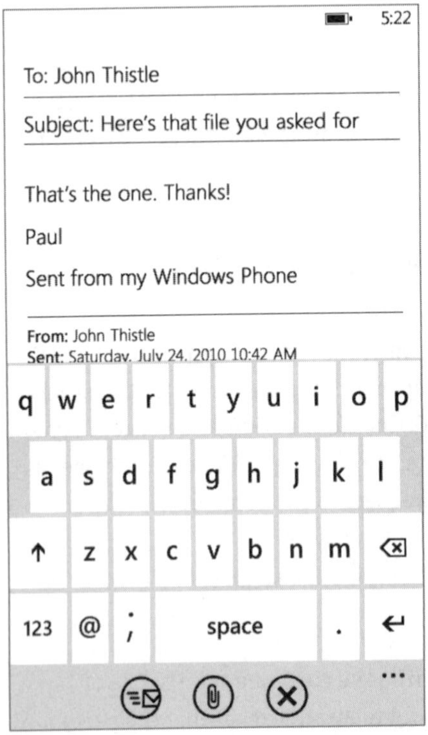

FIGURE 10-19: When you respond to an e-mail message, you can edit the To: line, Subject, and message body, and optionally add an attachment.

FIGURE 10-20: A new mail message.

From this screen, you can specify the following:

▶ **Message recipients:** In the top "To:" line, you can specify one or more contacts (or arbitrarily entered e-mail addresses) that will receive your e-mail message.

You can specify contacts in one of two ways. First, you can simply start typing an address or name and Windows Phone will provide auto-complete suggestions, based on the contents of your contacts lists, as shown in Figure 10-21.

FIGURE 10-21: If you start typing in the To: line, Windows Phone will auto-complete contact suggestions.

Second, you can choose a contact from your People hub, which aggregates all of your contacts from multiple sources into a single list. To choose a contact, tap the tiny Add ("+") button at the right end of the To: line. This will trigger the Choose a Contact screen shown in Figure 10-22.

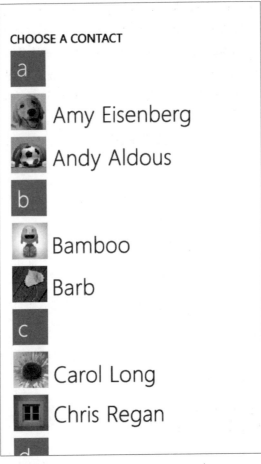

FIGURE 10-22: From this screen, you can choose one recipient at a time.

From this screen, scroll around as usual and tap on the contact you want. If the contact has two or more configured e-mail addresses, you will be prompted to pick the e-mail address you want as well.

If you want to specify multiple recipients, you can repeat that process as many times as necessary. Note, however, that it's also common to put some recipients in the optional CC: or BCC: fields instead. These options are described later in this section.

▶ If you have second thoughts about a particular recipient, just tap his or her name in the To: line and choose Remove from the pop-up menu.

▶ **Subject line:** Here, you can construct a pithy, one-line description of your e-mail message. This should be short and to the point. For example, I prefer to receive e-mails with subjects such as "You are the man" instead of more long-winded subjects such as "Your stance on Apple and its products is both uninformed and incorrect, so allow me to set you and the record straight, you knuckle-dragging moron." (Opinions vary.)

▶ **E-mail body:** Here, you can type and type and type to your heart's content. The e-mail body can be as long as you need it to be, and consist of multiple paragraphs.

▶ **Attach a picture:** From the New E-mail screen, you can attach a picture only—sorry, no documents or other file types—by tapping the Attach button in the Application Bar. This will trigger the display of a Choose Picture screen, from which you can navigate through the various local photo galleries on your phone (see Chapter 5 for details). You can optionally take a picture with the phone's built-in camera if you'd like, and attach that instead.

> ▶ What you can't do here is use flowery styles, such as italicized or bolded text, or inline graphics. Mail sends plain text e-mails only, sorry.

NOTE You can repeat this action to attach multiple pictures.

TIP So what if you do want to send a document or other file via e-mail? Don't worry, you can do so, you just can't do it from here. To send a Word document, for example, just use the Send functionality that's built into Word Mobile—as described in Chapter 12—and choose an e-mail account as the destination. Similar functionality can be found throughout Windows Phone and is thus discussed, where appropriate, throughout this book.

▶ **Priority:** Buried in the More menu, the Priority option lets you set the priority level of the e-mail to High, Normal (the default), or Low. Don't abuse this. And what the heck, try using Low Priority, if only because no one else does.

▶ **CC and BCC recipients:** Also hidden in the More menu is the Show CC and BCC option. When you toggle this option on (by tapping it), two new fields, CC: and BCC:, are added to the e-mail message between the To: field and the Subject. They work similarly to To: in that you can tap them to add recipients, but they behave a bit differently. Recipients you add to CC, for "carbon copy," are visible to everyone who receives the e-mail, as are the To: recipients. The difference is that the CC recipients aren't considered the main target of the e-mail but are rather being included, or "CC'd," as a convenience, so that they know what's going on.

BCC, meanwhile, stands for "blind carbon copy." Anyone included on this list will receive the e-mail normally, but won't be visible to the other recipients, whether they're in the To: or CC: list.

Sending and Receiving Mail

By default, Mail is configured to poll your e-mail account and sync the phone-based display with your e-mail server on a set schedule. You can tap the Sync button in the Application Bar at any time to trigger a manual synchronization between the phone and the server. But it's possible that the sync schedule isn't optimally configured. If you'd like to check this, please refer to the section "Configuring Mail and E-mail Accounts" later in this chapter.

Viewing Other Folders

I mentioned briefly at the beginning of the chapter that the Mail application displays the contents of your mail service's Inbox folder, filtered in various ways across the top pivots, by default. Some people heavily utilize a folder-based e-mail management system, however, and may have important e-mail stored in other folders. If this is the case, you'll need to navigate out of the Inbox to view other folders.

Here's how you do so: From any main mail view, tap the Folders button. This will display a screen like that shown in Figure 10-23: You'll see only those folders you've already accessed from the phone (Inbox, by default) and an option, Show All Folders, which does exactly what it sounds like it would do.

When you tap Show All Folders, the Folders view expands to show all of the available e-mail folders on the server. This view will vary from service to service, since each e-mail service provides a slightly different folder structure. And of course, you may have made your own folders in a bid to better organize your life. At the very least, you should see folders similar to Outbox, Sent Items, Deleted Items, and so on.

To view e-mail in a different folder, just tap it. If this is the first time you've done this, you will be prompted with a link, Sync This Folder. Tap the link and the contents of the folder will be synced to your phone. Additionally, when you visit the Folders screen in the future, that folder will show up with Inbox, without you needing to display all folders.

FIGURE 10-23: The Folders screen lets you navigate to another e-mail folder on your e-mail service's server.

Searching for E-mail

Thanks to the integration of Microsoft's Bing search functionality—which I examine in more detail in Chapter 9—you can use the phone's dedicated Search button to search for e-mail while in any folder view. To do so, just tap the Search button. When you do, a search box appears at the top of the screen and a virtual keyboard pops up so you can type in your query (Figure 10-24).

> **NOTE** Searching is for the current folder only. If you wish to search for e-mail in a different folder, you'll need to navigate there first, as described earlier.

From this search box, you can search for the names of people who have sent you e-mail ("John," "Paul," or whatever), subject text, or e-mail body text. And the search results get whittled down as you type, helping you find exactly what you need.

Working Offline

In those rare instances when you're totally disconnected from any network—either a 3G data network or a Wi-Fi wireless network—you can still use Mail. That's because the contents of your inbox (and, optionally, other folders) are synced with the phone and can still display when you're disconnected, or offline. So you can still create new e-mails, respond to e-mails, triage e-mail, and perform other actions. The changes will take place on the phone only, but when you connect online again, these changes will be synced back up to the server, automatically.

FIGURE 10-24: Search your inbox at the tap of a button.

CONFIGURING MAIL AND E-MAIL ACCOUNTS

As you know, each e-mail account you configure for Windows Phone is accessed from a different version of the Mail application. So if you have configured multiple e-mail-type accounts, you will have multiple Mail applications in All Programs, with names like Gmail, Hotmail, Outlook, Yahoo! Mail, and so on (or whatever names you may have used). This has some interesting ramifications in day-to-day use—that is, you must access different applications to read all of your mail—but it also means that you have multiple e-mail accounts to configure. And if my experience with Windows Phone is any barometer, you're going to want to take the time to do this right.

The reason is simple: When you create an e-mail account (or any account that includes access to an e-mail service), Windows Phone applies default values to various options. And these options may not be optimally configured for your needs. So you are going to want to take the time to walk through these steps, once each for each of your configured e-mail accounts. It's a bit monotonous if you have multiple accounts. But you'll agree it's worth it when you discover, say, that one of your accounts isn't even automatically downloading mail to the phone.

You can configure an individual e-mail account in one of two ways. The most obvious is to navigate to All Programs, Settings, Email & Accounts, and then pick the account you wish to modify.

You could do it like this, but there's a better way.

Or, instead of that first way, you can manually launch one of your e-mail accounts, either via its Start screen-based live tile, or from within the All Programs list. Then, tap the More button and choose Settings. This will display the E-mail Account Settings screen shown in Figure 10-25.

Why go through this convoluted process? Because this screen has a single, additional option you won't find if you try to configure the account through the E-mail & Settings interface: Use an E-mail Signature. If you want to change this from the default option—Sent from Windows Phone—or, more likely, just want to turn it off, you can do so right here. You never would have found this option if you had gone with Plan A.

With that out of the way, tap the giant Sync Settings button. This will display a more complete Settings screen. (In fact, it's the one you would have seen if you ignored my advice.) This has a wide range of configurable options, much of which is obvious. But there are a couple options that are quite important and quite possibly are misconfigured. These are:

> **Download new content:** This option determines how frequently the phone synchronizes with the e-mail server. The possibilities vary here from

account type to account type. For example, for Yahoo! Mail, you can only choose between every 15 minutes, every 30 minutes, hourly, every 2 hours, and manually. (And, oddly, for Yahoo! Mail, *every 2 hours* is the default.)

More sophisticated e-mail services—those that offer "push" e-mail support through Exchange ActiveSync and similar technologies—will offer an additional choice, *as items arrive*. This is the optimal choice for these types of accounts, which include Windows Live, Outlook, and Google.

▶ **Download e-mail from... :** This option determines how far back to go when syncing with the server, and the further back you go, the bigger your bandwidth and storage requirements are. Available choices include the last 3 days, the last 7 days, the last 2 weeks, the last month, and any time. (Not all accounts will offer all of these choices, however.) For most account types, the default is *the last 7 days*.

FIGURE 10-25: E-mail Account Settings.

Once you've evaluated and potentially changed the settings for one account, you'll want to do the same for each configured e-mail account. You'll probably find, as I have, that each is configured a bit differently, depending on the source, and that you'll need to do some tweaking.

SUMMARY

In my testing of Windows Phone, I've found the Mail application to be one of the system's strong points. I do understand the need for a unified inbox, and hope that Microsoft will provide such an update in the future. But even in its current form, Mail provides all of the mobile e-mail functionality most people will need, including its superior triaging capabilities, which put it on par with my previous smart phone favorite, the iPhone.

Where Windows Phone goes beyond the iPhone is in its more efficient use of onscreen real estate and its liberating and efficient text-based interface. E-mail is at heart a textual experience and by forcing the UI to get out of the way, Microsoft has created a solution that is unique in the mobile space. Like much of Windows Phone, it's not perfect. But Mail is easily the most productive mobile e-mail solution I've found, and a key differentiator for this new platform.

CHAPTER 11

Tracking Your Schedule with Calendar

In keeping with its powerful Exchange and Windows
Live–based calendar solutions, Microsoft has provided a new calendar application for

Windows Phone users as well. The Windows Phone Calendar provides a vastly simplified

experience compared to these other more full-featured calendars, one that is both more

at home in the device's relatively tiny form factor and more in keeping with the modern

computing mantra of simplicity.

I examine the Calendar experience in this chapter, and explain how it works

within the Windows Phone way of doing things, including pop-up and lock screen

notifications, the customized Start screen button, and the streamlined calendar

views in the application itself. When it comes to managing your schedule, Windows

Phone is an excellent choice.

CONNECTED CALENDARS

Windows Phones have had calendars since, well, before they were phones, actually. So it's not surprising that your Windows Phone ships with an excellent calendar app that, get this, is called Calendar.

> **NOTE**   Throughout this chapter, when I use the term *Calendar* (with a capital "C"), I'm referring specifically to the Calendar app in Windows Phone and not to calendars in general.

Calendar isn't just any calendar app, however. It's a *connected* calendar, one that is designed to work in concert with one or more online calendars. These online calendars include Microsoft's Exchange, of course, but also a new generation of standards-based web calendars like those offered by Apple, Google, and others. And yes, for you Windows Live fans out there, Calendar works just fine with Microsoft's free consumer-oriented calendar, Windows Live Calendar (which is sometimes confusingly called Hotmail Calendar). If you set up a Windows Live ID as I recommended early on in the book—and you did, right?—then you already have a Windows Live Calendar.

What Calendar *doesn't* work with are PC-based calendars in Microsoft Outlook, Mozilla Sunbird, and other applications. Nor does it work with non-standards-based calendars, like that provided by Yahoo currently. For the former case, the reasoning is simple: Aside from media sync with the Zune PC software, Windows Phone offers virtually no interaction with the PC. So if your data is locked away in some individual application, it's time to move into the 21st century and get your schedule up in the cloud.

Given this, I'll assume that you are at least using Windows Live Calendar together with Windows Phone's Calendar app. You can of course, use other calendars as well (or, shame on you, *instead* of Windows Live Calendar).

General Features of Connected Calendars

Before diving into Calendar, I want you to take a moment to understand some of the benefits of using a connected calendar.

> ► **Useful:** Connected calendars allow you to create, edit, and maintain scheduling information, such as events, meetings, and appointments, so you can easily organize your schedule. You can also create multiple calendars within any given connected calendar solution, so if you want to overthink things and create separate calendars for work, personal, and other categories, you're free to do so.

NOTE Well, you're free to do so on the web. One important limitation of Windows Phone's Calendar app is that it can *only* sync with the primary calendar in any connected calendar solution. So while you can indeed connect Calendar to multiple calendar solutions, it will only "see," and sync with, the primary calendar in each.

CONNECTIONS, NOT SILOS

As it turns out, you can use Calendar without connecting it to any external (web-based calendars) as a sort of standalone application. I don't recommend this for many reasons, but the most obvious is that if you do so, the content you store in Calendar will be locked inside the phone and be inaccessible from anywhere else. So if you lose the phone or are without it when you need to access some schedule information, you're out of luck. Don't silo your data: Make sure you connect your phone to at least one account with a decent online calendar—I recommend either Google Calendar or Windows Live Calendar, as both are free and work well—so that you can always access your schedule data no matter where you are.

- ▶ **Shared:** With a connected calendar, you can share parts or all of your schedule with others. Most connected calendars offer at least some form of privacy controls so that you can determine who you share with and what you share. You can also invite other people to events in your calendar.

- ▶ **Mobile:** Thanks to mobile device integration, and two-way over-the-air synchronization, you can access your calendar on the go, using your smart phone or other connected device. This can happen via dedicated, feature-rich apps, like Calendar, or through mobile web clients.

NOTE You may have heard the term *push* used with e-mail, contacts, and calendars. Yes, Windows Phone does support push. This means that instead of requiring software on the phone to arbitrarily poll the e-mail, contacts, or calendar databases, these servers will instead "push" information to connected clients whenever needed. So if there's a schedule change or a pending event, your phone-based calendar will be updated immediately. And push isn't just faster: It's also better for device battery life.

▶ **Notifications and reminders:** Connected calendars can be configured to provide you with reminders about upcoming events in your schedule. These calendars typically have a default reminder set, but you can set your own. And you can be reminded in different ways, too, by e-mail, perhaps, a notification pop-up on your Windows desktop, or with a text message.

▶ **Desktop sync:** In addition to working with mobile devices, connected calendars can be used in tandem with powerful PC-based applications, such as Microsoft Outlook or Windows Live Mail (which, despite its name, offers calendaring functionality, too).

▶ **Free (usually):** Most connected calendars—including Google Calendar and Windows Live Calendar—are absolutely free, though you will sometimes see web ads if you access them from your PC's web browser. Some connected calendars— Microsoft Exchange and Apple's MobileMe, for example—are not free, however. In my experience, it doesn't make sense for individuals to pay for this kind of functionality since the free options are so good (and are in fact superior, in many cases). But if you have to use Exchange because of work, no worries: It works just fine with Windows Phone.

▶ **Free calendars:** One of the more underappreciated side effects of the open web standards used by connected calendars is that there are a host of free and useful calendars out there. And you can *subscribe* to them via your own calendar. There are calendars for local weather, holidays, sports team schedules, and much more.

> **TIP** For the record, a connected calendar is a calendar that conforms to the iCal, or iCalendar, standard, which specifies "interoperable calendaring and scheduling services for the Internet." Those who back iCal propose that all calendars should use a single, open standard for interoperability purposes. It's a great idea and works well in the real world. You can find out more about the iCal format on the IETF Web site (`ietf.org/rfc/rfc2445.txt`).

Using Windows Live Calendar

As noted previously, Microsoft's connected calendar is called Windows Live Calendar. Shown in Figure 11-1, Windows Live Calendar is pretty representative of the connected calendar world, with day, week, month, and agenda views, support for multiple calendars, calendar subscription and publishing functionality, and sharing features.

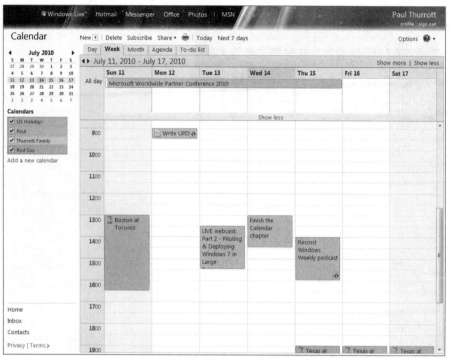

FIGURE 11-1: Windows Live Calendar.

Windows Live Calendar is also available in a mobile web version (Figure 11-2) that is accessible from smart phone-based web browsers like those found on the iPhone, Android, and, yes, Windows Phone. And you can access it from desktop applications in Windows, such as the aforementioned Outlook and Windows Live Mail.

Back in Chapter 1, I explained why it's important for Windows Phone users to create and configure a Windows Live ID that is connected to all of the various social networks and other online services of which you're a member. And in Chapter 2, you learned how to log on to this account with your Windows Phone, opening up the various experiences on the device to all of your connected data. This ID is also associated with a Windows Live Calendar, and since you connected your phone to your Windows Live ID, the Calendar app on the device is already populated with whatever scheduling information is available in your primary calendar in Windows Live Calendar.

As you use Calendar (on the phone) to access Windows Live Calendar (on the Web), you will be viewing live information, of course. But when you make changes on the phone, those changes will be reflected back in the web version of the calendar. The reverse is also true, of course: Any change you make in Windows Live Calendar will be reflected in Calendar as well.

▶ As a free web calendar aimed at consumers, Windows Live Calendar is a decent solution, one that gives Google Calendar a run for its money. (Google Calendar is still considered the best of the connected calendars, so I'll understand if you stray.)

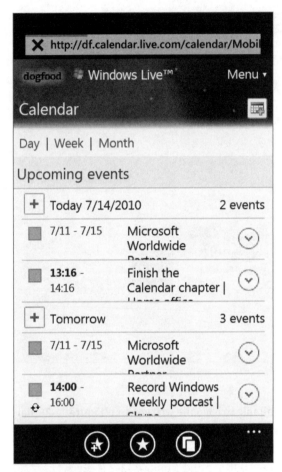

FIGURE 11-2: Windows Live Calendar in mobile web guise.

Windows Live Calendar is pretty straightforward and I assume that anyone with a smart phone has spent at least a bit of time with some calendaring solution. That said, here are a few things you might want to do with Windows Live Calendar before accessing the service on your phone.

▶ **Consider creating different calendars:** I happen to prefer using a single calendar (imaginatively named *Paul*) for all of my own events, but you may want to create different calendars for different categories of events (such as the aforementioned *work* and *personal*). How you do this is up to you, of course, as everyone has a different style of working. But each calendar can have its own color in the web-based version of Windows Live Calendar (and in various desktop clients and on the phone), which can help you understand the type of event just by glancing at it. You create a new calendar by clicking Add a Calendar in the Windows Live Calendar task pane to bring up the interface shown in Figure 11-3.

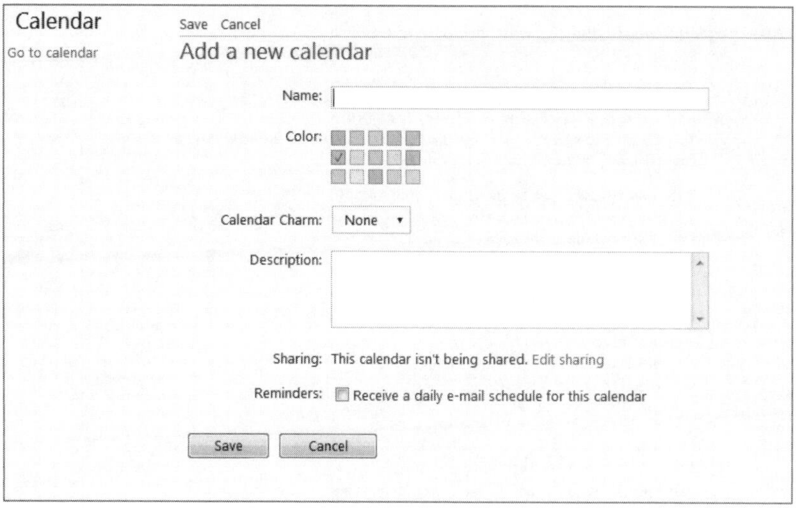

FIGURE 11-3: Adding a new calendar.

Of course, as I mentioned previously, you can only access your primary calendar from the Windows Phone Calendar app. While I feel that Microsoft will correct this strange limitation quickly, you can work around this by creating secondary accounts at Windows Live or Google Calendar specifically for multiple calendars. Then, you can configure each account to sync only calendars with Windows Phone, providing you with multiple, free calendars, all in one device. It may sound a bit tedious, but you only have to do it once, and then you can access the calendars from the single UI on your Windows Phone.

▶ **Configure calendar sharing:** Windows Live Calendar supports numerous sharing options on a per-calendar basis. To access the sharing interface (Figure 11-4), click on the calendar name in the Windows Live Calendar task pane and then click Edit Sharing.

The default setting is Don't Share This Calendar (Keep It Private). But you can optionally configure the calendar so that it is shared only with those you specify, via your contacts list, or, preferably, through a view-only link.

You can also make your calendar public. I do not recommend this, unless of course you want to publicize when you're not home so someone can more easily rob your house.

There are three link types offered up by Windows Live Calendar: HTML, ICS, and RSS. Most calendar applications expect the ICS version of the link.

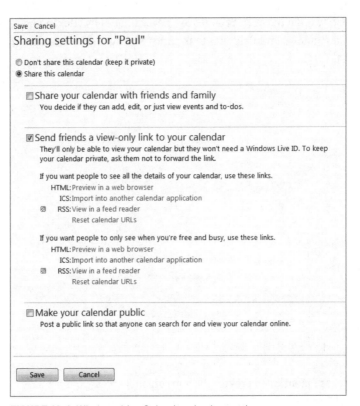

FIGURE 11-4: Windows Live Calendar sharing settings.

▶ **Subscribe to other calendars:** As noted previously, there are numerous public calendars available out there, and you could easily subscribe to them if you only knew where to look. As it turns out, there are many online calendar resources. One of the best is Apple's iCal Library (www.apple.com/downloads/macosx/calendars). This library includes professional sports schedules, worldwide holidays, movie openings, and more. Another excellent resource is iCalShare (www.icalshare.com), which lists even more calendars to which you can subscribe, in a bewildering array of categories.

Using sites such as these, you can browse different calendars until you find one to which you'd like to subscribe. I'm a Red Sox fan (who isn't?) and as you might expect, there are a number of calendars devoted to the schedule of Boston's major league baseball team. In Figure 11-5, you can see that I added the Red Sox team schedule to my Windows Live Calendar. You add calendar subscriptions by clicking the Subscribe link at the top of Windows Live Calendar. (I also gave it an appropriate color: Red.)

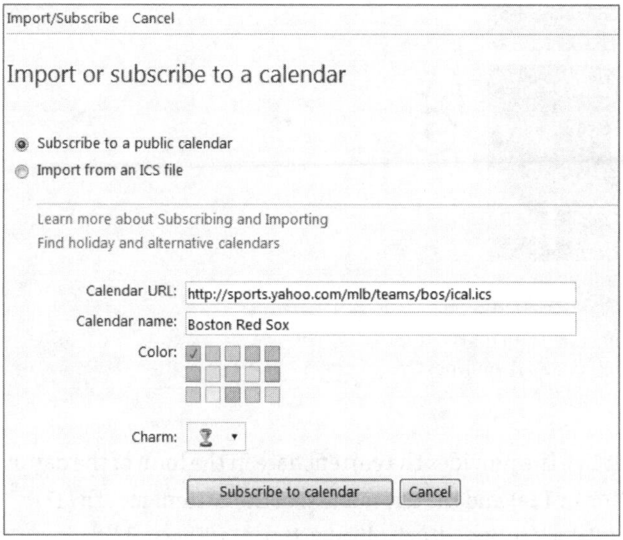

FIGURE 11-5: By subscribing to public calendars, you can find out about upcoming events you care about.

Okay, that's the fun stuff. It's time to jump onto the phone and see how this all plays out on the go.

GLANCING AT YOUR SCHEDULE ON THE GO

A shortcut to the Calendar app is pinned to the Windows Phone home screen by default and is afforded a rare "double-wide," rectangular (rather than square) live tile. That's because the Calendar live tile displays textual information about your next appointment, right on the tile. This works a bit differently from the simpler notifications you may have seen on other live tiles. So instead of a number (1, 2, 3, or whatever) representing the number of upcoming appointments, the live tile will actually provide details about the next event, as shown in Figure 11-6.

The Calendar live tile provides three discrete pieces of information about your next appointment. These are:

- **Subject:** The name you've given to the appointment.
- **Location:** Where the appointment is occurring.
- **When:** The time, or time frame, for the appointment.

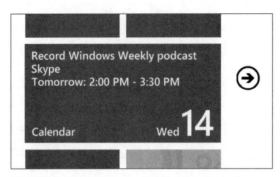

FIGURE 11-6: The Calendar live tile is particularly expressive, with detailed information about your next scheduled event.

Additionally, the Calendar live tile provides the current date in the form of the day of the week (abbreviated, like Mon or Tue) and the day number of the current month (17). So if it is Monday, June 17, the Calendar live tile will display Mon 17. (These abbreviations may differ if you've configured Windows Phone for a non-U.S. locale.)

Combined with the details of your next appointment, that's an awful lot of useful information. But Microsoft feels that your calendar is *so* important that it also supplies glanceable appointment information right on the Windows Phone lock screen. So even if you haven't logged onto your device yet, you can still find out a bit about upcoming events just by glancing at the screen.

Amazingly, this information is only slightly less detailed than what you can see on the Calendar live tile. Looking at the Windows Phone lock screen, you'll see the time and date in very large letters, centered on the screen. And at the bottom of the screen, in small letters, you'll see the number of missed calls/voice mails and unread e-mails, next to phone and mail icons, respectively. Between these two elements, in even smaller letters, you will see information about your next appointment. This includes the Subject and When fields, so it's pretty expressive. You can see an example of this in Figure 11-7.

NOTE In Windows Mobile 6.5, Microsoft created a nifty lock screen that would allow you to unlock the screen and go directly into the phone, calendar, messaging, and other experiences. Unfortunately, this useful interface is not available in Windows Phone. Instead, you can view time, date, calendar, phone/message, and e-mail information, but when you unlock the screen you are brought directly to the new home screen.

FIGURE 11-7: Information about your next appointment is available right on the Windows Phone lock screen.

USING CALENDAR

The glanceable stuff is interesting, but eventually you are going to want to actually use the Calendar application. Fortunately, it's a full-featured affair, and while the interface has been perhaps over-simplified in a way that is common to Windows Phone, you'll find virtually everything you need—from a scheduling perspective—within.

NOTE There is one obvious "weirdism" to the Calendar user interface. Where the Mail UI has a text-friendly black on white color scheme, Calendar goes in the opposite direction, offering white (and colored) text on a black background. If you opt for a white background in your Windows Phone theme, however, Calendar does utilize black (and colored) text on a white background too. (For clarity, I'm using the black on white theme for the screenshots in this book.)

When you launch Calendar for the first time, you should see something similar to Figure 11-8.

The UI is straightforward. On the top is the pivot, which consists of just two options, Day and Agenda. These correspond to the two default view options. In the center, largest part of the screen, you will see the actual calendar, and this interface changes according to which view you select.

On the Application Bar at the bottom of the screen, there are three buttons. They are:

> **Today:** Tap this and the calendar will display the current day and, if possible in the current view, the current time.

> **New:** This launches the New Appointment interface, which I examine in just a moment.

> **Month:** Tap this third button and Calendar will switch to a full-screen Month view, shown in Figure 11-9, which dispenses with the pivot and Application Bar controls. Note that there is tiny, illegible text on each day that has an appointment.

To scroll back and forward in time through the months, simply flick your finger up (back) and down (forward) on the calendar (not left or right as you might imagine).

TIP While in this Month view, you can tap any day on the grid to "zoom" into that date. It will then display that date in either Day or Agenda view, depending on whatever view you used last.

You will need to tap the Back button to return to the normal Calendar views.

There is also a fourth, hidden option, Calendars, which can be accessed by tapping the More (...) button. This interface, shown in Figure 11-10, lets you manage which calendars to display and which color to assign to each calendar.

For each calendar, you'll see a separate On/Off switch and a color option. Available colors include mint, indigo, purple, magenta, pink, tangerine, brown, chocolate, grass, gold, teal, and ocean. Or you can simply leave it on the default, automatic, which matches the color of the calendar to the accent color used in the system theme you've configured.

FIGURE 11-8: The Windows Phone Calendar app.

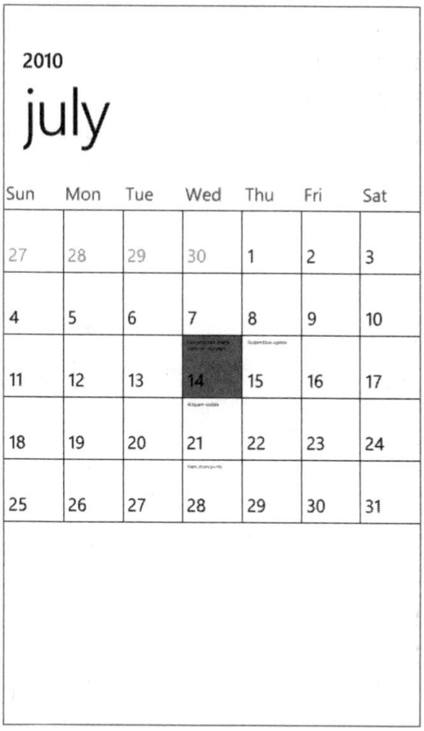

FIGURE 11-9: Calendar's full-screen Month view.

NOTE In the interests of simplicity, Calendar does not include some common desktop/web calendar views like Week or Work Week. Calendar also does not, curiously, reorient its display when the phone is held in landscape mode. You know, where a Week-type view would make particular sense. Maybe in the next version.

Back in the main calendar display, you can switch into Agenda view, by simply swiping right on the top pivot. Agenda view, shown in Figure 11-11, is a more textual, list-like way of examining your schedule. It provides the same options as Day view, and you can scroll down to view future appointments and click on appointments to view more information.

TIP Like other Windows Phone applications, you can launch Calendar using Windows Phone's integrated voice command functionality. To do so, hold down the Start button on the phone and say "Open Calendar." Try to say something like "new appointment," however, and you'll find yourself searching for "Newell Pointman" or similar. Some things are best left to more traditional interfaces.

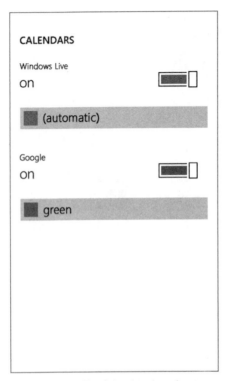

FIGURE 11-10: The Calendars interface.

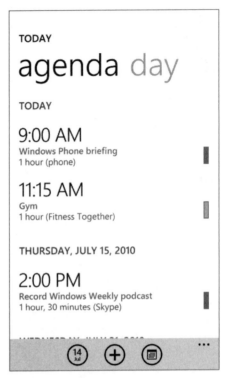

FIGURE 11-11: Agenda view.

CALENDAR DOESN'T SUPPORT TASKS

There is one major (and obvious) feature missing from Calendar. It doesn't support tasks from Exchange, or what Windows Live Calendar calls To-Do items. Again, maybe this is something Microsoft will add in v2, but for now, this is a glaring functional hole.

Oddly enough, because I switched to Google Calendar years ago, before that solution offered any sort of tasks functionality, I stopped separating "tasks" from "appointments." This isn't the solution you may be looking for, but it has worked for me, and coincidentally works fine with Windows Phone because all of my tasks are configured as appointments.

WORKING WITH APPOINTMENTS AND REMINDERS

At some point, you're going to need to work with specific appointments. And as you might expect, Calendar offers some useful functionality around creating and viewing appointments, as well as how you can be reminded about pending appointments.

Creating a New Appointment

To create a new appointment directly on the phone, tap the New Appointment button on the Calendar Application Bar. Doing so launches the New Appointment interface, which is shown in Figure 11-12.

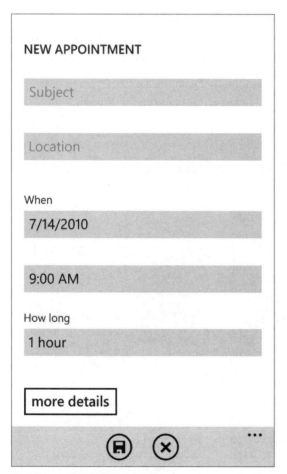

FIGURE 11-12: The New Appointment interface.

This interface provides the following fields, each of which maps to a specific bit of information about the appointment you're creating:

▶ **Subject:** This is the name of the appointment you're creating and will typically be short and descriptive, like "Meeting with Mark" or "Lunch with Steph."

▶ **Location:** Like the Subject, this field can be filled with short, descriptive text, usually the location (an address or more vague location) or, in the case of a phone call, the phone number and other call information.

▶ **Account:** This field is very important, and pertains to the calendar to which you'd like to add the appointment. When you tap this item, the view will expand to show the configured account types that include calendar support (Windows Live, Google, Outlook, and so on). If you have only one calendar account configured, the Account field will not be present.

▶ **When (Date):** The first When field will be filled with a date. When you tap this field, the Windows Phone date picker appears, as shown in Figure 11-13.

To pick a date, scroll up or down individually on the Month, Day, and Year items. As you select each item, a range of boxed options will magically appear (Figure 11-14).

▶ Subject and Location may look small, and indeed they should be filled with only small amounts of text. But these text boxes can be filled with an inordinate amount of text if need be. I don't recommend doing so. But it's there if you need it.

FIGURE 11-13: Calendar utilizes a full-screen data picker so you can select the correct date for a new appointment.

FIGURE 11-14: The date picker lights up when you select individual items.

- ▶ **When (Time):** Like the Date field, the Time field provides a sliding "picker" UI, though this time of course it's a time picker with individual Hour, Minute, and AM/PM items. It works identically to the date picker.

- ▶ **How long:** This field determines the duration of the appointment. When tapped, the How Long interface appears. As shown in Figure 11-15, you can choose between various durations, including 0 minutes, 30 minutes, 1 hour, All Day, and more.

- ▶ **More Details:** Tapping this button reveals several additional fields. These include:

  - ▷ **Reminder:** Here, you can specify when the phone will remind you about the appointment in question. By default, the reminder is set to 15 minutes, meaning *15 minutes before the start of the appointment*. But you can set this to any one of a number of values between None and 1 week.

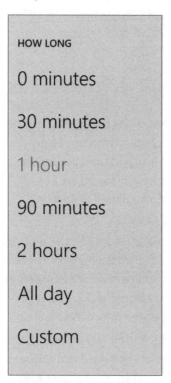

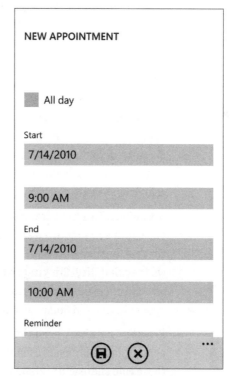

To specify appointment start and end times on different dates, tap the Custom item. The When fields will be replaced by separate sets of Start and End fields, as shown in Figure 11-16.

FIGURE 11-15: How long will the appointment last?

FIGURE 11-16: It's a bit ponderous on the phone, but you can specify start and end times on different dates.

▷ **Occurs:** This field determines if an appointment recurs which, by default, it does not. However, in some cases, you may want an appointment to recur on a regular basis. For example, perhaps you go to the gym at the same time every Monday. Several possibilities are available, including Once (the default), Every day, Every weekday, Every *day of the week* (where *day of the week* is the day of the week of the original appointment, such as, *Wednesday*), Day *number* of every month (where *number* is the day number of the original appointment, such as *14*), or every *Month number* (where *Month* is a month name like *July* and *number* is the month number of the original appointment, that is, *7*).

> **TIP** Can you see what's missing here? That's right: It's not possible to configure more complicated recurrences. For example, maybe you actually go to the gym at the same time every Monday, Wednesday, and Friday. You wouldn't be able to set up that appointment in Windows Phone easily, because you'd have to set up a different recurring appointment for each set of Monday, Wednesday, and Friday appointments. If you do have more complex recurrence needs, consider making the appointment at the calendar service in question, rather than on the phone. Outlook and Google Calendar, for example, could handle this more complex type of occurrence more readily. (Tellingly enough, Windows Live Calendar could not.)

▷ **Status:** Here, you can configure your status during the time that the appointment is taking place. This can be set to Free, Tentative, Busy (the default), or Out of Office. This field is important if you intend to share your calendar with anyone else, especially coworkers who might need to schedule shared appointments and would need to know your availability.

▷ **Attendees:** This field provides an Add Someone button. When you tap this, you can specify required and optional attendees for the appointment, and these attendees will receive an e-mail invitation so that they can confirm their availability. Clicking either option will launch a contact picker so you can choose attendees from your address books. Attendees you pick appear in the Add Someone button when you're done.

▷ **Private:** This check box is left unchecked by default, meaning that appointments are public ("not private") by default and can be shared with those who share your calendar. Marking an appointment as private means that it will not be shared, even with those who do share your calendar.

▷ **Notes:** Where the Subject and Location fields are typically used with only small amounts of entered text, Notes is a virtually unlimited text box that you can fill with whatever text-based appointment details you like.

To save a new appointment, tap the Save button in the Application Bar. (It resembles a floppy disk for some reason.) To cancel an appointment, tap Cancel (X). If you've entered data in any field and attempt to cancel the appointment, Calendar will warn you that you're about to lose whatever information you added.

Once the appointment is saved, it appears in the current calendar view. As shown in Figure 11-17, a new appointment shows the Subject and Location in Day view.

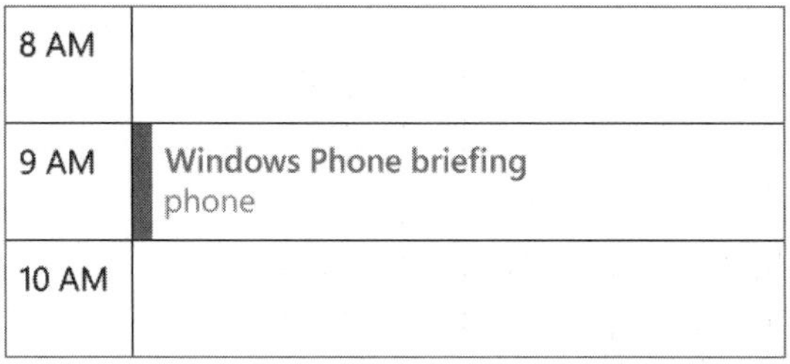

8 AM	
9 AM	Windows Phone briefing phone
10 AM	

FIGURE 11-17: Appointments provide a bit of detail at a glance.

If you switch to Agenda view, you'll also see the duration. Both views provide color coding so you can tell with which calendar the appointment is associated. And Agenda view uses a colored rectangle next to each appointment to indicate both the calendar to which the appointment belongs and whether you're free (outlined rectangle) or busy (filled-in rectangle).

Accessing Existing Appointments

When you access an already-created appointment—by tapping it in either Day or Agenda view—you receive a slightly different view. That is, instead of a screen full of entry fields, you see a read-only version of the appointment like that shown in Figure 11-18. In this view, you will see whatever fields were filled out for that appointment.

There are two major options here, beyond simply checking up on the appointment. You can edit the appointment by tapping the Edit Application Bar button (it looks like a pencil); doing so brings up the Edit Appointment screen, which looks and works just like the New Appointment screen except that all of the previously filled-in data populates the appropriate fields. Or you can delete the appointment, by tapping the Delete button (which looks like a trash can).

FIGURE 11-18: You get a cleaner, easy-to-read display when you view an appointment.

Dealing with Reminders

Reminders work exactly as expected. If you have an appointment for which you've configured a reminder, that reminder will surface at the top of the Windows Phone screen—turning on the phone if needed—and chime. (You can find out how to configure whether to play a chime in the next section.) This pop-up reminder will resemble Figure 11-19, and will appear regardless of what you're doing with the phone.

You have two choices here: Snooze and Dismiss. If you tap Snooze, the reminder pop-up will disappear and then reappear in 5 minutes. If you tap Dismiss, you will not be reminded anymore.

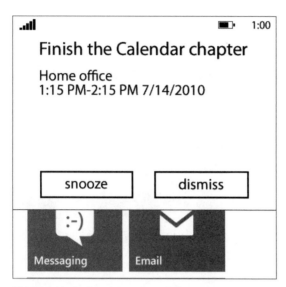

FIGURE 11-19: Appointment reminders appear over whatever else you're doing with the phone and need to be handled in some way.

CONFIGURING CALENDAR

You may expect there to be any number of Calendar configuration options in the Windows Phone Settings interface. Oddly enough, that's not the case. And if you visit Settings and then Applications, you'll discover that Calendar isn't even listed. But there is in fact one Calendar-related setting you can configure. You just need to know where to look.

To find it, navigate instead to Settings and then Ringtones & Sounds. This is shown in Figure 11-20.

Scroll down near the bottom of the list and you'll see an option called Play a Sound for... Appointment Reminders (Figure 11-21). This is checked by default, meaning it is enabled, but if you don't want appointment reminders to trigger a sound when fired, you can uncheck this option.

Note, too, that the global Vibrate option (on by default, and at the very top of this list) applies to appointment reminders as well.

▶ Curiously there is no way to assign a particular sound to an appointment reminder.

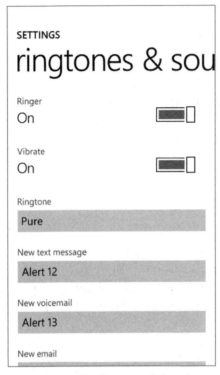

FIGURE 11-20: The Ringtones & Sounds Settings interface.

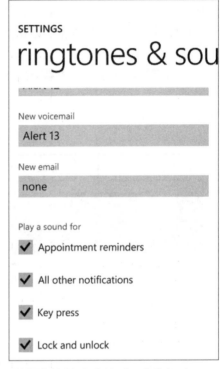

FIGURE 11-21: A single, lonely Calendar-related option can be found at the bottom of this screen.

SUMMARY

The Calendar application in Windows Phone is a decent solution, offering support for multiple connected calendars, a few basic view styles, generous appointment capabilities, and reminders. It's also a great Windows Phone citizen, with simple views on the Lock screen and Home screen, and integration with the device's native voice command feature.

More important, perhaps, Calendar is just part of a wider range of productivity solutions on Windows Phone that make this solution an ideal companion for both consumers and business users. In addition to Calendar, you can configure multiple e-mail accounts of almost any kind, configure the People hub with an integrated contacts list derived from multiple services, and view and edit Office documents via the Office hub.

Combine these capabilities further with the other exciting entertainment experiences on the phone and you arrive at something truly exciting. Point being that Calendar is just part—a good part, but just part—of the bigger puzzle that is Windows Phone.

CHAPTER 12

Getting Work Done on the Go with Office Mobile

With its Office 2010 family of products, Microsoft has advanced its best-selling office productivity solutions beyond the PC desktop with web-based Office Web Apps as well as a new generation of its Office Mobile, which runs on Windows Phone. The idea is to allow customers to be as productive as possible, no matter where they are, and no matter which devices they're using.

This isn't the first version of Office that Microsoft has released for its smart phone OS, of course. But it is the most full-featured so far. Thanks to a new emphasis on the tasks that make the most sense for mobile devices—note taking, over-the-air connectivity with your workplace's document repositories, and excellent word processing document, spreadsheet, and presentation viewing capabilities, along with basic editing functionality, Office Mobile is a great companion for any Microsoft Office user.

It also takes advantage of the unique capabilities of today's Windows Phones, with touch and gesture support, integration with the virtual keyboard and its on-the-fly suggestion functionality, and a cool new hub-based interface. So Office Mobile looks and works like an exemplary Windows Phone app.

In this chapter, you'll examine the Office hub, its OneNote Mobile, Word Mobile, Excel Mobile, PowerPoint Mobile, and SharePoint Workspace Mobile components, and how you can access and sync documents via a SharePoint 2010–based document repository. And for those readers using Microsoft's SkyDrive-based Office Web Apps, I'll explain how you can access your cloud-based documents from that service as well, albeit in more limited form.

INTRODUCING THE TINIEST MEMBER OF THE OFFICE FAMILY

Originally dubbed Pocket Office (as in, "Is that an Office in your pocket or are you just happy to see me?"), Microsoft's mobile version of Office debuted a decade ago as part of the Pocket PC platform. Originally, it consisted of Pocket Outlook, Pocket Word, and Pocket Excel, and over the years PowerPoint and OneNote applications were added as well. Eventually, the Pocket moniker was dropped in lieu of the more professional sounding name Office Mobile.

PRODUCT BUNDLING IS OKAY WHEN YOU DON'T HAVE A MONOPOLY

Since the first release, Microsoft has always shipped some version of Office Mobile with each Pocket PC/Windows Mobile/Windows Phone version. Why bundle such applications with its mobile software when it doesn't do so with traditional, PC-based versions of Windows? Likely for two reasons: First, Microsoft has never owned the dominant mobile platform and, thus, hasn't had to worry about antitrust-related product bundling issues. Second, by the time Office did appear on Microsoft's mobile platform, a number of decent office productivity solutions were already available, including DataViz's popular Documents to Go.

Prior to Windows Phone, Office Mobile was delivered as a traditional set of Windows Mobile–type apps, with the exception of Outlook, which was (and still is, in Windows Phone) divided into separate mini-applications for e-mail, calendaring, and contacts management.

> **CROSSREF** I cover e-mail in Chapter 10, calendaring in Chapter 11, and contacts management (via the all-new People hub) in Chapter 4. If you're coming to Windows Phone from a previous Windows Mobile version, these experiences have all changed pretty dramatically. And while the other Office apps described in this chapter should be largely familiar, the way you access them—via the new Office hub—is decidedly Windows Phone–centric as well.

On Windows Phone, Office functionality is provided via a hub, or panoramic experience, that spans across several screens. As you can see in Figure 12-1, when viewed as a single entity, the Office hub is a sweeping, widescreen experience with multiple sections, or columns, each providing its own unique Office related functionality.

FIGURE 12-1: The Office hub, seen as a single panoramic entity.

The Office hub provides the following sections, from left to right:

▶ **OneNote:** Right up front and center, and imbued with new importance as a result, is the OneNote Mobile experience, which provides you with quick access to notes and note-taking functionality.

▶ **Documents:** From here, you can create new Word documents, Excel spreadsheets, and PowerPoint presentations. You can also access existing documents of these kinds that are stored on the phone.

▶ **SharePoint:** If you utilize a SharePoint document repository at your work-place, you can configure your phone to automatically connect to that server so that you can easily view, edit, and work offline with documents between your phone and work.

SKYDRIVE INTEGRATION?

If you're not toiling away in an enterprise sweatshop, you may be surprised to learn that the Office hub doesn't provide a SkyDrive section so you can access your Office Web Apps–based documents in a seamless fashion. I was surprised by this as well, but as you'll see later in the chapter, you can still download, view, and edit SkyDrive-based documents from the Office hub, over the air. It's just not particularly seamless.

WHAT YOU CAN—AND CAN'T—DO WITH OFFICE MOBILE

As you might imagine, given the constrained environs of a typical Windows Phone screen, Office Mobile doesn't provide much competition for the PC-based versions of Office, or even the Office Web Apps for that matter. But it wasn't designed for that purpose. Instead, Microsoft sees Office Mobile as a companion for the Office user on the go, and it's best, I think, to understand this fact and what that means when it comes time to actually use Office Mobile on Windows Phone.

That is, you need to be realistic about the capabilities of this solution and under-stand what it is that it can and cannot do.

What You Can Do

Office Mobile is a great way to view Office documents—and from now on, unless I specify Word documents explicitly, I'm referring to Excel spreadsheets, PowerPoint presentations, and OneNote notes here as well—even rich Office documents, on the go. If all you're looking for is a document reader, Office Mobile is a fantastic solution, and it's compatible with even the very latest document formats used by the PC appli-cations in Office 2010.

Office Mobile is also a decent solution for editing Office documents, even rich Office documents, on the go. One of the issues with this functionality is that Office Mobile cannot accurately display some of the more complex document layouts supported by modern Office application versions. But as you'll see in a bit, you can generally work around these issues, and it does a great job of retaining underlying formatting even when these elements aren't accurately rendered onscreen. If what you need to do is read a document and make light edits, Office Mobile works quite well.

Office Mobile is a great solution for synchronizing Office documents between your phone and your work-based SharePoint document repositories. It also respects and understands enterprise-oriented Information Rights Management (IRM) technology, which is used to secure documents, electronically, from prying eyes.

If you are a OneNote user—and it's very clear that Microsoft intends to make you one—or just someone who likes to take notes frequently, OneNote Mobile for Windows Phone is a first-class note-taking solution.

> **NOTE** It's worth mentioning, too, that some functionality has been lost since Windows Mobile. You can no longer directly sync device-based notes with notes on your PC, and vice versa. That's because Microsoft has designed Windows Phone to not utilize Windows Mobile Device Center (or any other productivity application) for tethered PC-to-phone sync. But you can still sync notes to the PC indirectly, through Windows Live SkyDrive. I'll show you how later in this chapter.

What You Can't Do

So that's what Office Mobile can do for you. What about its limitations?

Office Mobile is somewhat lacking for those that wish to access SkyDrive-based Office documents and completely lacking if you want to sync them between the Web and your phone.

If you want to create new Word or Excel documents, Office Mobile is a decent solution that lacks only the more complex formatting options that are available on the Web and on the PC. However, if you save these documents externally to the phone, you can later edit them again in Windows or on the Web and add complex new formatting easily enough.

If you want to create new PowerPoint presentations on the go, you're out of luck: You cannot create a new presentation with PowerPoint Mobile. (That said, you could of course create basic, empty presentations and save them to the device as templates for future presentations. It does support Save As.)

USING THE OFFICE HUB

In previous Windows Mobile versions, the available Office Mobile applications were accessed individually. That is, you could find and launch Word Mobile, Excel Mobile, PowerPoint Mobile, or OneNote Mobile (or the Outlook-based e-mail, calendar, and contacts solutions) individually. In Windows Phone, that is no longer the case. In fact, aside from the e-mail, calendar, and contacts solutions built into Windows Phone, there are no individual Office applications outside of the Office hub. So if you want to access any Word, Excel, PowerPoint, OneNote, or SharePoint Workspace functionality on Windows Phone, you'll need to do so through the Office hub.

PINNING THE OFFICE HUB TO YOUR START SCREEN

The Office hub is not pinned to the default Windows Phone Start screen, so if you don't have an Office hub live tile, you may want to add it. To do so, navigate to All Programs (via the right arrow button on the Start screen), locate Office 2010, and then tap and hold. In the pop-up menu that appears, choose Pin to Start. An Office hub live tile will be added to the bottom of the Start screen, and if you wish you can of course move it to any position on the screen.

As noted previously, the Office hub consists of four sections, and provides access to five Office Mobile experiences: OneNote Mobile, Word Mobile, Excel Mobile, PowerPoint Mobile, and SharePoint Workspace Mobile. I discuss each of these solutions in turn in the following sections.

Taking Notes, Capturing Ideas, and Syncing with Mobile OneNote

If you're not familiar with Microsoft's excellent note-taking solution, OneNote, then you might be a bit shocked to see that the mobile version of this app is highlighted in the first section, or column, in the Office hub. But that's by design: Microsoft feels that OneNote will one day rank among the most frequently used Office applications (the top two today are Word and Outlook), based on usage trends and rapid uptick with certain demographics, like students. Another part of the strategy of making that happen, of course, involves giving it a key place of honor in the Office hub on Windows Phone.

This makes sense when you consider OneNote's mission: It's an idea processor, if you will; a way to jot down ideas that will later be used in full-fledged documents, such as Word documents or PowerPoint presentations. On the phone, OneNote is a wonderful tool for taking quick notes, which can include lists, pictures, and even voice clips recorded through the device's microphone. These notes can be also be synced back to Windows Live SkyDrive, Microsoft's free cloud storage solution, and then from there synced to PC-based versions of OneNote as well.

Remember, too, that in Windows Phone the various Office Mobile applications cannot be run individually. There's no way to launch Word Mobile, Excel Mobile, PowerPoint Mobile, SharePoint Workspace Mobile, or OneNote Mobile individually. Instead, you access these apps through a single interface, the Office hub. And since OneNote Mobile is the most phone-centric of all these solutions, it really does make sense that it would be the first thing you see. Chances are you're there *because* of OneNote Mobile.

Now, what were you so shocked about again?

TAKING NOTES WITH ONENOTE MOBILE

To get started with OneNote, open the Office hub and tap the New Note button. This will display a new and empty note, as shown in Figure 12-2.

From here, you can select the title field to add a title, or just start typing text-based notes. OneNote works as expected with the virtual keyboard and provides a small variety of formatting styles via the Format menu item (More, and then Format in the Application Bar). As shown in Figure 12-3, you can add or remove bold, italic, underline, and strikethrough styles, and add (yellow only) text highlighting.

> **NOTE** All OneNote Mobile formatting controls are toggles. So the first time you tap, say, the Highlight format, it will enable yellow highlighting, and that format will be applied to all subsequently typed text. To disable this format, open the Format page again and tap Highlight again.

Where OneNote Mobile really excels is in its creation of lists. You can create a basic numbered list quickly and easily by tapping the List Application Bar button, and as you can see in Figure 12-4, this list type will auto-number each line as you tap Enter.

You can also create bulleted lists, though this isn't accessible via a top-level Application Bar button. To start a bulleted list, you must instead tap More and then Bulleted List.

OneNote lists are also toggles. You select the option once to enable a list and then select it again when you're done with the list.

FIGURE 12-2: An empty OneNote note.

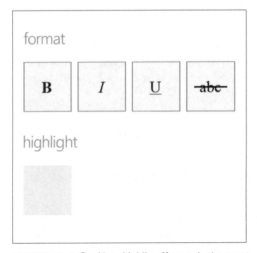

FIGURE 12-3: OneNote Mobile offers only the most basic of text formatting.

From the More menu, you will also find other simple editing controls such as Undo, Redo, Increase Indent, and Decrease Indent.

To arbitrarily move the text insertion cursor around on the OneNote writing surface, tap and hold your finger anywhere on the screen. After a second or two, an I-beam cursor will appear above your finger, so it can more easily be seen, as shown in Figure 12-5.

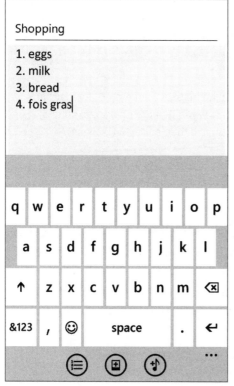

FIGURE 12-4: OneNote Mobile's real strong suit is quick list making.

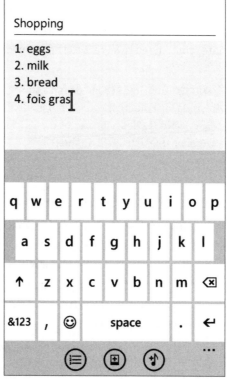

FIGURE 12-5: It's a bit funky at first, but you can move the text insertion cursor around easily once you figure out how.

Now, move your finger around, noting that the I-beam cursor moves with it, albeit just a bit above your finger. Position the I-beam cursor—*not* you finger—where you want to insert text and let go. The normal text insertion cursor will appear in that location.

> **NOTE** OneNote Mobile works only in portrait mode; if you rotate the Windows Phone device into a landscape viewing mode, OneNote won't rotate with it. This is true of Word Mobile and Excel Mobile as well. PowerPoint Mobile, conversely, *only* opens in landscape mode.

▶ *If you ever want to look at a note without the virtual keyboard taking up such a huge slice of valuable onscreen real estate, just tap the device's Back button. Now you can view the note in almost full screen mode. (The Application Bar is still visible.)*

ADDING A PICTURE TO A NOTE

OneNote Mobile also provides a simple way to add a picture to a note. Just tap the Picture Application Bar button. Windows Phone will navigate to the Pictures hub and allow you to choose from any pictures that are stored on the phone. These include pictures taken with the device's camera (Camera Roll), pictures you've downloaded from the Web (Saved Pictures), or pictures you've imported from your PC.

What it does not include, unfortunately, is access to connected pictures that otherwise display in the Pictures hub, and you won't see those pictures appear in this interface. If there is a picture you've found online that you'd like to add to a note, you'll need to save it to the phone first.

> **NOTE** OneNote Mobile doesn't offer anything in the way of picture formatting, sizing, or editing. If you need this functionality, you'll need to sync the note to SkyDrive (as described later in this chapter) and then edit it in OneNote Web App or OneNote 2010 on the PC.

ADDING A VOICE CLIP TO A NOTE

Text notes are all well and good, but when you're out and about with your phone, you oftentimes don't have time to hunker down, look at the screen, and type detailed notes. In such a case, a voice clip might make more sense.

To add a voice clip to a note, simply tap the Audio Application Bar button. When you do, the audio recording interface shown in Figure 12-6 appears, allowing you to speak into your microphone.

FIGURE 12-6: OneNote Mobile lets you make voice recordings, which can be added to notes as clips.

When you're done recording, just tap Stop. The voice recording appears as a small icon in the note page with a short text description. If you tap this icon, OneNote Mobile will ask you if you'd like to open the attachment. Tap Open to play the recording in Windows Phone's built-in media player.

SAVING NOTES

One of the neat things about OneNote Mobile (and, really, all versions of OneNote) is that you don't have to worry about saving notes: They're saved automatically. So if you tap Back to get out of a note, OneNote Mobile will automatically save it, using the title as the name.

SYNCING NOTES WITH WINDOWS LIVE SKYDRIVE

While Office Mobile conspicuously doesn't offer a seamless way to access Word documents, Excel spreadsheets, or PowerPoint presentations via Microsoft's consumer-oriented Windows Live SkyDrive cloud storage solution, it does provide a way to automatically sync OneNote-based notes between OneNote Mobile on Windows Phone and SkyDrive.

Additionally, thanks to similar functionality in the Windows-based version of OneNote 2010, you can also add your PC to the sync-fest. So notes you create in any of the three environments—OneNote 2010 on the PC, OneNote Web App on SkyDrive, or OneNote Mobile on Windows Phone—can be automatically synced between the three environments. And it's super-simple to set up.

To configure OneNote Mobile for live syncing, launch the Office Hub. If it's not already visible, pivot to the OneNote section and tap the All button. This will display the Pages screen, which lists all of your on-device OneNote notes, as shown in Figure 12-7.

Next, tap the Refresh Application Bar button. If this is the first time you've done this, OneNote will prompt you with the message shown in Figure 12-8, offering to sync your notes with SkyDrive.

Click Yes to establish automatic sync with Windows Live SkyDrive. OneNote Mobile will connect to the online service and attempt to sync your device-based notes to the Web.

When the first sync is completed, OneNote will display a new section called Notebooks. Pivot to this section, and you will see that OneNote Mobile has also created a new web-based notebook called Personal (Web), as shown in Figure 12-9.

From here, you can drill down into the notebook, and open individual notes. More important, you can create new notes, which will automatically sync to the Web.

To ensure that this is working, browse to office.live.com from your PC's web browser and log on to your Windows Live ID if required. As you can see in Figure 12-10, there will be a new OneNote notebook named Personal (Web).

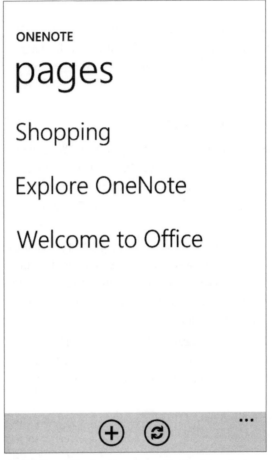

FIGURE 12-7: The OneNote Pages display lists all of your available notes.

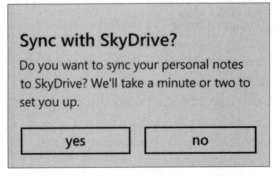

FIGURE 12-8: Would you like to sync device-based notes with SkyDrive? Yes, yes, you would.

FIGURE 12-9: Web-based notebooks can easily be accessed from Windows Phone once you set up syncing with SkyDrive.

FIGURE 12-10: A synced notebook, seen from the full Web.

And if you open up this notebook, you'll see the individual notes you've created and edited on the phone.

Any changes you make on the Web will sync back to the device (and vice versa). This includes edited notes, of course, but also other changes you may make. For example, if you rename a note or note section on the Web, those changes will be synced back to Windows Phone as well.

If you're not a OneNote user yet, OneNote Mobile may be enough to turn you into a convert. But the desktop version of this application (Figure 12-11) is even more powerful, and it can be easily configured to automatically sync with Windows Live SkyDrive as well. When you combine these three solutions—OneNote 2010 on Windows, OneNote Mobile on Windows Phone, and SkyDrive on the Web—you get the best of both worlds. Or of three worlds. Or something.

If you're not seeing the changes, simply tap the Refresh button on the Notebooks display. Many changes require you to first close a note before syncing occurs.

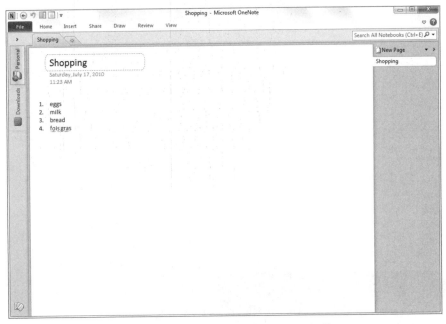

FIGURE 12-11: The desktop version of OneNote can also automatically sync your notes via SkyDrive.

Telling Your Story with Word Mobile

Where OneNote Mobile offers only basic editing features, Word Mobile, Microsoft's Windows Phone–based word processing solution, turns things up a notch with more formatting controls and additional capabilities. If OneNote seems a bit too limiting, or you simply must open a Microsoft Word document on the go, Word Mobile is the place to turn.

I assume you're familiar with word processing basics, so I want to explore how Word Mobile (Figure 12-12) expands on the text editing capabilities in OneNote Mobile.

WHICH TO USE: ONENOTE MOBILE OR WORD MOBILE?

You should also pause to consider the handful of ways in which OneNote Mobile is superior to Word Mobile. While it is relatively straightforward to add rich media such as pictures and audio files to Word documents in the desktop version of Word, you cannot do so in Word Mobile. OneNote Mobile, by contrast, does support inserting voice clips and pictures in notes. It also provides bulleted and numbered lists, two features that display properly in Word Mobile but can't be added by the application.

FORMATTING TEXT IN ADDITIONAL WAYS

Because word processing documents are meant to be seen, and aren't just notes or background material for other documents, Word Mobile includes some additional text formatting capabilities when compared to OneNote Mobile. It also includes a dedicated Format Application Bar button, which provides access to this functionality.

When you tap the Format button, the Format screen appears. In addition to the formatting abilities found in OneNote Mobile, Word Mobile adds Grow Font and Shrink Font buttons for increasing and decreasing the size of the text, respectively; two additional highlight colors (green and red); and three font colors, brown, lime and red.

WORKING IN OUTLINE VIEW

Word Mobile also sports an Outline view mode, where the display splits in half, showing the actual Word document on the top and the structure of the document, with indented headings, on the bottom. This is shown in Figure 12-13.

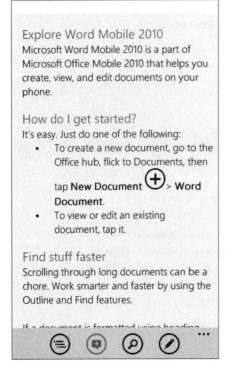

FIGURE 12-12: Word Mobile.

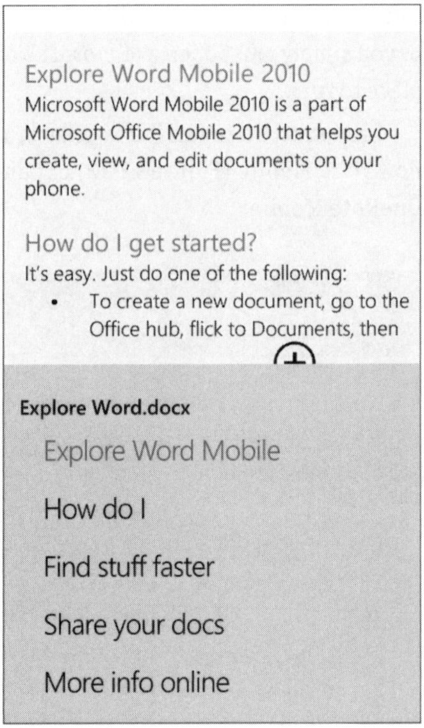

FIGURE 12-13: Word Mobile's Outline view.

In Outline view, you can quickly scroll through the sections of the loaded document. To jump to a location in the document, just tap on a heading in the Outline view pane.

Tap the device's Back button to exit Outline view.

ADDING AND REVIEWING COMMENTS

While Word Mobile doesn't support the full set of Track Changes functionality that's available in the desktop version of the product, it does supply one useful and related bit of functionality: The ability to add inline comments. With this tool, you can literally make a comment about the text you're reading and then when a co-worker or other collaborator views the comment, they can optionally act on it, or delete it.

To add a comment to a Word document, navigate to the place where you'd like to make the comment and then position the cursor in the appropriate place in the document. (Remember: Tap and hold until the I-beam cursor appears, and then position.)

Then, tap the Comment button. A comment edit box will appear as shown in Figure 12-14, allowing you to type a comment. When you're done, tap Back.

FINDING TEXT IN A DOCUMENT

Word Mobile supports the ability to find text in the currently loaded document. Curiously, you use a dedicated Find Application Bar button for this purpose and not the device's Search button.

If you're familiar with the Find on Page functionality in Internet Explorer (see Chapter 8), you'll immediately grok Word's Find feature. Just tap the Find button and then enter the text you wish to find in the text box. When you hit Enter, Word will highlight the first instance of the found text, as shown in Figure 12-15, and provide a new Next button so you can navigate to subsequent matches.

Tap Back to exit this view.

▶ The Find functionality is a bit limited. There's no Previous button, just Next, so you can't navigate backwards through the document. And Find doesn't highlight other instances of the search term simultaneously. So only the currently selected result will appear highlighted.

Explore Word Mobile 2010
Microsoft Word Mobile 2010 is a part of Microsoft Office Mobile 2010 that helps you create, view, and edit documents on your phone.

I have a comment to make about this.

q w e r t y u i o p

a s d f g h j k l

↑ z x c v b n m ⟨×⟩

&123 , ☺ space . ↵

FIGURE 12-14: Word Mobile lets you comment in a Word document.

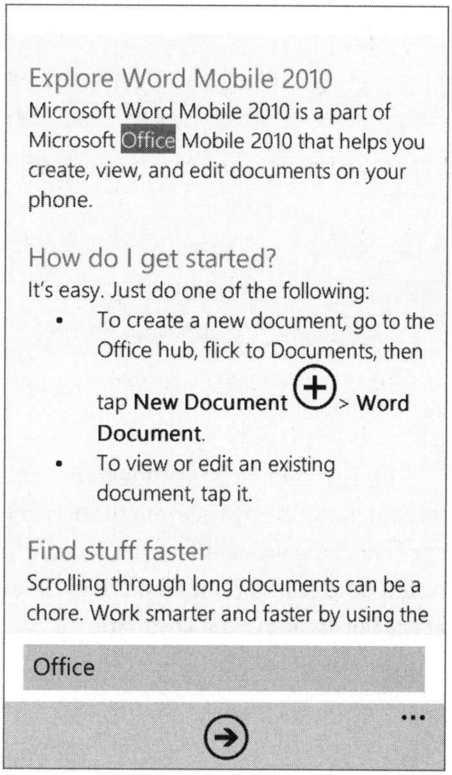

Explore Word Mobile 2010
Microsoft Office Mobile 2010 that helps you create, view, and edit documents on your phone.

How do I get started?
It's easy. Just do one of the following:
- To create a new document, go to the Office hub, flick to Documents, then tap **New Document** ⊕ > **Word Document**.
- To view or edit an existing document, tap it.

Find stuff faster
Scrolling through long documents can be a chore. Work smarter and faster by using the

Office

⊙   ...

FIGURE 12-15: You can easily find text within a Word document.

CORRECTING SPELLING

Word Mobile offers a useful automatic spell checking feature, which resembles the automatic spell checking on desktop versions of Word (and other Office apps): When you misspell a word, you'll see a red squiggly line underneath it (Figure 12-16).

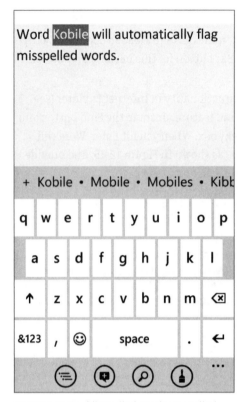

FIGURE 12-16: Misspelled words are called out for correction.

You can even add words to the phone's built-in spell checker. Simply highlight a misspelled word (tap and hold), and then tap the "+" button at the front of the suggestions list that appears.

This feature works in tandem with the Windows Phone auto-correct functionality, which works any time you're entering text on the phone. The difference is that spell checking will mark words you may have missed. To correct the spelling, tap the errant word to highlight it and then choose one of the auto-correct words that appear at the top of the virtual keyboard.

WHAT'S MISSING FROM WORD MOBILE

There are a few missing bits of functionality here. For example, while Word Mobile is smart enough to flag misspelled words, it can't help with grammar.

And oddly enough, Word Mobile on Windows Phone is missing a few features that were available in Word Mobile for Windows Mobile. Chief among these are formatting features such as text alignment and word count.

Crunching Numbers with Excel Mobile

Excel is famous around the world for its number crunching prowess, and Excel Mobile continues that tradition in the smart phone space, offering a way to create, view, and edit spreadsheets on the go. Excel Mobile is shown in Figure 12-17.

FIGURE 12-17: Excel Mobile 2010.

> **NOTE** In Excel lingo, a spreadsheet is technically called a workbook, and it can contain one or more worksheets, which are presented as tabs in desktop versions of Excel. As you'll see in a moment, these elements are presented a bit differently in Excel Mobile.

Here are some of the things you can do with Excel Mobile. (And really, I mean *some*. Though Excel Mobile provides just a tiny portion of the capabilities of the desktop version of Excel, it is a surprisingly rich application with all kinds of excellent functionality.)

ACCESSING DIFFERENT WORKSHEETS

If you're familiar with the Outline view in Word Mobile, you may be interested to know that Excel Mobile supports the same Application Bar button. But in Excel, Outline view works differently: Rather than let you navigate around a Word document by headings, in Excel Mobile it provides a way to navigate between the different worksheets in the currently loaded workbook.

Excel's Outline view can be seen in Figure 12-18.

Excel Mobile also provides a Find button that works just like the Find function in Word Mobile.

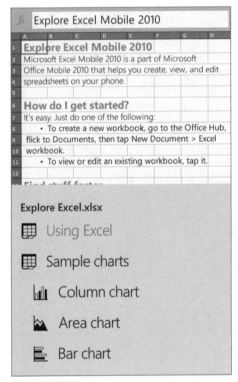

FIGURE 12-18: Move between worksheets using Outline view.

CREATING AND NAVIGATING AROUND A WORKBOOK

When you create a new Excel workbook in Excel Mobile, you get a blank workbook with three worksheets. To see this, tap the Outline Application Bar button.

Like Word Mobile, Excel Mobile supports simple Comment and Find functions. These work nearly identically to their Word cousins and are largely obvious. You can also perform basic housekeeping tasks such as Send (via Messaging or an e-mail account), Save, and Save As.

To select a cell, just tap it.

To edit the contents of a cell, select the cell and then tap the formula bar, which is a text box at the top of the screen. From here, you can type in text or numbers, or tap the Function button ("fx") to make the cell display the result of a function.

To select a range of cells, first make sure that the virtual keyboard is not displayed. If it is, tap the device's Back button. Then, tap and hold on the cell that will be at the start of the selected range. Tap Select Cells from the pop-up menu that appears, and then drag away from that cell and select the cell range you want; you must drag your finger across the screen. If you're doing it right, it will resemble Figure 12-19.

WORKING WITH FUNCTIONS

Excel Mobile includes several built-in functions, including SUM, AVERAGE, COUNT, MAX, and MIN, and via an Advanced option, many others. You apply functions as you do in the desktop version of Excel: Choose a cell, tap the Function button, and then select the function from the list (Figure 12-20).

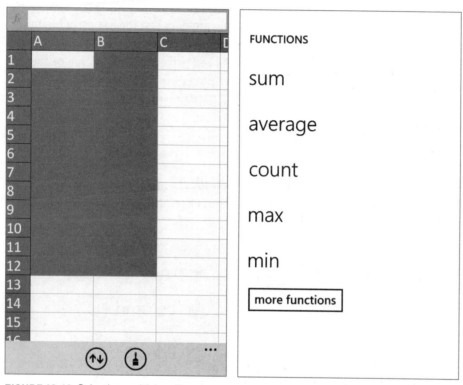

FIGURE 12-19: Selecting multiple cells.   FIGURE 12-20: Excel Mobile functions.

Then, Excel fills out the function in the formula bar, explaining in the process which variables you need to define. You can tap individual variable and then cells to fill out the formula. Or just use your editing skills to type it in manually. When you're done, tap the Enter key on the virtual keyboard and Excel Mobile will run the function, providing the correct calculation in the selected cell (Figure 12-21).

As with desktop versions of Excel, these calculations are live, so if you edit the value of a cell that is involved in a function calculation, the calculated cell value will change accordingly as well.

FORMATTING CELLS

Excel Mobile provides some basic formatting features that are similar to the format functions in Word Mobile, but with some differences. The font color options are identical, but instead of text highlighting, Excel Mobile provides a fill color, which in the context of Excel performs the same basic function: That is, it fills the background of the currently selected cell with the chosen color (red, yellow, or green).

On the text formatting front, Excel Mobile provides just the basics: bold, italics, and underlining. But it also has three commonly used number formatting types: date, accounting (that is, money or "dollar"), and percent. That way, you can select a cell, or a range of cells, and apply a formatting style accordingly.

Note that you can apply these formats to individual cells or to a range of selected cells.

Missing are some variations on these styles. You can choose date, but not how the date is styled, for example, and accounting but not a specific currency.

WORKING WITH CHARTS

To create a chart based on data in a worksheet, select a range of cells and then tap the More Application Bar button and then Insert Chart. This causes the Insert Chart screen, shown in Figure 12-22, to appear.

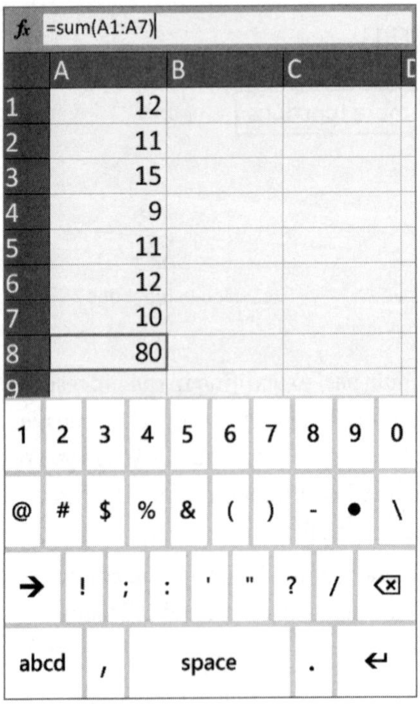

FIGURE 12-21: I can add!

FIGURE 12-22: Excel Mobile supports a number of different chart types.

Select a chart type from the list. Excel Mobile will create a new chart worksheet to accommodate the chart. A simple pie chart is shown in Figure 12-23.

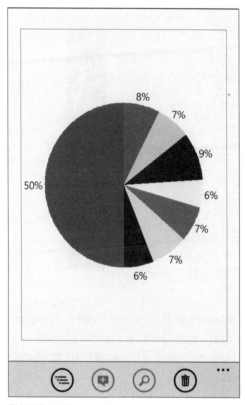

FIGURE 12-23: A pie chart.

NOTE You can't really style or format the chart in any way once it's created.

Okay, that's enough Excel Mobile. As I noted earlier, there's a lot going on there, and if you're an Excel guru, you may be surprised by how much this capable little mobile app can do.

Viewing and Editing Presentations on the Go with PowerPoint Mobile

PowerPoint Mobile is a bit different from the other Office Mobile apps in that you can't actually create a new, blank presentation on the device. Instead, you can only download, lightly edit, and save existing presentations on the device. It's also the only Office Mobile application to work in landscape (rather than portrait) view. In fact, it only works in landscape view. PowerPoint Mobile is shown in Figure 12-24.

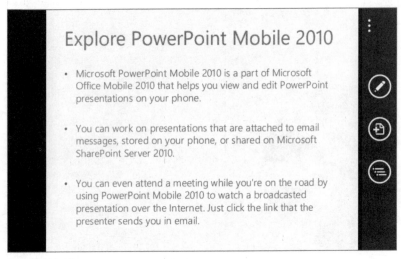

FIGURE 12-24: PowerPoint Mobile 2010.

Because of this landscape orientation, PowerPoint Mobile works a bit differently than the other Office Mobile apps tool. The Application Bar is actually hidden by default, for example. To display it, tap near the right edge of the screen. (If you don't access it quickly, it will auto-hide again.)

PowerPoint Mobile provides only a few simple options, and is in fact quite limited. These include:

- ▶ **Edit:** If you enable Edit mode, you can move between text boxes in each slide and edit the text. When you select a text box, PowerPoint moves into a strange editing view where the virtual keyboard takes up about 80 percent of the screen (Figure 12-25). When you're done editing, tap Done.

    You can also navigate between slides, move slides, hide slides, and add notes while in edit mode. These options are all available from the Application Bar that appears while you are in edit mode.

- ▶ **Notes:** Like the desktop version of PowerPoint, this tiny mobile PowerPoint lets you associate text notes with each slide in a presentation. Tap the Notes Application Bar button to enter this mode and add notes to the current slide.

- ▶ **Outline view:** Like other Office Mobile apps, PowerPoint Mobile supports an Outline view, and in this case it lets you navigate to individual slides easily via a list of slide titles.

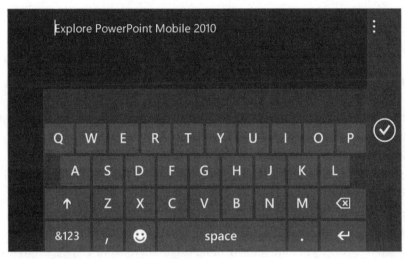

FIGURE 12-25: PowerPoint's editing mode.

And that's about it. PowerPoint Mobile is significantly lacking even when compared to the version that shipped earlier for Windows Mobile. That app offered support for editing and adding different transitions and animations, presentation playback options, and more. It also provided a way to use your smart phone as a smart presentation device, working in concert and wirelessly with a PC-based presentation. Maybe Windows Phone users will be so blessed in a future update.

ACCESSING ONLINE DOCUMENTS

If you believe as I do that the future of computing is both mobile and connected, then it stands to reason that Microsoft's mobile platforms and various connected services probably have a lot to offer in the way of integration. And that's certainly true enough, as you're learning throughout this book: Windows Phone connects to an amazing array of Microsoft and third-party services, and these connections are in many ways what makes Windows Phone so exciting.

When it comes to accessing Office-based documents in the cloud, however, Microsoft's consumer-oriented and business-based tools take decidedly different approaches. One is seamless and automatic, but priced according to the needs of businesses. The other is free and available to all, but is unfortunately limited as well.

Let's start with the free one.

Using Windows Live SkyDrive

Windows Live SkyDrive is Microsoft's online storage service and it provides everyone with a Windows Live ID with free access to 25GB of web-based storage. That sounds like a lot—because it is—but Microsoft really does do everything it can to prevent users from accessing that storage efficiently or easily. For example, Microsoft provides no way to access SkyDrive storage via the Windows Explorer interface in desktop versions of Windows, preventing users from dragging and dropping files between their PC and the cloud.

Likewise, on Windows Phone, there's no integrated, seamless way to sync documents between your phone and SkyDrive. Oddly enough, Microsoft does provide this functionality for the business-oriented SharePoint service, however. Why the disparity? Simple: Whereas SkyDrive is free, corporate customers pay Microsoft a lot of money, directly or indirectly, in order to use SharePoint. Thus, their lives are made easier.

> **NOTE** I explain how SharePoint/Windows Phone integration works in the next section.

So in the world of the haves and have-nots, SkyDrive users are decidedly in the have-not camp. But that doesn't mean you can't access SkyDrive-based documents from Windows Phone. You just have a bit more work to do. Here's how to make it happen.

CONNECTING TO YOUR SKYDRIVE-BASED DOCUMENTS

The first step is to connect to your SkyDrive-based document repository, which can be found at office.live.com on either the PC or the phone. You'll need to use Internet Explorer to access this site, and then log on with your Windows Live ID if it's not already set to auto-logon.

> **TIP** On the PC, you also gain access to the Office Web Apps at this address, web-based versions of Word, Excel, PowerPoint, and OneNote.

What you'll see here will vary depending on whether you've ever used or customized the site. If you're new to SkyDrive from an online document perspective, it will be empty but for a few stock folders like Personal and Shared. Otherwise, you'll see a list of folders and documents like that shown in Figure 12-26.

> **NOTE** If you've never used SkyDrive before, it will be worth adding a few documents to the site from your PC's browser. You can do this by copying preexisting documents from your PC to the site, using SkyDrive's uploading functionality, or by using Office Web Apps to create some new documents. That way you'll at least have something to work with.

VIEWING A SKYDRIVE-BASED OFFICE DOCUMENT IN THE BROWSER

To view a Word, Excel, or PowerPoint document in a scaled-down, read-only mode, navigate through the SkyDrive interface and then tap on the appropriate file. It will display right in the browser, using a very limited version of the Office Web Apps, as shown in Figure 12-27.

FIGURE 12-26: SkyDrive can be used to store and organize Office documents.

FIGURE 12-27: It's possible to view Office documents with the mobile version of Internet Explorer.

VIEWING A SKYDRIVE-BASED OFFICE DOCUMENT WITH OFFICE MOBILE

The ability to view Office documents directly in the browser is a good one, but it's limited in that complex documents—especially Excel spreadsheets and PowerPoint presentations—don't display in very high fidelity. To overcome this, and view the document in a more capable Office Mobile application, you can download it to the phone.

To do so, click the prominent Download link at the top of the page that's displaying the Office document. This will trigger the interesting display shown in Figure 12-28. Then you can tap the icon as instructed to download the file.

From here, you can of course view the document in a much higher fidelity environment than is made available through Internet Explorer. If you tap the Back button, however, you'll return back to IE, and the document will not be saved to the phone.

SAVING A SKYDRIVE-BASED OFFICE DOCUMENT TO THE PHONE

You may want to save the document to your phone, however. To do so, tap More and then Save As. This will display the Save to Office Hub screen shown in Figure 12-29. Rename the document if needed and then tap Save.

FIGURE 12-28: Office documents can also be opened, over the air, and viewed in an Office Mobile application.

FIGURE 12-29: You can also save documents, locally, to the phone.

To see that the file is saved, tap Start and then launch the Office hub. If you scroll over to the Documents section (Figure 12-30), you'll see that the saved document is now at the top of the list.

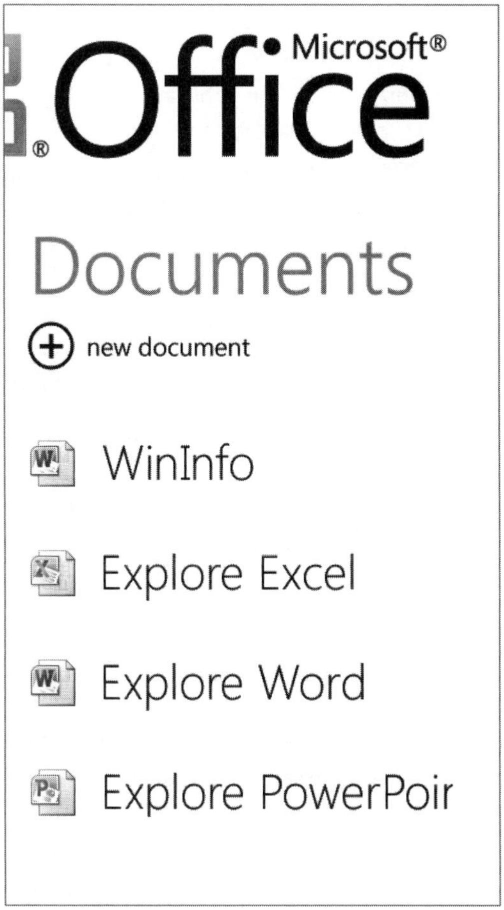

Office Microsoft®

Documents

(+) new document

 WinInfo

 Explore Excel

 Explore Word

 Explore PowerPoir

FIGURE 12-30: Saved web-based documents can be found in the Office hub's Documents list.

WINDOWS PHONE/SKYDRIVE INTEGRATION— WHAT YOU CAN'T DO

This is where Windows Phone/SkyDrive integration, such as it is, falls apart somewhat. On the PC version of the SkyDrive web site, for example, it's very easy to upload documents from the PC to the web site. But there's no such capability on Windows Phone.

So how does one get a document on Windows Phone into SkyDrive?

(continues)

(continued)

You can't do it directly, unfortunately. If you don't mind making this a mind-numbing affair and can use your PC to do part of the work, however, you could make it happen.

Here's how: E-mail the document (or documents) in question to your Windows Live account. Then, open your e-mail on the PC, either via the web-based version of Hotmail, or whatever e-mail application you prefer, and save it to the PC. Then, using the SkyDrive file uploading interface in Internet Explorer, upload the file(s) to the Web.

By this doing this, you miss out on all of the good parts of synchronization—the automation, and even version control and file check-outs—but at least it works. My hope is that Microsoft will make SkyDrive integration as seamless as is SharePoint integration in the future. Cross your fingers.

Using SharePoint

For those few users who have access to a SharePoint document repository, the Windows Phone picture is considerably brighter, and certainly more seamless, than it is with Windows Live SkyDrive. That's because Microsoft has built an incredible SharePoint client right into the Office hub.

SharePoint, for those who aren't aware, is one of the most successful platforms Microsoft has ever created. It's a server product that installs on top of modern Windows Server versions, providing collaboration and web-based publishing functionality to business users. In fact, SharePoint is a jack-of-all-trades type solution, which is part of the reason for its huge success: Businesses use SharePoint to create web sites, web portals, intranets and extranets, content management systems, wikis, blogs, and other types of web-based content sites.

Another, equally important aspect of SharePoint's success in the corporate world is that it's *self-servicing*. This means that information workers who wish to set up a site for document collaboration or other purposes can do so immediately, via a simple web-based interface, and without having to grovel to busy administrators and IT professionals who are probably already busy with other tasks. Using a simple delegation model, admins can configure SharePoint once and then leave the company's workers free to go about their business.

I'm not going to provide a thorough SharePoint overview here. You either have access to SharePoint or you don't. If you do, you're in luck, because Windows Phone has incredible SharePoint integration functionality. If you don't, you can look to this integration as a clue to what future SkyDrive integration could look like. Indeed, from the perspective of users, SkyDrive and SharePoint work similarly in terms of document storage and access. Why Windows Phone ships with vastly superior Share-Point integration is unclear.

Here's what you can do with SharePoint on Windows Phone.

WARNING Windows Phone offers Office 2010–level functionality and is designed to work with the most recent version of SharePoint, which at the time of this writing is SharePoint 2010. It's possible that Microsoft may later update Windows Phone to work with older SharePoint versions, but for now SharePoint 2010 is the only option.

SITES, LIBRARIES, AND LISTS, OH MY

I don't want to get too bogged down in SharePoint terminology, but what the heck. When I think in terms of "documents stored in SharePoint," my mind immediately translates that into "document repositories" because that's really what these things are. That said, SharePoint geeks—and yes, they are out there—will point out that SharePoint has its own set of names for things. These include, among others, SharePoint *sites* (accessed just like web sites with browsers, and also via dedicated client software), *libraries* (a collection of server-based documents), and *lists* (sets of SharePoint-specific lists such as announcements, parts lists, and so on).

▶ *You may need to ask your administrator or help desk for the correct URL. Normally SharePoint URLs follow the normal http://servername form. But if you have trouble connecting try the form http://servername/?Mobile=1 instead.*

CONNECTING TO A SHAREPOINT SITE

The SharePoint client on Windows Phone is called SharePoint Workspace Mobile, and it is exposed as a prominent part of the Office hub. In fact, it occupies fully 50 percent of the Office hub panorama, or the two rightmost sections, or columns.

If you haven't yet connected to a SharePoint site, you can do so now by tapping the Open URL button. Then, type in the address of your SharePoint Server. You'll be prompted for a username, password, and domain as well.

> **WARNING** SharePoint Workspace will prompt you to save your SharePoint password so that you won't need to enter it every time you access the site on the go. This is okay to do, but only if you are already locking your device. You don't want someone who steals or finds your phone to gain access to your company's private information.

When you make the connection, SharePoint Workspace will list the various server-based libraries and lists that are available to you. This is shown in Figure 12-31.

To investigate what's available, navigate into one of the libraries or other locations. There, you'll see a list of documents, like that shown in Figure 12-32.

From here, you can do a number of things, including those tasks listed next.

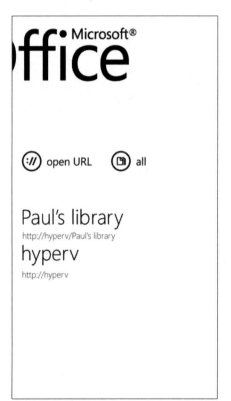

FIGURE 12-31: You're connected. Now you can access SharePoint documents on the go.

FIGURE 12-32: SharePoint documents, accessible on Windows Phone.

BOOKMARKING A LOCATION AS A LINK

Available via the More menu, Bookmark This Link will create a bookmark, or shortcut, to the current SharePoint location in the SharePoint Workspace Links list.

It will also be added to SharePoint Workspace's second section, or column, which includes a list of recently accessed SharePoint locations. (This new item will appear under the bookmark that was automatically created for your SharePoint server when you first made the connection.) The bookmark works just like a live tile or an Internet Explorer Favorite; when you tap it, you go right to that location.

To view the SharePoint Workspace Links list, tap All.

DOWNLOADING A SHAREPOINT-BASED DOCUMENT

To download a document from SharePoint to your phone, tap and hold on the name of the document to display the pop-up menu seen in Figure 12-33. Then, tap Download Now.

FIGURE 12-33: Tap and hold to see options related to individual SharePoint documents.

In place below the document name, you'll see a message that the document is downloading until, eventually, the message changes to "Downloaded." You can now access this document at any time from the SharePoint Workspace Mobile section of the Office hub; the first pane provides a list of recently accessed documents.

VIEWING A SHAREPOINT-BASED DOCUMENT

To view a document in the current SharePoint library, simply tap it in the list. SharePoint Workspace will connect to the server, download the document, and make it available for viewing.

> **NOTE** If you attempt to open a SharePoint document that was edited elsewhere (either in the SharePoint Office Web Apps interface, or via a PC-based version of Word, Excel, or PowerPoint) since it was first opened on the phone, you will be prompted to open the new version of the document instead.

EDITING A SHAREPOINT-BASED DOCUMENT

Downloaded documents can also be edited. In Word Mobile or PowerPoint Mobile, tap the Edit Application Bar button to begin editing. In Excel Mobile, editing can begin immediately.

> ## SAVING CHANGES TO A SHAREPOINT-BASED DOCUMENT
>
> If you do make changes to a SharePoint-based document and exit that document, you'll be prompted to save the document. If you choose Yes, the changes will be saved to the document on the server (that is, to the original, actual document) as well as to the local copy. And if this is the first time you've done so, you'll be prompted to enter a username for yourself as well.

> **NOTE** In case it's not obvious, any server-based files that you edit on the phone will be synced with the server, automatically. If you are offline—such as when you're on a plane—when you make the edits, those changes will be synced back to SharePoint when you reconnect.

▶ Anytime you view or edit a SharePoint-based document, a copy of that document is downloaded, locally to the phone. A list of recently accessed documents is maintained in the first of the two SharePoint Workspace sections in the Office hub.

SENDING A LINK TO A CO-WORKER

If you've edited a SharePoint-based document and would like to contact a co-worker—perhaps someone you're collaborating with at work—about the changes, you can do so right from within SharePoint Workspace Mobile.

To do so, tap and hold on the document name in library view. When the pop-up menu appears, tap Send Link. Windows Phone will display a Send From screen, and you can choose between Messaging (standard SMS text messaging) or any of your configured e-mail accounts. In either case, a web URL to the edited document will appear in the message automatically.

KEEPING CERTAIN FILES AVAILABLE WHILE OFFLINE

You can mark individual documents on SharePoint so that they are always available offline, which in this context means, "when you're not connected to the server." That way, you can ensure that you have an offline copy to work on should you be in a disconnected state.

To do so, browse a SharePoint library and find the document you'd like to mark. Then, tap and hold on the document name and choose Always Keep Offline from the pop-up menu that appears. This will ensure that the document in question is kept on the phone. But fear not: Changes you make to this offline document will still be synced to the server. So if you're connected when the changes occur, it will be synced immediately. Otherwise, changes will sync when you are later connected.

CONFIGURING OFFICE MOBILE

If you take a peek at the Settings interface for Office (which is listed as Office 2010, go figure), you'll find a couple of useful items to configure. These include:

- ▶ **Username:** Office Mobile is supposed to pick up the name of the registered phone user but has never actually done that in my experience. If you haven't yet configured this information—Office Mobile will ask you if it needs it—you can do so here.

- ▶ **SharePoint:** There are numerous options related to SharePoint Workspace Mobile, including a way to clear the cache and thus delete all temporary SharePoint files and history, a simple file conflict management interface, a way to configure the phone for Forefront Unified Access Gateway (UAG, Microsoft's server-side security product—your administrator can provide this information if it's needed), and more.

▶ **OneNote:** Here, you can determine whether OneNote Mobile automatically syncs notes with Windows Live SkyDrive. It's a simple On/Off option, and when it's set to On, notes will sync anytime you open a note page, save a note page, or open a note section.

SUMMARY

Office Mobile is in many ways the quintessential Windows Phone solution. Rather than provide you with multiple, discrete applications, Microsoft has instead provided a panoramic Office hub from which you can take notes and sync them with the Web, create and edit Word documents and Excel spreadsheets, view and edit PowerPoint presentations, and sync, over-the-air, with online SharePoint repositories.

Office Mobile is also curiously limited in some ways on Windows Phone, even in ways that its predecessor, running on the antiquated Windows Mobile system, was not. The reasons for this are varied and tied in large part to Microsoft's desire to deeply simplify (some would say *oversimplify*) its new mobile platform. But the reality is that Office Mobile is missing some curiously obvious features as a result. Hopefully, the software giant will fix these issues over time.

Ultimately, Office Mobile is exactly what Microsoft promised, however: a great mobile companion for Office users, especially those who have fully embraced the company's latest Office version for Windows, Office 2010, and the new Office Web Apps and online storage capabilities of Windows Live SkyDrive and SharePoint 2010. It's not perfect, but it does represent an important step forward toward a future that deeply integrates the PC desktop, the cloud, and the phone.

CHAPTER 13

Making Calls and Using Voicemail

I know what you're thinking: Hundreds of pages and several chapters into the book and I'm finally getting around to discussing how Windows Phone is, of all things, a *phone*? It seems like a fair criticism at first, but face it: With expensive monthly data plans, computer-like processing power, and a wealth of third-party applications and related capabilities, most people are using the "smart" parts of smart phones more than the phone parts. In fact, it shouldn't surprise you to discover that, according to a recent survey of smart phone users, making phone calls isn't even one of the top five activities people do when alone with the devices. Heck, even texting—the subject of the next chapter—is more popular than making and receiving calls.

But fear not, phone fans. Windows Phone makes and receives phone calls. Of course it does. In fact, with the benefit of years of experience with this type of core capability, Microsoft has engineered Windows Phone with first-class phone features. It includes integrated voicemail, speakerphone, call forwarding, and call waiting capabilities; integrates with hands-free Bluetooth headsets; and offers a wealth of ringer and vibration options, too. It's even smart enough to mute the currently playing song or game volume so you can focus on that important call, and then make sure that everything goes right back to where it was when the call is over.

Heck, someone has to say it: When it comes to actual phone functionality, Microsoft has put the *smart* in smart phones.

CONFIGURING CONTACTS ACCOUNTS

As you know, there are various account types you can configure for Windows Phone. These account types differ in various ways. One of these accounts, your primary Windows Live account, is special because it determines which web services are connected to your phone through the Messenger social feed. This account also connects to a wide variety of Microsoft offerings, including Zune, Xbox Live, Windows Live Photos, Find My Phone, and more.

Beyond this special default account, Windows Phone supports configuring any number of other accounts comprising different account types. I discuss these account types more completely elsewhere, but I want to do a quick recap so you can understand which of these account types do offer contacts support because this functionality is the basis for your phone's People hub and thus the integrated address book you'll use when making and receiving phone calls.

Account types that include contacts support include:

▶ **Windows Live:** This account type can be configured as your primary account (e-mail, contacts, calendar, photos, feeds, and more) or as a secondary, "normal" account with e-mail, contacts, and/or calendar. You must have at least one Windows Live account, which functions as your primary account. But you can configure multiple other Windows Live accounts as well.

▶ **Facebook:** Windows Phone explicitly supports Facebook accounts, but you have no control over what gets synced. If you enable Facebook support, Windows Phone will link to the service's contacts, photos, and feeds. You cannot enable just some Facebook features, and you have no control over, say, which contacts get synced. It's all or nothing.

- ▶ **Outlook:** Designed for Exchange-type servers, this account type works with e-mail, contacts, and/or calendar data. But it's not just for Exchange. In fact, the Outlook account type will work with any account that uses a technology called Exchange ActiveSync (EAS) on the back end. And that's a surprising number of services, including Gmail/Google Calendar, Microsoft's Hotmail, and many others.

- ▶ **Google:** Microsoft explicitly supports Google's Gmail (for e-mail and contacts) and Google Calendar because the services are so popular, but it's not much harder to configure this account type using the Outlook option. Behind the scenes, the accounts are configured the same way, using EAS.

MAKING AND RECEIVING PHONE CALLS

On Windows Phone, the functionality that you might typically associate with a phone—that is, the ability to make and receive phone calls—is provided via an application called Phone. So it's really no different from any other built-in application—like Mail, Calendar, or whatever—though it is designed to run side by side with other applications when necessary, a feature tech experts call *multitasking*.

MULTITASKING AND WINDOWS PHONE

Indeed, there is some confusion about whether Windows Phone supports multitasking. It does. In its original shipping form, however, only those applications provided by Microsoft on the phone will support this functionality, and the software giant has pledged to open up support for true third-party multitasking over time. What multitasking means to you is that you can perform certain tasks simultaneously. For example, if you're playing music (or an audio podcast) through the Zune software in Music + Videos and switch to another (non-game) application, the music will keep playing. That's multitasking. Likewise, you can talk on the phone and perform other tasks. And if you're using another app and the phone rings, you can answer it without disturbing what you're doing. Other forms of multitasking are more subtle. For example, Internet Explorer will continue loading web pages or downloading a file in the background while you do other things.

You can access Phone in various ways, but the most obvious is via the prominent Phone live tile, which is situated at the very top of the Start screen, as shown in Figure 13-1.

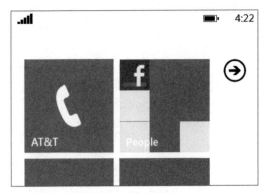

FIGURE 13-1: The Phone live tile.

▶ *If the phone is in Airplane Mode, the Phone tile will report "Phone off" because it is not connected to a cellular network.*

This live tile provides the name of the wireless network provider to which you're connected, but it can also provide other status information as well. If you've missed one or more phone calls, for example, the tile will display the number of missed calls next to the phone icon. And if you have one or more voicemails waiting, a small voicemail icon (that looks like a roll of recording tape) will appear below the phone icon.

When you tap the Phone live tile, the Phone application launches. As shown in Figure 13-2, Phone is a single screen application, but unlike many other built-in applications, it doesn't include any pivots. Instead, you're presented with a Call History list and then some other options that are made available via Application Bar buttons.

Call History is exactly what it sounds like: It presents a list of the contacts, voicemail, and other numbers you've called and been called from. Calls you've made are noted as Outgoing and calls that have come in to you are marked as Incoming. Missed calls are highlighted with the phone theme's accent color so they visually stand out, as shown in Figure 13-3.

You scroll through the Call History list as you would any other list in Windows Phone.

To call a contact or other entry in this list, just tap the phone icon next to the appropriate entry. If you tap the entry name, and that entry is a contact, you will navigate to the contact's contact card instead.

From this Phone screen, you can also access your voicemail, bring up the phone keypad to make a manual call, or access your aggregated contacts list in the People hub. Since they are all such important tasks, I want to cover each one separately.

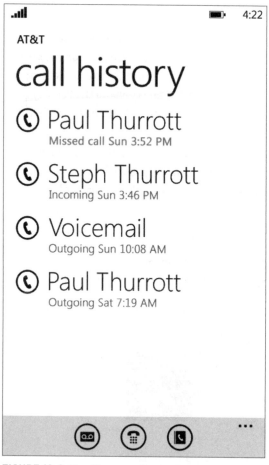

FIGURE 13-2: The Phone application is pretty basic, with a single screen interface.

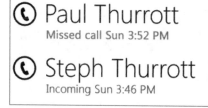

FIGURE 13-3: Missed calls really stand out in the Call History list.

Calling a Contact

Contacts integration is obviously a key aspect of the phone experience on any smart phone. In Windows Phone, this works as expected: You can browse through your list of contacts in the People hub and then tap a Call Number link in order to call that person. Or you can simply access the Phone application directly, and then tap the People button to access this same interface. That is, you're brought directly to the All list in the People hub, which is shown in Figure 13-4.

Using your newly developed Windows Phone navigational skills, scroll down the list (or use the letter shortcut buttons) to find the contact you wish to call. Then, tap on that person's entry in the list. You'll be shown that person's contact card, which should resemble Figure 13-5.

FIGURE 13-4: The All list in the People hub is directly accessible from the Phone app.

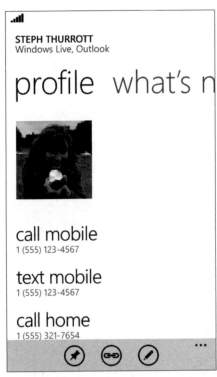

FIGURE 13-5: Most contact cards will include one or more phone numbers with prominent Call links.

Many of your contacts will have one or more phone numbers associated with their contact card. And each phone number will be exposed via a Call Number link, such as Call Mobile, Call Home, Call Work, and so on. Pick the location you wish to call and tap that entry. When you do, the Windows Phone call overlay appears, as shown in Figure 13-6. Note that this overlay appears over the current screen.

FIGURE 13-6: The Windows Phone call overlay.

From here, you can use the phone normally to complete the call. When the call is over, you can tap the End Call button to hang up.

You may have noticed that the call overlay has two additional buttons, Keypad and More Options. I examine them next.

Using the Keypad

There are two ways in which you will typically access Phone's keypad. You may be making a call and need to enter a string of numbers, such as when you're accessing a phone menu and you need to tap 1, 2, or some other number to make a choice. Or you may need to manually dial a phone number because it's not in any of your contacts lists.

To access the keypad while making a call, just tap the Keypad button in the call overlay. The overlay will expand to cover the entire screen, presenting an onscreen virtual keypad with large keys (Figure 13-7).

If you want to dial a phone number manually, you can also access the keypad directly. To do so, run the Phone app and then tap the Keypad Application Bar button. (It's the one in the middle that looks like a cute little phone.) When you do, Phone presents a large keypad like that shown in Figure 13-8. But this time you have a couple more options.

> ▶ First, you're able to manually call another phone, just like grandma would have done 30 years ago. (Well, not exactly. We require area codes now, but you get the idea.) That is, you can just type in the number and then tap Call

When you're using the phone and interacting with the keypad simultaneously, it's often useful to use the phone's speakerphone too, so you can hear what's going on while you tap away. Speakerphone functionality is covered later in this chapter.

to make the call. If the number you type isn't associated with one of your contacts, the call overlay won't report a name, because it doesn't know which name is associated with that number. Instead, it will just display the number, as seen in Figure 13-9.

> **NOTE** Phone even makes an old-fashioned phone sound when you type a phone number in this way.

FIGURE 13-7: The keypad as part of the call overlay.

FIGURE 13-8: When you use the keypad to manually dial the phone, you have some additional options.

FIGURE 13-9: Sometimes Windows Phone just doesn't know the owner of a particular phone number.

▶ Optionally, you can also use this keypad to save a new phone number. To do so, type in the number but then tap Save instead of Call. You'll be presented with the Choose a Contact screen shown in Figure 13-10. From here, you can apply this phone number to an existing contact (perhaps by replacing an out-of-date number) or create a new contact.

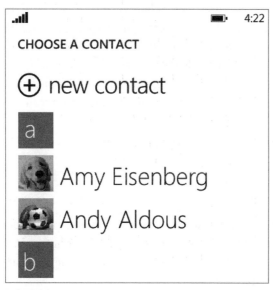

FIGURE 13-10: You can optionally save a new phone number to an existing contact or create a new contact.

Using More Options

While in a call, you may find that you want to perform some other action, such as use the phone's speakerphone, mute the call, place the call on hold, or make a second call without hanging up on the first. All of these actions can be accomplished via the More Options button, which appears as a down-pointing arrow button in the call overlay (that is, you will only see this choice while in a call).

To access these options, tap the More Options button. The call overlay will expand with the options shown in Figure 13-11.

The next sections examine each of these options.

USING THE SPEAKERPHONE

By default, phone calls utilize the small speaker located above the screen, and you need to place the phone next to your head in order to hear properly. But in certain circumstances—such as when you're interacting with the keypad—you may need to hear the call and do other things on the phone at the same time. And in such cases, the speakerphone is exactly what the doctor ordered.

To access speakerphone mode, tap the Speaker button under More Options in the call overlay. The Speaker button will be highlighted to visually indicate that this feature is on, and the phone's speaker(s) and microphone will operate a bit differently. Now, instead of placing the phone next to your head, you can place it somewhere in front of you. (In fact, if you place it next to your head, it will be uncomfortably loud.) Instead of using the tiny phone speaker above the screen, your phone will utilize the larger speaker (or speakers, depending on your device) for sound output. And the internal microphone will expand its range to account for the presumed distance between your mouth and the phone.

Speakerphone works like a toggle. To disengage this feature, just tap the Speaker button again.

PLACING A CALL ON MUTE

If you wish to mute your end of the call—that is, prevent anyone else on the phone call from hearing anything from your phone—you can tap the Mute button instead. When you do, the Mute button is highlighted and the text On Mute appears in the call overlay, as shown in Figure 13-12.

FIGURE 13-11: The More Options button lets you access additional in-call functionality.

FIGURE 13-12: A muted phone call.

Note that muting a call does not mute sounds coming *into* your phone. This is by design: Mute is for those times when you need to listen in, perhaps during a conference call, but you don't want others to be disturbed by the background noise around you.

Mute is also a toggle: Just tap it again to unmute the call.

PLACING A CALL ON HOLD

When you want to mute both ends of a phone call, you can place it on hold. This won't hang up the call. Instead, neither party will hear anything until you remove the hold. To toggle this feature, tap the Hold button (Figure 13-13).

MAKING A SECOND CALL... WITHOUT HANGING UP ON THE FIRST

Finally, Windows Phone supports an interesting feature, Add Call, which lets you temporarily place the current phone conversation on hold so you can call another number and start a second conversation. Once both calls are connected, you can switch back and forth between them. (What you can't do here is start a conference call where all three parties are connected simultaneously.)

Here's how it works. While in a call, tap the More Options button on the call overlay. Then, tap Add Call. The current call will be placed on hold, as denoted by a small ON HOLD overlay that appears at the very top of the screen, as shown in Figure 13-14.

The main part of the display has changed to the Phone app's Call History list. From here, you can pick a contact or number from the list, tap the Keypad button to manually type in another phone number, tap the People button to choose a contact from the People hub, or even tap Voicemail to listen to your voicemail. (I discuss voicemail a bit later in this chapter.)

> Mute and Speaker are not mutually exclusive. You could enable both and have sound come out of the external speakers while your own sound input is muted.

FIGURE 13-13: Place a call on hold, just like the cable company does every time you call.

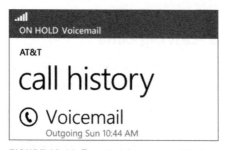

FIGURE 13-14: To switch between calls, the first call must be placed on hold first.

FIGURE 13-15: The small call overlay lets you switch between two different (but unconnected) phone calls.

However you do it, you'll eventually find yourself in another call. You'll notice that the small call overlay stays at the top of the screen. This allows you to switch between the two connected calls; just tap the overlay to switch (Figure 13-15). Once one of these two calls ends, the small overlay will disappear and you will return to the normal phone display.

Doing Something Else While on a Call

As mentioned earlier, the Phone application can multitask, meaning you are free to do something else while talking on the phone. To see what this experience is like, put the call on speakerphone (you don't want to be rude) and tap the Start button. The

FIGURE 13-16: The small call overlay also lets you use other phone applications while talking on a call.

phone will navigate to the Start screen, but as you can see in Figure 13-16, a small call overlay will display at the top of the screen, providing you with access to the full-sized call overlay. Just tap this overlay to return to the normal overlay.

Otherwise, continue navigating around the system. You can check your e-mail, browse the Web, search with Bing, look at your calendar, and perform many other tasks while talking on the phone. Eventually, of course, you may want to end the call. When that happens, just tap the small call overlay and then tap End Call. It's that simple.

Receiving Calls

Many of the calls you engage in will of course come from others. And how Windows Phone reacts to these calls differs slightly depending on what you're doing at the time.

If the phone is off (locked) and a call comes in, the screen will come on and the phone will chime with the incoming call sound. Displayed at the bottom of the screen will be the text INCOMING CALL along with the phone number that is calling. If that number is in one of your contacts lists, the name of the caller will also display, and if available, their contact photo. This is shown in Figure 13-17.

At the bottom of this lightly bobbing screen is the text Slide Up. If you do slide the screen up, you'll see two buttons, Answer and Ignore. I assume their use is obvious, but if you do nothing, the phone will eventually stop trying, and the caller will have a chance to leave a voicemail.

If you're using the phone when a call arrives, the screen is slightly different. You get the same name, number, and photo display, but the Answer and Ignore buttons are immediately available, and there's no need to slide up the screen (Figure 13-18).

FIGURE 13-17: Wake up! It's an incoming call.

FIGURE 13-18: Pardon the interruption, but you have a phone call.

If you're already on a phone call and another call comes in, you get the incredible screen shown in Figure 13-19. Here, you are alerted about the incoming call, but you get three choices: Answer, Ignore, or End Call + Answer. Again, these are pretty obvious. But it's still a pretty impressive screen.

▶ If you're listening to music when a call comes in, the music will fade out and pause. After the call is over, the music will automatically start up again and fade back in so you're not startled. Nice!

FIGURE 13-19: Now, that's going to require some thought.

Handling Missed Calls

Nobody's perfect, and sometimes calls go unanswered. Maybe you were busy and didn't hear the phone. Or you were away from the phone. Or maybe you're just on AT&T. Whatever the reason, calls get missed. There's no need to point fingers.

> **NOTE** If you explicitly ignore a call by tapping an Ignore button, this section does not apply: This section is about calls you missed, not ignored. That said, when a call comes in, you could literally ignore the phone. In such a case, you have indeed missed the call because you didn't interact with the phone at all.

So you pick up your phone later. What do you see?

When you miss a call and turn on your phone, you'll see a number next to a small phone icon in the lower-left corner of the lock screen. The number you see indicates the number of missed calls.

When you unlock the phone and view the Start screen, the Phone tile will likewise show a number, which again indicates the number of missed calls. When you tap the tile, the Phone app loads as usual, but this time you will have one (or more) missed calls right at the top of the Call History list. You can then decide whether to call back or, if they left a voicemail, perhaps you could check that out next.

Speaking of checking on voicemail . . .

USING VOICEMAIL

Windows Phone offers basic voicemail functionality through its Phone application. You can call your voicemail at any time by tapping the Voicemail Application Bar button. This number is configured automatically by your wireless carrier, though as you'll see in a moment, you can manually change the number if required as well. Likewise, the audio interface to voicemail will vary from carrier to carrier and isn't Windows Phone–specific. When you do call voicemail, the call overlay automatically expands the keypad, as shown in Figure 13-20, because it's likely that you'll need to respond to a voice menu while interacting with the voicemail system.

A number of things happen when you receive a new voicemail. Typically, you will have received a missed call as well, so the missed call counter on the lock screen and Phone tile on the Start screen will both increment by one. When Windows Phone detects that a new voicemail has arrived, it will chime and display a small overlay at the top of the screen announcing the arrival. And on both the lock screen and

FIGURE 13-20: When you dial voicemail, Windows Phone automatically expands the keypad.

the Start screen, a small voicemail badge will be added to the phone icon, indicating that at least one voicemail has arrived.

In the Phone app, the Voicemail Application Bar button will also change, adding a number to indicate how many voicemails you now have waiting. This is shown in Figure 13-21.

FIGURE 13-21: This is the only place in the phone where you can visually confirm how many voicemails are waiting.

WORKING WITH BLUETOOTH

In addition to the normal, built-in phone functionality, Windows Phone also supports Bluetooth, which is used, primarily, to connect the phone with small, wireless headsets that combine an earpiece with a microphone. Bluetooth is an industry standard for creating wireless connectivity between devices over very short distances only, and at relatively slow speeds, so it's no competitor to Wi-Fi or 3G-style wireless connectivity. But it's become a staple of the cell phone and now smart phone businesses, in large part because of the convenience and low cost of wireless headsets.

The way that Bluetooth interacts with different device types is formalized by a set of Bluetooth *profiles*. With regards to phones in general, and Windows Phone specifically, there is one that is particularly relevant: a Bluetooth profile for communications and control between phones and hands-free headsets.

That said, Windows Phone does support the latest Bluetooth version (Bluetooth 2.1 + EDR) and the following specific Bluetooth profiles:

- **Hands-Free Profile (HFP) 1.5:** This is typically used for hands-free interfaces in automobiles.

- **Headset Profile (HSP):** The most common BT profile, HSP provides support for wireless headsets.

- **Advanced Audio Distribution Profile (A2DP) 1.2:** This provides high quality mono and stereo audio playback over Bluetooth.

- **A/V Remote Control Profile (AVRCP) 1.0:** This allows a Bluetooth device to be used as a remote control. Windows Phone supports only the most basic remote control features (play, pause, stop, and so on).

- **Phone Book Access Profile (PBAP):** This allows a Bluetooth-compatible device to exchange address book (contacts) data with another Bluetooth-compatible device. It is typically used with car kits so that contact names can appear on the in-car display.

To connect, or *pair*, a Bluetooth headset with Windows Phone, navigate to All Programs, Settings, and then Bluetooth. In this simple interface, first ensure that Bluetooth is on. Once that is enabled, the settings page will display a "Searching" message.

Tap the On/Off switch on your headset to start the pairing (or, follow the instructions provided with the device, as they can vary from headset to headset). The Bluetooth headset will show up in the Bluetooth settings page, first with the generic name Headset, and with the note "tap to pair."

If you wait a few seconds, the headset will communicate its real name to Windows Phone, and the generic name will be replaced by that real name in the found devices list.

Tap the name of the headset to begin pairing. The note under the device's name will change to "connecting."

After a few more seconds, the devices will pair and the device name will appear as "connected," as shown in Figure 13-22.

Most hands-free headsets work in a similar fashion. If the device is on and paired with the phone and a call comes in, you can quickly press the On/Off button on the headset instead of tapping the Answer button on the phone's screen. This will route the call through the headset instead of the phone's microphone and speaker.

Otherwise, you can alternate between the phone's built-in hardware and the headset. If you answer the phone via the software's Answer button, you can later transfer the call to the headset by quickly pressing the headset's On/Off button.

> When Bluetooth is enabled, a small Bluetooth logo will appear at the center top of the phone's screen.

FIGURE 13-22: Pairing a hands-free headset with Windows Phone.

> **WARNING**   Bluetooth usage can impact the phone's battery life, so if you're not using this functionality, or you're out and about without the headset, it's a good idea to disable Bluetooth via the Bluetooth settings page.

CONFIGURING PHONE AND VOICEMAIL

Because the phone functionality is so integral to Windows Phone, you're going to want to make sure it's configured correctly. There are, oddly, a number of separate interfaces for this, including some in the expected Settings area. But you can also configure certain phone-related features on the fly. I examine all of these possibilities here.

Changing Phone Features on the Go

Some phone features can be changed immediately, on the fly, including volume, which affects the ringer as well as the volume of phone calls. You can make this change easily enough: Just tap the Volume Up or Volume Down button on the phone to change the volume. However, when you do this, you may notice a new overlay appear over the top of the screen. This overlay, shown in Figure 13-23, provides a visual representation of the current volume level as well as some other information.

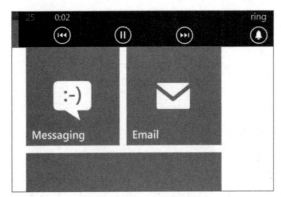

FIGURE 13-23: The volume overlay lets you configure the volume, media playback, and the ringer on the fly.

In the center of this overlay are some media playback controls that relate to the phone's media playback software, which I discuss in Chapter 6. But there's another item here, on the right side of the overlay, where you can toggle the phone's ringer between Ring and Vibrate (by default). In this configuration it's normally set to Ring. But if you tap this button, it will change to Vibrate.

So that provides a simple way to quickly switch between ringing and vibrating: Just tap a volume key and then tap the Volume button in the onscreen volume overlay. It's the perfect solution for those times when you need to quickly turn off the ringer. But what if you want to switch to a third mode, Silent? In this case, the phone would neither ring nor vibrate. To understand the secret behind this feature, read on: It can be found in the Ringtones and Sounds settings page, which is described shortly.

Phone and Voicemail Settings

For a deeper set of phone and voicemail related settings, head over to All Programs, Settings, Applications, and then Phone. You'll see a screen similar to that in Figure 13-24.

FIGURE 13-24: Phone (and voicemail) settings.

From this interface, you can view and often configure a wide range of options. These include:

▶ **Phone number:** Because your phone number is determined by your wireless carrier, you can't of course change this yourself. That said, if you are on a GSM-type wireless network such as those used by AT&T, you can implicitly change your phone's phone number (and other capabilities) by swapping out the SIM (Subscriber Identity Module) card. CDMA-type networks, such as the ones provided by Verizon Wireless, do not use SIM cards and instead program phone information directly into the device.

▶ **Voicemail number:** This number is configured by your wireless carrier. But you may need to change it at some time, perhaps because you are using a third-party voicemail service such as the one provided by Google Voice. This field can be edited, unlike the phone number field.

▶ **Caller ID:** Caller ID is a phone service that identifies callers, either with a number, a name, or both. You can use this field to determine how you show up when you call others. The possible choices are to show your caller ID (name and number) to everyone you call (the default), to no one, or to just your contacts. Note that some people block calls that do not provide caller ID information, however. So if you choose No One, you may find that some of your calls do not complete.

▶ **Call forwarding:** This is another phone service that lets you automatically forward all calls to your number to another number of your choice. This option is set to Off by default; if you change it to On, you will be prompted to enter a new phone number. That number can be literally any phone number, valid or not, yours or not.

▶ **International assist:** This feature, enabled by default, corrects some common dialing mistakes, especially for international calls. For example, if this feature is enabled, you can dial a phone number in the United States without affixing a 1 to the front of the number. And if you're out of the country, or dialing another country from the United States, this feature will automatically add some dropped country codes and other commonly forgotten numbers. Put simply, there's no good reason not to leave this on.

▶ **SIM security:** If you or your wireless carrier has previously configured your phone's SIM card (available only in GSM devices) with a PIN code for security

[handwritten margin note:] ▶ Caller ID and call forwarding features must be explicitly supported by your wireless network. If they are not, these features will be grayed out and inaccessible.

reasons, you can use this option to unlock the SIM and use it with your phone. Most U.S.-based SIM cards do not utilize this functionality by default. (Note: This option cannot be used to enable PIN-based security on your SIM card.)

Ringtones and Sounds

In addition to the phone-related settings discussed previously, Windows Phone provides a separate Ringtones & Sounds settings page in Settings. Shown in Figure 13-25, this interface lets you configure a number of phone-related features, including the ringer and vibrate features and which ringtone plays when a call comes in.

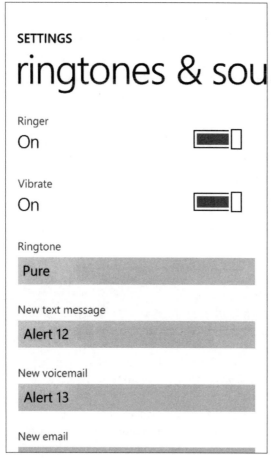

FIGURE 13-25: In Ringtones & Sounds settings, you can find a few other features related to the phone.

Both Ringer and Vibrate can be toggled between on and off states independently. This differs somewhat from the Ring/Vibrate toggle in the volume overlay that I discussed previously. But they actually do work in concert. The trick is understanding how these features interact.

- ▶ **Ringer On, Vibrate On:** In this default setup, both the ringer and vibrate features are enabled. So when you receive a phone call, the ringer will sound (using the ringtone specified by the Ringtone option that's also found on this page), and the phone will vibrate. When you tap a volume button to bring up the volume overlay, you can then toggle the ring state between Ring (which will ring and vibrate) and Vibrate (which will only use vibrate).

- ▶ **Ringer On, Vibrate Off:** In this configuration, only the ringer is enabled. If you receive a call, a ringtone will sound, but the phone will not vibrate. And if you access the volume overlay, you can toggle the ring state between Ring and Silent.

- ▶ **Ringer Off, Vibrate On:** In this configuration, the phone will vibrate (but not sound a ringtone) when a call comes in. If you access the volume overlay, you can toggle the ring state between Vibrate and Ring.

- ▶ **Ringer Off, Vibrate Off:** In this setup, the phone will not make any sound or vibrate when a call arrives. (However, the incoming call display will still take over the screen to indicate that something is happening.) From the volume overlay, you can toggle the ring state between Silent and Ring.

Additionally, this settings page also lets you choose between several pleasing ringtones via the Ringtone field.

BLUETOOTH CHIMES

Many hands-free, Bluetooth-based headsets provide their own audible call notifications that work outside of the phone's functionality. So if you are using such a headset and have the ringer and vibrate features both turned off, it's possible that your headset will still provide some kind of sound-based indication when a call is coming in. This does make some sense: Generally, you would turn off the phone's ringer and vibration capabilities in situations where silence was required. But no one is going to hear your in-ear headset making a chime.

SUMMARY

Most people who receive a phone call on Windows Phone will know exactly what to do the first time it happens and could muddle their way through accessing voicemail, speakerphone, and other phone features. But the key to taking advantage of all of the phone features this system provides is to understand that they're there, and how they work in the real world. Hopefully this chapter has pointed you in the right direction.

Of course, Windows Phone is more than just a phone. And in the next chapter, I examine more of this platform's support for traditional mobile phone features, including its ability to send and receive text and multimedia messages.

CHAPTER 14

Text and Multimedia Messaging

We've all seen them. The millennial generation, hunched over tiny keyboards, typing away rapidly with their thumbs. If you didn't know any better, you might assume these youngsters were retreating into an insular world in which they only interact with online services or their phone. Well, prepare for a shocker: These people are actually far more social than any generation before them, and what they're really doing is keeping up with their friends and family—as well as many people they barely know—via a number of communications services on their phones.

Windows Phone supports virtually every modern communications technology imaginable, and generally does so in fairly unique and innovative ways. But the most often used communications feature on any phone, perhaps, is messaging, where you send either text or multimedia messages over the air to others in your contacts list. Messaging is the number one activity for many with smart phones, and it explains why all the major wireless carriers have separate messaging plans in addition to call (cellular) and Internet (data) plans.

Most important, you don't need to be a 20-something hipster to become a messaging savant. In fact, messaging is a key skill for anyone with a smart phone, regardless of their age. You can keep in touch with your kids, using a language and communication model they know and appreciate. And grandparents can use it just as effectively to share photos of their families with others. So don't be worried that you won't ever be able to type *War and Peace* on that tiny virtual keyboard. No one's asking you to. But you may be surprised at how useful this feature is, and how well implemented it is on Windows Phone. In fact, for many people, messaging is a far more important feature on a smart phone than making and receiving actual phone calls. It's time to see what all the hubbub is about.

UNDERSTANDING MOBILE MESSAGING

Modern mobile messaging technologies date back to the early 1980s as the very first part of what became the international standard called the Global System for Mobile Communications (GSM). Yes, *that* GSM, the mobile phone carrier standard that's used by AT&T in the United States and most mobile carriers around the world. At the time, GSM was an offshoot of the European Conference of Postal and Telecommunications Administrations (CEPT), an industry body responsible for radio communications, telecommunications, and postal matters, of all things.

This initial mobile messaging technology, still in heavy use today, is called Short Message Service (SMS), though most of us simply call it *text messaging*. As that latter moniker suggests, SMS is all about text, and when you think back to the archaic technologies available in the early 1980s, you can see why. Text messaging is so basic, and so popular, that it has been adopted by virtually all mobile operators, regardless of the underlying technologies they use. And it's estimated that almost 80 percent of all mobile phone subscribers use this technology in some capacity. In 2008, over 4 *billion* SMS messages were sent worldwide.

Today, SMS messages are one of two very common messaging types that are available on smart phones. The other is MMS, for Multimedia Messaging Service. MMS expands on SMS in several ways. First, it expands on a limitation in early SMS implementations, allowing for text messages that are longer than 160 characters. Second, and more obviously, it provides for the sending of multimedia in messages. These can include pictures, videos, and audio files.

Under the hood, MMS works a bit differently than SMS and is in fact based on the attachment system employed by traditional e-mail systems. It also features an understanding of whether the receiving phone in a conversation can even handle MMS attachments. If it can't, the message is usually delivered to a web site and a link to that site is sent to the phone. That way, recipients can try and view the sent content using their device's web browser. Or they can write down the information and try it on their PC.

THE COST OF MESSAGING

SMS is so prevalent, in fact, that most wireless carriers bill for it separately, alongside phone calls and data plans. These three features constitute the primary expenses associated with a smart phone bill, and while messaging is usually the cheapest of the three—even for those with unlimited messaging—it can add up. And that's an important fact to note: You pay for messaging, so this is a feature you want to be careful not to abuse, unless you've opted for an unlimited plan.

It's also a feature you could probably opt out of altogether if you think you won't be sending a lot of messages. But I recommend against this for a few reasons. First, there's nothing to prevent others from sending you messages, and if you're not on even a basic messaging plan, you'll pay for each incoming message whether you want to or not. Second, messaging may surprise you. It's amazingly useful, and a terrific way to keep up with others. It's often quicker and easier than a traditional phone call.

Whatever you do, check with your wireless carrier about messaging costs before proceeding. It's important to understand what you're getting into.

NOTE   Mobile messaging is becoming more common and accepted every day. I recall receiving my first SMS message in 2003, and being confused at the new sound my phone had made. After reading the rather lengthy message, which instructed me to meet a friend at a certain place and at a certain time, I then issued my own first-ever SMS reply: I tapped the letter "K" (as in "OK") and hit Send. It's been downhill ever since.

MESSAGING ON WINDOWS PHONE

Modern smart phones can handle both SMS and MMS messaging with ease, of course. So if your friends, family and other contacts are using Android, iPhone, or Windows Phone–based phones, you should have no problem sending and receiving messages between any of them. In fact, from the perspective of today's smart phone users— including those on Windows Phone—these devices simply support messaging. No one really thinks of them as separate SMS and MMS services, because both messaging types occur through a single experience. And on Windows Phone, logically enough, that experience is called Messaging.

> **NOTE** Windows Phone does have some limitations when it comes to MMS-type messages. For example, though you can take videos with the device's built-in camera, Windows Phone does not support the sending of videos via MMS. Likewise, there's no way to send audio files via MMS either.

Using the Messaging App

The Messaging app is typically accessed from the Messaging live tile on the Start screen. Shown in Figure 14-1, this live tile will reflect the number of unread messages, if any, by placing a number next to the messaging icon.

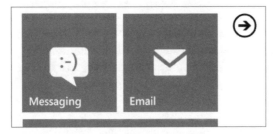

FIGURE 14-1: The Messaging live tile.

As for the Messaging application itself, it looks and works much like the Mail application, but with one big difference: Instead of offering multiple views on a pivot, Messaging offers an even simpler, single-screen experience, consisting of the Conversations list shown in Figure 14-2.

The Conversations view is sorted from top to bottom with the most recent conver- sation at the top. Compared to Mail, you'll find another difference: Each contact with whom you've conversed via messaging gets only a single conversation. So you won't see multiple entries for the same contact, even if the conversations you've had with them occurred over time.

Sending a Message

To send a message, tap the New toolbar button. This triggers the new conversation screen shown in Figure 14-3.

FIGURE 14-2: The Messaging application is as simple as a Windows Phone app gets, offering just a single-screen experience.

FIGURE 14-3: A new conversation can consist of one or more recipients, a message, and, optionally, an attachment.

From here, you can perform the following tasks related to sending messages within a conversation:

- ▶ **Choose one or more recipients:** In the To: line, you can add one or more recipients. This can be done in three basic ways.

  - ▷ You can simply begin typing a name, in which case, Windows Phone will auto-suggest contacts, on the fly, as you type. This is shown in Figure 14-4.

▷ You can tap the Choose a Contact ("+") button to the far right of the To: line in order to view the Choose a Contact screen and pick from your contacts list.

▷ You can just type in a mobile phone number directly. If this number is already in your contact list, it will auto-fill to the name of the contact. If not, the number will remain in the To: line (and will work fine, assuming it's a valid mobile number).

FIGURE 14-4: As you type in a name, Windows Phone will match what you type against your aggregated address books.

▶ **Type a message:** You'll see a blank text box right above the virtual keyboard with the text "Type a message" inside: When you tap this, the box becomes highlighted and you can begin typing a message.

FIGURE 14-5: Windows Phone will automatically split long messages into 160 character missives that will work with any phone system.

Your message must technically fit within 160 characters. However, if you exceed this limit, Windows Phone will automatically split the message into multiple parts, and send each separately. This is shown in Figure 14-5.

Note that if you type in a web address, Windows Phone will automatically turn that text into a clickable hyperlink. It's pretty smart about this too, so even truncated web addresses such as microsoft.com are correctly detected. This works for both incoming and outgoing messages.

▶ **Send an individual message:** You can send what you've already typed at any time by tapping the Send toolbar button. When you do, the text you've typed is sent as its own message, and you'll see it visually detached from the message box as shown in Figure 14-6.

FIGURE 14-6: Individually sent messages appear as unique messages within a conversation.

Each message can contain only one picture. If you want to send more, just tap Send to send the current message and start a new one.

▶ **Attach a picture:** At any time, you can tap the Attach toolbar button to add a picture to your message. When you do, the Choose Picture screen appears (Figure 14-7), providing a way to browse between the various pictures you have stored in your phone. (Note that you can send only local pictures, and not pictures that are stored in web-based photo galleries.) You can combine text and a picture in a single message. Note, however, that the picture always appears "above" the text no matter which order they were added.

WARNING Some wireless carriers don't support the sending of media content. If this is the case, you may see a message like the one shown in Figure 14-8. If you do see this message and think it to be in error, you should contact your wireless provider.

FIGURE 14-7: Browse through your local photo galleries for a picture to send.

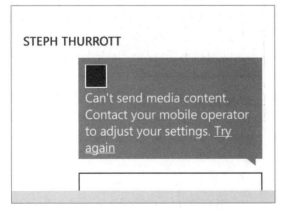

FIGURE 14-8: No MMS for you!

▶ **Remove a picture:** If you inadvertently attach the wrong picture and haven't yet sent it, you can tap the new Remove toolbar button ("-") to remove it. Note that this button replaces Attach, and if it's too late, the Attach button will have returned.

Receiving Message Responses

When other people reply to your text messages, or send you new text messages, you can be notified in different ways. If you're already in the Messaging application, for example, and in a conversation with someone, and that person replies to a message you sent, their response will appear inline, as shown in Figure 14-9.

Whereas your messages in a conversation abut up to the right of the screen, the responses you receive will be flush to the left of the screen.

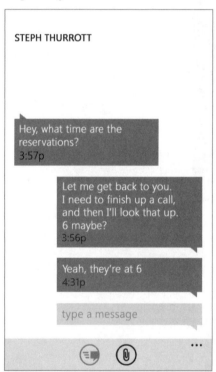

FIGURE 14-9: Messages from others are staggered a bit visually so you can tell who sent what.

Depending on what was sent, you can perform different actions as well. Text can simply be read onscreen; there's nothing further to do. If the other person sent you a photo, however, you can tap that photo to view it full screen, and zoom with a double-tap or pinch. To save a sent message to your phone, hold and tap on the image and choose Save to Phone from the pop-up menu that appears.

And while Windows Phone can't send audio or video messages, it has no trouble receiving them. These types of messages arrive as a link (Figure 14-10). To listen to an audio message, or view a video message, just click the link and the content will play in Windows Phone's full-screen system media player.

You can, of course, also reply to these messages with more text or photo messages of your own.

STEPH THURROTT

(No subject)
recording62337.amr
Expand message
6:07p

FIGURE 14-10: Audio and video messages appear as links in Messaging.

Receiving Messages While You're Doing Something Else

Oftentimes you will find that messages arrive when you're not using the phone or when you're outside of Messaging, doing something else. In each of these cases, Windows Phone notifies you of incoming messages, giving you a chance to reply immediately or at least see what's happening.

If a new message arrives when the phone is locked and off, Windows Phone will play a notification sound and light up the screen, showing the lock screen. At the top of this screen, you'll see a notification toast, or overlay, displaying the text part of the message and who sent it (Figure 14-11).

From here, you'll need to unlock the phone to view the text message in Messaging and, potentially, reply. (If you try to tap the toast, the lock screen will instead bob up and down, indicating what you must do.)

If you are doing something else with the phone when a message arrives, Windows Phone will again play a notification sound, and will again display the notification toast, overlaid on top of whatever screen you're currently viewing. This time, however, the toast is interactive: If you tap the overlay, Windows Phone will navigate directly into the correct conversation in Messaging. Nice!

In a nice touch, Windows Phone navigates directly to the Messaging app when you unlock the screen, but only if you do so while the notification toast is visible. (Otherwise, it returns to where you were in the phone when the screen became locked.)

Managing Conversations and Messages

You can go back and review conversations at any time by loading Messaging and tapping on individual messages. You can also use this as an opportunity to send a new message to someone you've already communicated with in this fashion. And if you attempt to start a new conversation with a person for which there's already a stored conversation, Windows Phone will simply add your new messages to the existing conversation. Again, you can't have multiple conversations with the same person.

Over time, as you conduct more and more conversations via messaging, you'll discover that the Conversations list in Messaging will become clogged up with conversations that you either don't care about anymore or simply don't need any more. Either way, it's easy to delete individual conversations. Just tap and hold on the doomed conversation and choose Delete from the pop-up menu that appears, as shown in Figure 14-12.

FIGURE 14-11: Messaging notification toast appears at the top of the lock screen if the phone is off or locked.

FIGURE 14-12: You can delete entire conversations with a single tap.

Windows Phone will ask if you're sure you want to delete the entire conversation from your phone.

Interestingly, you can also delete individual messages from within conversations. To do so, open a conversation and tap and hold on the message you'd like to delete. Then, tap the Delete choice. Again, Windows Phone will ask you if you're sure, as shown in Figure 14-13.

FIGURE 14-13: Windows Phone will prompt you before deleting conversations or messages.

▶ You can use this tap and hold action on a message to forward a particularly pithy message along to someone else, too. Instead of choosing Delete, just tap Forward. This will create a new conversation, using the chosen message as a new message within that conversation.

CONFIGURING MESSAGING

The Messaging app supports very little in the way of configurable options. Via the Messaging Settings interface (Figure 14-14), which you can access via the More menu from within the application or through the normal phone Settings interface, you can see just a handful of choices.

FIGURE 14-14: Messaging settings.

These choices include:

▶ **SMS delivery confirmation:** Off by default, this option can be enabled if you wish to receive a confirmation notification every time a message you send is successfully received on the other end. This can get a bit annoying, of course, and isn't supported by all wireless carriers.

▶ **SMS center number:** To send text messages, your phone must be configured with a valid SMS messaging center number. Generally, this number will be automatically configured by your wireless carrier and shouldn't be edited.

> **TIP** But if you don't have a text messaging plan and still want to send text messages, you can check out any one of a number of free message center numbers that are available in countries around the world. One such list can be found at www.smsfre.com/SMS-Mesaging-Centers.htm.

BEYOND MESSAGING

In addition to the built-in Messaging application in Windows Phone, various third-party developers will no doubt create dedicated instant messaging (IM) applications as well. These applications will integrate with PC-based IM solutions such as Windows Live Messenger, AOL Messenger, Yahoo! Messenger, Google GTalk, and others, providing yet another avenue for communicating on the go with others from Windows Phone.

Instant messaging works just like SMS and MMS messaging except that it uses the data connection on your phone and thus will be held against your data consumption limits instead of your text messaging limits. This can have both positive and negative connotations depending on your service level.

It wasn't available for testing at the time of this book's writing, but Microsoft's Windows Live Messenger client for Windows Phone should be available by the time you read this. Messenger supports integration with your Windows Live contacts list, the Messenger social ("What's New") feed, and other Windows Live services. But most important from a messaging perspective, it also lets you send photos, just like Messaging.

You can find out more about Windows Live Messenger for Mobile, and Microsoft's other mobile application offerings, at explore.live.com/windows-live-mobile.

SUMMARY

While it's possible that the messaging capabilities in Windows Phone will be dramatically expanded by instant messaging solutions in the future, the built-in capabilities are already pretty exciting, with nice support for both text (SMS) and multimedia (MMS) messaging that works with all smart phones and many standard cell phones worldwide. Thanks to a dedicated Messaging application, you can easily text any of your friends, family, and other contacts, and receive messages from them while you're out and about. Messaging may be one of the very simplest applications included with Windows Phone, but it's also one that you'll find yourself using again and again.

Digging Deeper into Phone Configuration

As you've worked your way from feature to feature throughout this book, I've covered each individual application or system feature's Settings interface as required. But there are a number of configurable options in Windows Phone that don't fall neatly into set categories like Email or Calendar. But they're still important, and you still need to know about them.

So in this chapter, it's time to dig a little deeper and find the truly useful Settings interfaces that you might have otherwise ignored. I'm not going to step through every single interface, since many are obvious and many are covered elsewhere throughout the book. Instead, I am going to look at some key features we haven't really covered yet.

These include the following: locking the phone with a password and configuring what you can and cannot do while the phone is locked; determining what sounds, if any, the phone makes in response to certain events; properly using your Windows Phone on an airplane without worrying about inspiring the next disaster flick; configuring every single e-mail account type that Windows Phone supports and not just Windows Live–type accounts; navigating through the mess of region, locale, and language configuration choices that are possible in Windows Phone; syncing over Wi-Fi; and knowing when it's time to just give up, wipe the phone out, and start over again from scratch.

It's a motley list of topics, sure. But in the true spirit of the *Secrets* series of books, this is in some ways the most excellent chapter in the whole book. It's time to dig in.

CONFIGURING WHAT HAPPENS WHEN THE PHONE IS LOCKED

If I can offer up one piece of advice that's rooted in personal experience, it's this: Lock your phone with a password. Do it now, don't wait, and don't second guess the decision. Your phone is a highly personal device, chock-full of private and personal information. And it could also be full of your workplace's critical data, especially if you're syncing with work-based e-mail, contacts, calendars, and documents. Don't be a statistic.

LOCKING AND UNLOCKING THE PHONE

Locking the phone is easy, as is unlocking it when you want to use it. To enable a lock, navigate to All Programs, Settings, and then Lock & Wallpaper. From this interface, shown in Figure 15-1, you can change the wallpaper, which is nice and personalized, but not what you're concerned with right now. You can also configure some features related to locking the phone.

Windows Phone supports exactly one kind of password: a four-digit numeric PIN, similar to what you probably use with your ATM card. Heck, you can use the same PIN— security experts would cringe at such advice, but seriously, the important bit is that you remember it and that it's not immediately obvious to others.

To add a lock to the phone, switch the Password option to On. Then, type in the password/PIN you'd like to use. Windows Phone will prompt you to type it twice just to make sure you get it right.

Once you've set the password, check out the Screen Time Out option. This setting, which can be set to 30 seconds, 1 minute, 3 minutes, or 5 minutes, determines how long the screen remains active after you last tapped it. Once this time elapses, the screen shuts off (don't worry, the phone stays on) and the lock is activated.

The next time you wake up the phone—and on subsequent attempts as well—you'll be prompted to enter your password when you swipe up on the lock screen, as shown in Figure 15-2. Ah, security.

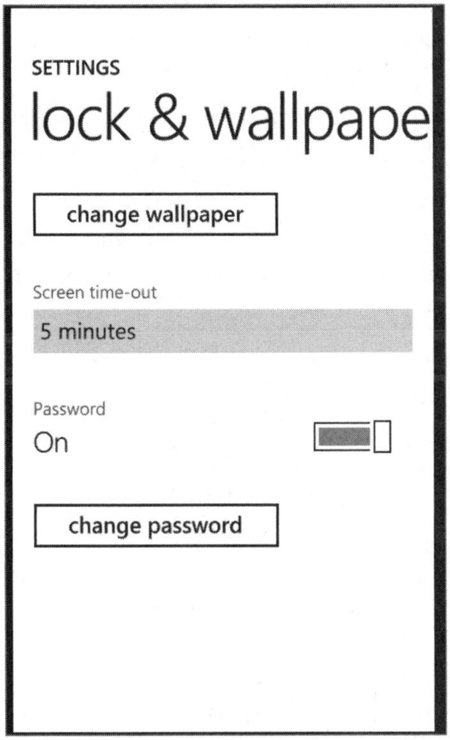

FIGURE 15-1: The Lock & Wallpaper settings screen.

FIGURE 15-2: A password-protected lock screen is a happy lock screen.

CONFIGURING LOCKED SCREEN SETTINGS

Okay, locking the phone down with a password is fairly obvious. But there are actually some additional features you can configure to work (or not) when the screen is locked. And these features can't be accessed from Lock & Wallpaper, so you really have to spelunk around to find them.

▶ The first is the phone's integrated camera. By default, you can configure the camera's on-device button to wake up the phone when pressed. But maybe you don't want that for some reason. (I happen to think it's both idiot-proof and convenient, but to each his own.)

To disable this feature, navigate to All Programs, Settings, Applications, and then Pictures + Camera. The very first option on this settings screen is Allow the Camera Button to Wake Up the Phone. If you would prefer this to be off, just change it to Off.

▶ The second is Windows Phone's incredible speech functionality. While the phone is on, you can hold down the Start button for a few seconds to trigger the speech interface; just speak a command—"open calendar," "call Steph at home," or whatever—and the phone will go off and do your bidding. All it's missing is a Cylon-like "by your command" reply.

By default, the speech feature won't work when the screen is locked. So if the phone is off and you hold down the Start button for a few seconds, nothing will happen. But if you navigate to All Programs, Settings, Speech, you'll find an option titled Use Speech When the Phone Is Locked. Just check that option and you're good to go.

Enabling speech when the phone is locked isn't as clear cut as the previous camera setting, however. That's because it's possible, depending on the design of your particular phone and your usage patterns, that the phone could inadvertently trigger the speech feature because the button was pressed while in your pocket or bag. You've heard of "butt dialing?" Welcome to butt speech command. My advice is to test this feature if you think it will be useful. And pay attention to any suspicious battery drain or angry crank call recipients.

▶ Finally, Microsoft offers a free service called Find My Phone that will help you recover a lost or stolen Windows Phone. This service is discussed in Chapter 16, but there are a couple of on-phone settings related to Find My Phone that might be of interest in the context of locking your phone.

That is, Find My Phone works best when it can actually *find* your phone. And while you can manually try to find a lost or stolen phone from the Web, seconds count. So if you navigate to All Programs, Settings, Find My Phone, you can enable two options.

▷ The first, Save My Location Periodically for Better Mapping, is a must if you think there's any chance you may lose your phone.

▷ The second, Use Push Notification, could be more problem than benefit. That's because pushing your location info from the phone can be battery intensive, especially if you're moving around a lot. So this could drain the battery prematurely.

You may be wondering what Find My Phone and locking the screen have to do with each other. From the Find My Phone web service, one of the things you can do is lock the phone's screen remotely. But you won't have to worry about that because you're already locking the screen. It's the right thing to do.

CONFIGURING SOUNDS

As a device designed explicitly for communications, Windows Phone sure does make a lot of sound. The list of events that will cause some form of alert or tone to emanate out the device is surprisingly long—new e-mail, voicemail, new messages, appointment alerts, new and snoozing alarms. Even taps on the virtual keyboard emit a small sound by default.

Sometimes it's too much. Fortunately, you can configure how or whether your phone makes sounds under certain conditions. You can do so on the fly using the volume overlay discussed in Chapter 13, but that only affects some sounds, and then only some of the time. If you want to get to the root of the problem, you need to visit the Ringtones & Sounds settings screen. It's shown in Figure 15-3 and can be accessed from All Programs, Settings, Ringtones & Sounds.

The following options are available from this screen:

▶ **Ringer:** This can be set to on or off.

▶ **Vibrate:** This, too, can be set to on or off.

> **CROSSREF** There is an interesting interplay between the phone's ringer, vibration, and the volume overlay. This is discussed in Chapter 13.

▶ **Ringtone:** This is the sound that occurs when the phone rings. You can choose from between several admittedly pleasant sounds. But Windows Phone doesn't (currently) offer a way to import or make your own ringtones. Given the big business that ringtones are these days, you have to believe that functionality is on the way.

▶ **New text message:** This is the sound that occurs when a new text (or multimedia) message arrives. As with ringtones, you're provided with several excellent choices, but it's a different set of choices, alerts instead of ringtones. And again you can't extend the list of choices with your own custom alerts.

FIGURE 15-3: Ringtones & Sounds.

- ▶ **New voicemail:** This option works the same as new text message, and utilizes the same selection of alert sounds. (Obviously, it's the sound that occurs when a new voicemail is detected.)

- ▶ **New e-mail:** Ditto for e-mail: This also uses the same list of alert sounds.

- ▶ **Play a sound for appointment reminders:** Here, you can toggle between on and off, via a check box. So there's no way to configure which sound is used for appointment reminders.

- ▶ **Play a sound for all other notifications:** Another toggle, and again with no way to choose the sound that plays.

▶ **Play a sound for key press:** This is one of the first things I disable when I'm configuring any phone. The audible feedback on key presses can be valuable when you're just getting used to the virtual keyboard. But eventually, you may find it annoying.

▶ **Play a sound for lock and unlock:** This toggle determines if a short, soft sound plays when you manually lock or unlock the phone. It will not sound if the phone auto-locks.

USING WINDOWS PHONE ON AN AIRPLANE

Many smart phones have a special master on-off switch for all wireless features called Airplane Mode, and in this regard Windows Phone is no different. It's so named because airlines prohibit the use of wireless equipment on a plane while it's taxiing or flying. But phone users would like to use their devices' non-network functionality, to play music or enjoy a game while in-flight. So Airplane Mode is born.

On Windows Phone, you access Airplane Mode in All Programs, Settings, and then Airplane Mode. In this interface, shown in Figure 15-4, you'll see a single Ringer on/off switch.

FIGURE 15-4: Airplane Mode.

In the On position, the phone's cellular (voice and data), Wi-Fi, and Bluetooth radios function normally and can be configured via their individual Settings interfaces (Cellular, Wi-Fi, and Bluetooth, respectively). So when Airplane Mode is disabled, you're free to enable or disable the other features independently.

When Airplane Mode is set to Off, all three of the radio types are shut down in unison. When the phone is in Airplane Mode, a tiny Airplane Mode icon appears in the status bar, as shown in Figure 15-5.

FIGURE 15-5: Airplane Mode triggers a helpful reminder status bar icon.

WARNING Oddly enough, you can *still* independently enable the cellular, Wi-Fi, and Bluetooth antennas after doing this, and the phone will remain in "Airplane Mode" if you, say, enable Wi-Fi. This is a poor design decision, in my opinion. Worse yet, I think it completely bypasses the entire point of Airplane Mode.

TIP Each of these radio settings, of course, impacts battery life, and as a general rule, you should disable any radio you're not going to use, since they will otherwise be unnecessarily draining the battery. Bluetooth is the simplest choice, since you either need it (as with a wireless, hands-free headset) or you don't. And if you don't, just turn it off, and leave it off. But even Wi-Fi is a candidate for disabling; if you're not regularly accessing Wi-Fi, just disable that feature and manually enable it when needed.

CONFIGURING ACCOUNTS

You may recall that you log on to your primary Windows Live account as part of the Day One experience. But most people have other accounts, too. These include accounts associated with e-mail, calendars, contacts, and other services, and they come from a variety of sources online.

NOTE And make no mistake, Windows Phone is all about connectivity: *Online* connectivity. Unlike with previous versions of Windows Mobile, there is no way in Windows Phone to "sync" a PC-based e-mail account through Outlook or some other deskbound e-mail client. All of the accounts you configure for Windows Phone must live in the cloud.

Windows Phone supports multiple account types, including explicit account types such as Windows Live, Outlook (Exchange), Facebook, and Yahoo!. But it also supports other account types implicitly through more advanced and complicated configuration interfaces. And it supports multiple instances of account types too, so you could configure, say, two different Google accounts if you wanted.

Further complicating matters, the available services in each account differ from account type to account type. So with all of that in mind, here are the different account types offered in Windows Phone.

▶ **Windows Live:** As discussed previously, everyone who uses Windows Phone will need a Windows Live ID. This is the key to having a great experience, but it's also required for certain phone features. So it's sort of a no-brainer, but the primary account also behaves differently from other accounts.

When you configure your primary Windows Live account on the phone initially, it connects to your contacts list, photos, and feeds, automatically, and behind the scenes. These features cannot be individually configured. You can, however, later enable e-mail sync on your primary Windows Live account if you'd like, from within the phone's Settings interface. And if you navigate to the Calendar app, you'll see that Windows Live calendar sync is enabled automatically. But you can turn off calendar sync from there if you didn't want that. One thing you cannot do is disable contacts sync on your primary Windows Live account. It's on, and there's no way to change that.

Of course, Windows Phone supports multiple Windows Live accounts, though the secondary accounts only offer e-mail, contacts, and calendar sync, and none of the feed and online services integration you get with the primary account. With a secondary Windows Live account, you can individually enable or disable e-mail, contacts, and calendar sync, so in this way, at least, it's actually more configurable than the primary account.

▶ **Exchange, Outlook, or Outlook Web Apps:** You use the Outlook account type to connect to Exchange Server accounts (which makes me wonder why it's called Outlook instead of Exchange). This includes Exchange Server, Outlook Web Access, and so on, but also any e-mail account that uses Exchange ActiveSync (EAS) technology on the back end. And that's a surprising number of account types, including Google (Gmail) and Windows Live (Hotmail).

What this means is that even though both Gmail and Hotmail are explicitly supported by Windows Phone with their own pre-built account types, you could in fact configure accounts of either type using the Outlook account type instead. And Outlook accounts can be configured to enable/disable e-mail, contacts, and calendar sync individually.

> **TIP** Because Google and Hotmail can both be configured using the Outlook account type, you could, for whatever reason, configure multiple Google or Hotmail accounts, where one account was configured via the Outlook account type and the other was configured using the Google or Windows Live account type, respectively. Why would you want to do this? No good reason, though you'd get a different live tile for each, and since Outlook offers a unique icon, they'd be visually differentiated.

▶ **Facebook:** Facebook is the only social networking (that is, non-e-mail-type) account you can connect to explicitly via the Windows Phone accounts interface. It's either on or off; if you connect to Facebook, it will sync all contacts, photos, and feeds. There's no way to configure this (such as, turn off contacts but leave the others on) and that somewhat lessens its value, in my opinion. For example, I'm happy to sync the Facebook photos and feeds, but would prefer not to sync contacts.

▶ **Yahoo!:** Of the preconfigured account types that support e-mail, Yahoo! is the most limited. That's because Yahoo! can be configured only for e-mail access. The connection is automatic, but if you check the settings, you'll see that it uses the IMAP protocol. There's no way to sync the Yahoo! calendar or contacts with Windows Phone.

▶ **Google:** Google's e-mail service, Gmail, can be configured via the Google account type as can the company's contacts and calendar services. (As noted previously, because Gmail/Google Calendar supports Exchange ActiveSync, you could optionally configure these accounts using the Outlook account type.)

▶ **Other Accounts:** With this account type, Windows Phone will attempt to automatically configure your settings. For most accounts, that means you'll only get e-mail access, and then only via whatever basic protocols may be supported on the server. But if you use an address with a supported account type (`gmail.com`, `live.com`, and so on), Windows Phone will properly configure it and give you the option to enable and disable whichever services are supported by that account type.

▶ **Advanced Account Setup:** This account type starts off like Other Accounts, but rather than try to auto-detect the server settings, it will step you through a more advanced manual configuration. After entering the username and password of the account you'd like to set up, you must choose between Exchange ActiveSync and Internet Email Account, the latter of which can be a POP3- or IMAP-based account only.

If you choose Internet Email Account, you will have a lot of data to fill out, including the incoming e-mail server address, account type (POP3/IMAP), the outgoing e-mail server address, and so on. It's not for the faint of heart, though arguably this was what most e-mail configuration experiences were like just a few short years ago.

WARNING Some general advice around advanced account setup: Don't use POP3 unless you absolutely have to and, even then, be sure to configure the account to leave mail on the server. Otherwise, if you lose or reset your phone, or it gets stolen, you could actually lose data. The beauty of modern e-mail account types—such as IMAP or those based on Exchange ActiveSync—is that the e-mail stays on the server and is thus device independent. Don't tie your e-mail—or any data—to just a single device.

CONFIGURING GMAIL USING THE OUTLOOK ACCOUNT TYPE

Most of the account configuration tasks are pretty straightforward. But you may be interested to know how you can configure one or more of your Gmail accounts using the Outlook account type instead of the Google account type. Here's how:

1. In Email & Accounts, tap Add an Account.

2. On the Add an Account page, tap Outlook.

3. Enter your full Gmail e-mail account address and password, and then tap Next.

4. After Windows Phone thinks for a bit, new User Name and Domain fields will appear. In the User Name field, re-enter your full Gmail e-mail account address (that is, **username@gmail.com** or whatever).

5. Leave the Domain field blank and tap Sign In.

6. Windows Phone will report that it can't find your account settings. Tap the Advanced button.

7. Now, enter **m.google.com** in the Server field. Leave the Domain field blank and tap Sign In. The new account will be created and will sync with the server.

MAKING REGION AND LANGUAGE CONFIGURATION CHANGES

When you first use your Windows Phone, you're asked to choose from between five languages—German, English (U.K. or U.S.), Spanish, French, and Italian—and the choice you make at that time determines the settings for a wider range of region, locale, and language options. These settings may not be ideal, depending on where you live, or your needs. Fortunately, there's a single Settings screen—one with a lot of choices—for further configuring these options. It's called Region & Language (Figure 15-6) and you can find it in All Programs, Settings, Region & Language.

FIGURE 15-6: Region & Language.

Among the various options available here are the following:

▶ **Display language:** This determines which language the Windows Phone user interface uses to communicate with you. This maps to the five (well, six, because U.K. and U.S. English are separate) initial language choices you initially selected from.

▶ **Region format:** This setting determines the default formatting used for dates and times, and it provides a vast range of locale choices to choose between. When you select a new value for this setting, the Short Date, Long Date, and First Day of Week settings described in this list change to match. However, you can still optionally change each of those settings individually. This is like a master switch that changes them all at once.

▶ **Short date:** Here, you can configure how short dates (such as 1/2/2010 for January 2, 2010) are formatted. There are a number of choices such as 1/2/2010, 1/2/10, 01/02/2010, and so on.

▶ **Long date:** This option configures how long dates are formatted, with choices such as Saturday, January 02, 2010; January 02, 2010; Saturday, 02 January, 2010, and so on.

▶ **First day of the week:** You can choose between any of the available seven days. The default is Sunday.

▶ **System locale:** This setting determines the default character set that is used to display letters, numbers, and symbols. Like region format, it provides access to a vast range of choices. (There are 16 different English choices alone.)

▶ **Browser & search language:** Here, you can optionally configure the web browser and Bing search language to be different from that configured with the display language choice. So if you want to use a U.S. English version of the Windows Phone software, but search the Web in French, go for it. (But understand that there are six different French locales to choose from.)

▶ *Many of these options require a device reboot before any changes take effect.*

WI-FI SYNC

This configuration is actually made from the Zune PC software, but since it is deeply tied to the overall configuration of the phone, I thought it would make sense to cover it here. Generally speaking, you connect your Windows Phone to the PC for just a few reasons: To sync photos taken with the phone's camera to the PC, to sync your

PC-based media collection to the phone, to install large software updates, and so on. Each of these actions requires you to physically connect the phone to the PC using a USB-based PC sync cable. But Windows Phone, like the Zune HD before it, supports a more automatic way to perform these same actions.

Microsoft calls this feature wireless sync, but since it can only work over a Wi-Fi wireless network, and not over cellular or Bluetooth connections, I think the name Wi-Fi sync makes more sense. Wi-Fi sync is brilliant in its simplicity: Since you most likely have a Wi-Fi-based home network, and since you most likely bring your phone home every night to charge it, chances are that your PC and phone will be in close proximity to each other, and connected (in the case of the phone, at least, wirelessly) to the home network. So instead of forcing you to explicitly tether the phone to the PC, you can instead just configure the phone to sync over Wi-Fi. And it will happen automatically, as long as you plug the phone into a wall outlet for charging.

Here's how it works.

First, you must connect your phone to the home network's Wi-Fi connection, and the phone's Wi-Fi functionality must be enabled. Then, connect your phone to the PC using the USB sync cable (if only for this configuration step), open the Zune PC software, and navigate to Settings, Phone, Wireless Sync, which is shown in Figure 15-7.

FIGURE 15-7: Wireless Sync in the Zune PC software.

This will trigger a short wizard (Figure 15-8). In the first and only step of this wizard, you must confirm the network that will be used for wireless sync. Each time your phone has been connected to wall power for at least 10 minutes and detects the configured Wi-Fi network, it will search out the syncing PC and begin syncing content in both directions automatically.

FIGURE 15-8: Configuring Wi-Fi sync.

Once the settings have been verified, the wizard will inform you that wireless sync has been configured and you're good to go. I don't recommend throwing out the sync cable, but chances are you won't have nearly as much use for it in the future: Simply charging your phone in the same room, or often just in the same house, as the PC is all you'll need to do.

NUKE IT FROM SPACE AND START OVER

While Windows Phone doesn't suffer from the "bit rot" that used to impact older desktop versions of Windows, every once in a while you may find yourself in a situation where you simply want to start over again with a clean phone OS devoid of all the media, apps, documents, pictures, and other gunk that's been piling up on there since day one.

Windows Phone does support a way to start over from scratch, a digital mulligan or do-over, if you will. But before going down this path, take some steps to ensure that everything on the phone is backed up somewhere. The simplest thing you can do is connect the phone physically to your syncing PC via a USB cable and let the Zune PC software copy everything from the device to the PC.

Here are some common data types to think about.

▸ **E-mail, contacts, and calendars:** Since your Windows Phone e-mail, contacts, and calendar accounts all live up in the cloud, there's not too much you need to do there, aside from ensuring that you know all the logon information (user names and passwords) and, for more complex account types, whatever required server settings.

▸ **Messages:** Your text messages and any pictures received via Messaging will be blown away when you wipe out the phone. There's no way to save messages per se, but you can of course save any pictures to the phone and then sync them to the PC.

▸ **Games and applications:** Any games and applications you've downloaded to the phone—paid, free, or trial—cannot be backed up, but then they don't need to be: You can simply download them at any time from the Windows Phone Marketplace, and you won't have to re-pay for any apps you've already purchased. If you have a lot of these apps, you may want to just jot down their names.

▸ **Pictures:** Pictures you've downloaded to the phone will need to be synced to the PC via the Zune software. Or you can individually "share" each picture, sending them off the phone via e-mail.

▸ **Purchased music:** Music you purchased from Zune Marketplace can be redownloaded, but it's easier to just sync it to the PC.

▸ **Documents:** Any Word documents, Excel workbooks, or PowerPoint presentations that are stored on the phone will need to be backed up. The quickest way to do this, perhaps, is to send them to yourself via e-mail: Just tap and hold each in turn in the Office hub and choose Send, and then your e-mail account from the pop-up menu. You won't need to do this for SharePoint-based documents. And if you are syncing your OneNote-based notes to Windows Live SkyDrive, you should be all set there as well.

When you're sure you've successfully accounted for everything of value on the phone, you're ready to nuke the device and start over. Navigate to All Programs, Settings, and then About and tap the Reset Your Phone button. You'll be asked to confirm this decision twice (Figure 15-9), and then Windows Phone OS will wipe out all of the data on the phone, reboot, and go through the Day One, out of box experience all over again. It's like getting a brand new phone.

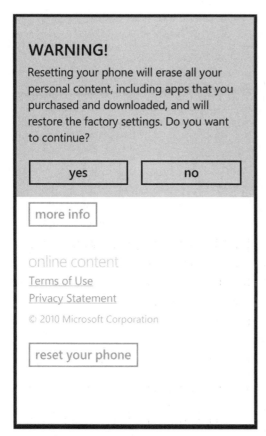

FIGURE 15-9: I'm sorry, Dave. But I can't let you do that.

SUMMARY

Windows Phone is a new platform with a new way of doing things. And as is so often the case, you sometimes really need to dig in deep to see what's possible. With Windows Phone, much of that hidden functionality is available only through the surprisingly powerful Settings interface.

This chapter highlighted some of the key secrets that lurk inside the labyrinthine interface. Next up, I examine some of the final secrets this new mobile platform has to offer, with regards to its interactions with the outside world. These include its interactions with both the PC and a growing host of unique new online services.

PC and Web Integration

Windows Phone is an interesting paradox. On the one hand, it's the most sophisticated and powerful smart phone available from any vendor. On the other, Microsoft has locked down Windows Phone in ways that are both perplexing and illogical. And this is as true of the device's interaction with the PC—or, more commonly, its lack of interaction with the PC—as it is with its integration with the Web.

You can work around some of these issues, but not others. So in this chapter, I'd like to focus on those things you *can* do, including accessing a much broader marketplace experience than is possible on the phone itself, finding those photos that the camera automatically copies online, figuring out a way to copy full-resolution versions of your phone's pictures to the Web in both manual and semi-automated fashions, and using a new Microsoft service called Find My Phone to catch a thief or, at the very least, recover a lost Windows Phone.

YOU CAN'T GET THERE FROM HERE

If you've owned any smart phone or digital camera, you know that you can connect it to your PC via a USB cable and download photos using your photo importing solution of choice. You can also access the device's onboard storage such as a mini-hard drive, copying content back and forth as needed. And if you've ever used a Zune HD or iPod, you know that these pocket media players can connect to powerful media devices such as the Xbox 360 or Sony's PlayStation 3 and provide access to their contents via your HDTV. It's the way you've come to expect things to work.

None of these scenarios are possible with Windows Phone, and it's all by design. Microsoft has locked down Windows Phone in ways that are both sensible and non-sensical, and while I expect that to change over time, for now you're stuck with the decisions Microsoft has made.

That means that, out of the gate at least, the only way to interact directly with your phone on the PC is via the Zune PC software. I have discussed this software elsewhere throughout the book—most thoroughly in Chapters 5 and 6, which deal with the phone's pictures and music/video capabilities, respectively—but there are a few more related Zune PC software issues to consider. So I am going to look at those first, before I head off into the clouds to show you what Windows Phone–oriented online services Microsoft offers. Oddly enough, you'll almost always need a PC to access these as well.

BROWSING AND BUYING IN THE MARKETPLACE

While Windows Phone offers decent access to Microsoft's various online stores directly from the device, if you're looking for the full range of online products and services, you're going to need to access these services from a PC. To understand the differences, consider for a moment what's available from the phone, where you get three primary marketplace experiences:

- ▶ **Apps Marketplace:** The Marketplace app on Windows Phone provides a front end to all of the on-device purchasing capabilities, including apps, games, and music.

- ▶ **Zune Marketplace:** Available on the Zune section of the Music + Videos hub, this marketplace provides access to Zune-based music only, and not any of the other Zune content.

- ▶ **Xbox Live Marketplace:** Via the Games hub, you can jump directly into the games portion of the marketplace.

This is all sounds pretty impressive until you realize what's available from the PC. Using the Zune PC software—which is used to synchronize digital music, videos, pictures, and other content between the phone and the PC, among other things—you can access a richer Marketplace experience, shown in Figure 16-1. And it's not just prettier. There's more stuff.

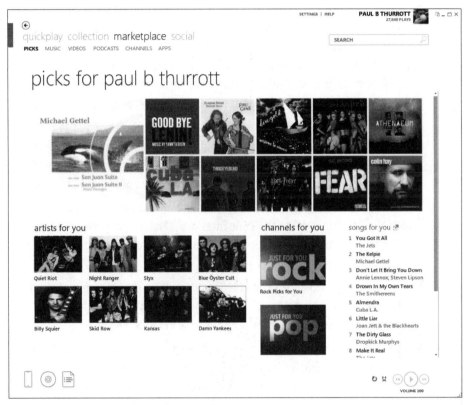

FIGURE 16-1: Microsoft's Marketplace, seen from the Zune PC software.

From a content perspective, you can buy and download the following types of content from the Marketplace:

▶ **Music:** Zune Marketplace offers over 7 million music tracks available for purchase, from over 20 different genres. And if you have a Zune Pass subscription, you can download almost any of those tracks to the PC, and from there sync them to the phone. (Zune Pass subscribers also get to download and keep 10 music tracks each month.) In the United States, most individual tracks cost $.99 to $1.29, and albums run roughly $10 to $12 for newer albums.

▶ **Music videos:** Zune Marketplace also offers thousands of music videos for purchase, from the same set of genre types as music. This includes the latest artists and songs as well as some staples from MTV's heyday in the early 1980s. Music videos run a wide gamut from a pricing perspective as well, though most are in the $2 range.

▶ **TV shows:** Microsoft offers TV content for purchase only—that is, there's no rental or streaming-only option—but the selection is pretty impressive. There are over 65 television networks represented in the marketplace and hundreds of individual shows, which range from currently run, A-list TV shows to back catalog shows from yesteryear. TV shows can be purchased by episode (for $2 to $3 each) or by the season (various prices depending on length and age).

▶ **Movies:** Zune's movie selection has gotten dramatically better over the years, and now offers a full selection of recent and back catalog movies, many of which are available for either purchase or rent. Again, prices vary widely, but brand-new movies typically go for $15 to $20 for purchase, or about $4 to $6 to rent.

▶ **Movie trailers:** If you're interested in upcoming movies, you can stream movie trailers directly from within the Zune interface. (There is, however, no download capability, and the playback quality is standard definition rather than HD.)

▶ **Podcasts:** Microsoft offers what I feel is the superior way to browse, download, and subscribe to both audio and video podcasts, and the selection on Zune Marketplace is excellent. If you know of a podcast that isn't available on Zune for some reason, no worries: You can subscribe via RSS feed as well.

▶ **Apps and games:** You can browse through the growing collection of Windows Phone applications (including games) in an interface that is decidedly more attractive and easy to use than on the phone. Zune Marketplace also provides access to Zune HD–based apps and games if you have that kind of device, too.

So the marketplace stuff is incredible on the PC. But it's not just the available types of content that make this solution so interesting. Microsoft watches your buying and listening habits over time and makes picks available to you through Zune Marketplace that could aid in the discovery of new music. There are custom channels, such as dynamic, downloadable radio stations you can sync with the phone, offering ever-changing playlists of music based on themes like top songs, fitness, and staff picks.

Zune Marketplace offers the ability to download or simply stream purchased movie content, and you can often choose between standard definition (SD) and HD for both rentals and purchases. In fact, purchased TV and movie content can be played at any time in the future, from any compatible device. This includes PCs (using the Zune PC software), Zune HDs, Windows Phones (after downloading and syncing), and even Xbox 360s. Most interesting, perhaps, is that you don't even need to download purchased TV shows or movies to watch them on the PC or Xbox 360; instead, you can simply stream them over the Internet. Microsoft supports instant-on streaming of 1080p content, too, so the quality is amazing.

There are other advantages, but you get the idea: Though the interactions you can have between the PC and phone are somewhat limited—and are indeed limited to the Zune PC software specifically—this is actually a benefit in some ways because that software is so full-featured and easy to use.

With that in mind, it's time to take a look at some of the ways in which you can take advantage of Windows Phone–specific content and features from the PC, using the Zune PC software.

Apps and Games

Microsoft does offer a decent Marketplace app on the phone, but the experience is better on the PC because of the additional onscreen real estate and the richer presentation allowed by that space. And as you can see in Figure 16-2, the Marketplace experience in Zune is particularly good when you're looking for new apps and games.

16-2: Apps and games for Windows Phone 7.

The interface here works much like other marketplace experiences in the Zune PC software. On the left, you'll find genres of apps, such as games, tools, lifestyle, and so on, and within those, sub-genres. (For example, the Games genre is divided into sub-genres such as Action, Music, Racing, Sports, Card, Board, Word & Puzzle, and more.)

Microsoft usually spotlights certain key applications, and offers lists of recommendations, top paid apps, top free apps, and new apps.

When you do select an individual application or game, you'll be presented with an interface like that shown in Figure 16-3. Here, you can find out more about the game, view its rating and reviews, expand screenshots of it, download it, and, if it's a paid app or game, buy it.

▶ Many paid Windows Phone apps and games will also feature a Try choice so that you can try out the selection on your phone and then purchase it later if you like it.

FIGURE 16-3: Individual games get their own page in the Windows Phone Marketplace.

Podcasts

▶ You can't even download new episodes of podcasts from the device, which seems like an odd limitation, especially for audio podcasts.

Windows Phone is an excellent solution for enjoying both audio and video podcasts. But there's no way to browse through the selection of available content on the device, and if you do find a podcast you like, you need to subscribe from the PC, because you can't do so from Windows Phone.

The Marketplace podcast experience, shown in Figure 16-4, provides a simple interface for finding content.

FIGURE 16-4: The Podcasts landing page in the Marketplace.

Once you do find a good podcast—like the excellent choice shown in Figure 16-5, you can download individual episodes or, better yet, subscribe. This will ensure that future episodes are automatically downloaded to your PC and, if configured properly, will automatically sync to your phone as well.

You can configure how podcasts are downloaded and organized via the Zune PC software's Settings interface, shown in Figure 16-6.

Equally important, however, is the Settings interface for the individual podcast, which can be accessed via Collection, Podcasts, and then Series Settings. From this interface, shown in Figure 16-7, you can also determine how the podcast is synced to your phone.

FIGURE 16-5: A landing page for an individual podcast.

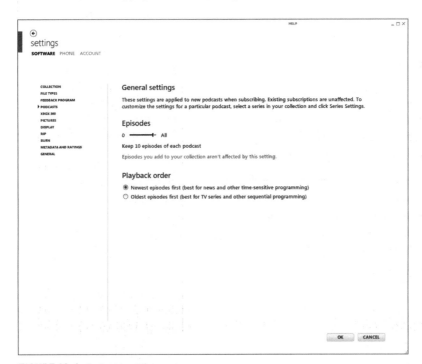

FIGURE 16-6: Podcast settings.

FIGURE 16-7: You can configure phone sync on a podcast-by-podcast basis.

Videos

TV shows, movies, and music videos cannot be downloaded directly to your phone. So you'll need to browse this content, purchase, rent, or download it using the Zune PC software, and then sync it to the phone. This can be surprisingly non-straightforward for two reasons.

First, some content requires you to choose between SD and HD versions, as shown in Figure 16-8. Only SD content will play on Windows Phone, so if you download an HD version of any video and try to sync it to your phone, you'll be given the SD version instead.

Renting is another issue. For reasons that are best left to the imagination, Microsoft requires you to choose which device you intend to watch a rented movie on, at the time of rental. You can choose to watch it on your PC, on a Zune HD device, or on a Windows Phone. (If you want to watch a rented movie on the Xbox 360, you must rent the movie from that console.)

You can't change your mind after the rental. So if you choose the HD version of a movie to be watched on your PC, you can't later try to sync that movie to the phone.

It will not work. And if you rent a movie for use on your phone, you will only be given the SD choice.

FIGURE 16-8: Movie rentals for the PC will support both HD and SD versions, but you can't use that rental anywhere else, including your phone.

WINDOWS PHONE ON THE WEB

As a connected communications powerhouse, Windows Phone offers some interesting on-device integration with various web-based services. But sometimes, you'll find yourself on a PC, and when you do, you'll gain access to some interesting Windows Phone–related web services. And these are things that only make sense from, or are only possible from, the PC web.

SkyDrive Camera Roll

In Chapter 5, I discussed how Windows Phone can optionally be configured to automatically upload photos taken with the device's camera to Microsoft's Windows Live Sky-Drive service. This web-based ("cloud") storage service provides 25GB of free storage to anyone with a Windows Live ID. And since you configured a Windows Live ID as part of your Windows Phone experience, this is just one of the many perks you received.

Windows Phone's use of SkyDrive isn't ideal: Automatically uploaded photos are not transferred at the full resolution of the original, in order to facilitate simple sharing and preserve bandwidth and, thus, your battery life.

That said, you may still want to access these picture duplicates from your PC's web browser in order to manage them in some way. For example, you can rename individual pictures, copy or move them, watch a slideshow, share them, or even download them to your PC. Of course, first you need to find them.

SkyDrive can be found at skydrive.live.com, but at this address you'll find all of your web-based files, including documents and notes as well as photos. As a short-cut, you can navigate directly to the photos section of SkyDrive, also called Windows Live Photos, by going to photos.live.com. This interface will look something like Figure 16-9. (You'll need to log on to your Windows Live ID to access either site.)

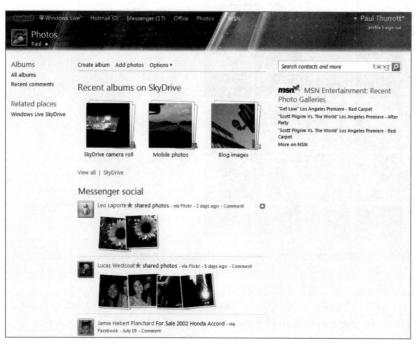

FIGURE 16-9: Windows Live Photos.

If you're familiar with the Pictures hub in Windows Phone, you may recognize some familiar elements here. The Recent Albums section at the top provides access to your own SkyDrive-based photo albums, as does the All Albums link on the left.

Below that, you'll see the Messenger Social list. This works like the What's New view in the Pictures hub, providing a timeline-based view of pictures posted online by your family, friends, and other contacts.

The photos that your phone uploads automatically to the Web can be found in the SkyDrive Camera Roll album. This may appear in the Recent Albums list right on the Windows Live Photos main page. If not, you can navigate to All Albums and find it there.

When you click on this photo gallery, you'll be provided with a view of all of the pictures your camera has automatically uploaded. This is shown in Figure 16-10.

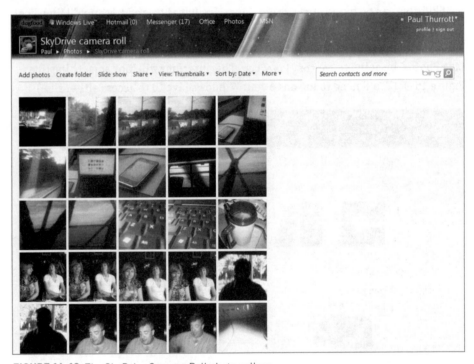

FIGURE 16-10: The SkyDrive Camera Roll photo gallery.

From here you can perform additional tasks. The most common reason to come here, I think, is to share uploaded photos with others. Each individual folder on Windows Live Photos (and SkyDrive, more generally) will have a specific permissions setting. You can edit these permissions on a per-folder basis, add specific people to the list of those that can view a folder's contents (by e-mail address), and send links to individual photos to others.

Uploading Full-Resolution Camera Photos to the Web

As I've harped on a number of times, the automatic photo uploading functionality in Windows Phone is, to put it kindly, lackluster. What you really want is a way to back up full-sized photos to the Web in an automated fashion. Microsoft doesn't actually offer such a thing. But they do provide a somewhat convoluted solution that comes pretty close. Sadly, it will require you to do a bit of work on the PC as well as on the Web. And this won't work directly from the phone. Here's how.

First, be sure to regularly download the photos from your phone to the PC using the Zune PC software, as discussed in Chapter 5. You don't need to delete the pictures from the phone when you do this, but you do need to stay on top of it, by manually downloading the camera pictures from the phone.

Second, make sure you have the latest version of Windows Live Essentials installed on your PC. This excellent and free suite of Windows applications can be found at get .live.com and includes two applications that are particularly relevant here.

The first is Windows Live Photo Gallery, which is shown in Figure 16-11.

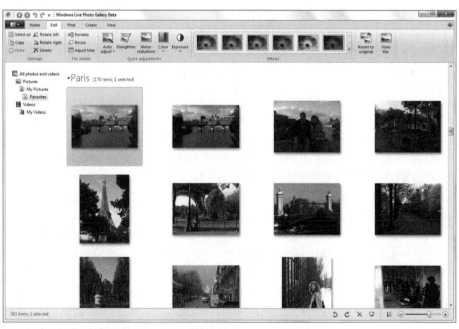

FIGURE 16-11: Windows Live Photo Gallery.

Photo Gallery performs a number of functions, including some first class photo editing features that are a must for anyone using Windows Phone's camera. You can also use this application to manually publish a folder full of photos up to a photo gallery (or "album") on Windows Live SkyDrive/Photos. This functionality, shown in Figure 16-12, is great if all you want to do is manually copy photos. But it won't help you in the future if you later add photos to a folder you already uploaded. That is, it's not automatic, and it won't later upload new files for you.

FIGURE 16-12: Photo Gallery lets you easily upload photos to SkyDrive.

▶ If you do use this feature, be sure to choose "Original" from the subtle Photo Upload Size drop-down list. Otherwise, you may inadvertently upload photos that aren't full sized.

Windows Live Essentials also includes a solution called Windows Live Mesh. This amazing utility performs a number of useful services, including remote PC access and limited application sync between PCs. But its primary purpose, and the reason you need to be interested in it here, is that Mesh also lets you sync folders of content between your PCs (if you have two or more) and SkyDrive.

PC-to-PC folder sync is what's known as peer-to-peer (or P2P) sync. And it's incredibly useful if you live in a multi-PC household and want certain content—favorite photos, your music collection, or key documents—synced between them. It's also mostly unlimited in that you can sync virtually any amount of content between PCs, using P2P sync.

▶ Windows Live Mesh is even compatible with the Mac, so if you have both PCs and Macs, this is an interesting solution for keeping files on those machines synchronized as well.

Syncing to the cloud using Windows Live SkyDrive is a bit more limited because of bandwidth and storage cost concerns. Here, Microsoft provides you with up to 2GB of storage only, and you can't upload incredibly large files. That latter bit won't be a huge concern for photos, though it's possible you'll run into the storage ceiling at some point. (As a reference, my own synced folder of favorite photos takes up only 1.1GB of space, and contains well over 600 photos.)

You can use Mesh to synchronize the photos taken with the camera on Windows Phone with SkyDrive. That way, as you copy more photos from the phone to your PC, they'll be automatically synced with SkyDrive and available there in full resolution versions.

First, you need to locate the folder that the Zune PC software uses for storing pictures copied to the PC. If you open up the Pictures library in Windows 7 (or the Pictures folder in Windows Vista), you'll see that there is a folder named From *Paul's Phone* (where *Paul's Phone* will be the name of your own phone). Inside of that folder, there could be a number of folders, but one will be named Camera Roll. You'll want to sync either From Paul's Phone or Camera Roll.

Now, launch Windows Live Mesh. This application, shown in Figure 16-13, provides a very simple way to sync individual folders, both between PCs and with SkyDrive.

To sync the folder, click the Sync a Folder link and then navigate to the correct location in the file system (usually C:*your username*\Pictures) and select either From *Paul's Phone* (where *Paul's Phone* will be the name of your own phone) or, inside that, Camera Roll (Figure 16-14). Click Sync.

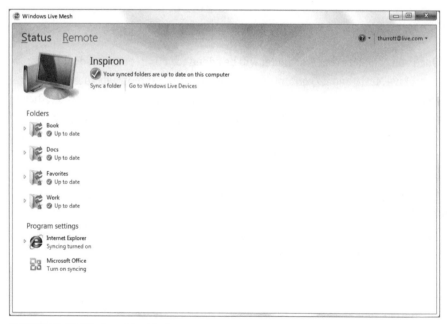

FIGURE 16-13: Windows Live Mesh.

Next, you'll be asked which devices—PCs, generally—you'd like to sync the folder with. But at the bottom of this list is a different choice, SkyDrive Synced Storage. If you choose this option, the folder will be synced to the Web.

FIGURE 16-14: Selecting the correct folder to sync.

Once you complete that, the folder will be added to your list of synced folders in Windows Live Mesh, and its contents will be synced to the appropriate locations. You can verify that the new folder is synced to the Web by visiting Windows Live SkyDrive. It can be found in a special location called SkyDrive Synced Storage. You get to that location by navigating to skydrive.live.com and clicking on the View Synced Folders link. Conversely, you could simply navigate directly to devices.live.com/Devices/SkyDriveSyncedStorage.

Either way, you'll see the folder you just synced, along with your other synced folders (if any), as shown in Figure 16-15.

Most important, perhaps, if you navigate into this folder, you'll see that your camera photos are there, and in their full resolution goodness.

> **NOTE** As mentioned previously, this is an interesting workaround, but you could eventually run into the 2GB storage limitation. That said, Microsoft will almost certainly enable full-sized photo copying from Windows Phone sometime in the future, and possibly even by the time you read this. So if we're all lucky, none of us will need to worry about this kind of thing in the first place.

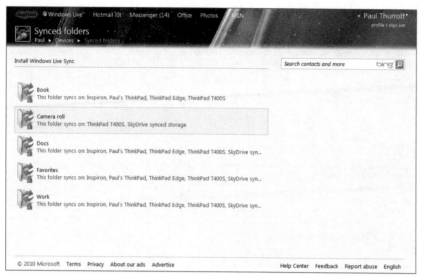

FIGURE 16-15: Synced folders in SkyDrive.

Find My Phone

Microsoft will offer a number of Windows Phone–specific online services, and my expectation is that the collection of these services will improve and grow over time. At launch, however, the most interesting service the company is offering is called Find My Phone. This service helps you recover a lost or stolen Windows Phone, and unlike similar services from, say, Apple, it's absolutely free.

Find My Phone, shown in Figure 16-16, can be accessed from `windowsphone.live .com/myphone`.

This service offers the following features:

▶ **Map it:** Tap the Map It link to see your phone in Bing Maps, as shown in Figure 16-17. It can be eerily accurate, especially if the phone is connected to a 3G data service.

▶ **Ring it:** Use this link to annoy a thief or, hopefully, simply locate a lost phone (Figure 16-18). The phone will play a somewhat piercing ringtone for about a minute.

▶ **Lock it and display a message:** This option locks the phone using a four-digit code you think up on the spot. This should prevent anyone from using it or accessing your private data, even if you don't normally lock the phone. You can optionally type a message that will display on the phone's screen that describes how to return your phone if somebody finds it, as shown in Figure 16-19.

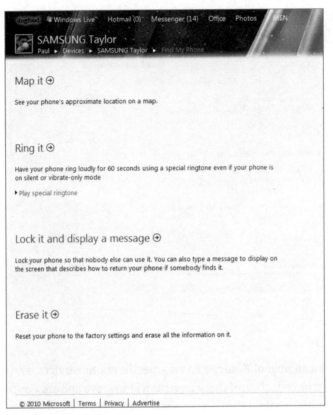

FIGURE 16-16: Find My Phone

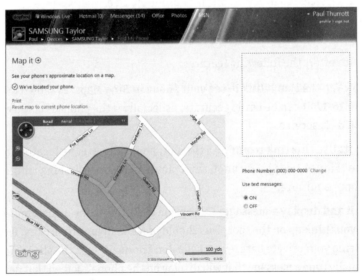

FIGURE 16-17: The Map It feature is, perhaps, a little too accurate.

FIGURE 16-18: Remotely ring the phone so you can find it when it's lost.

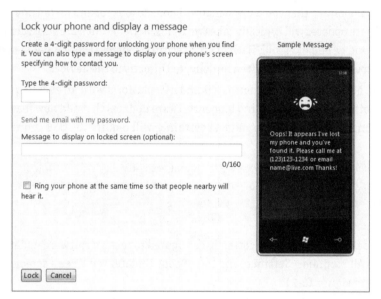

FIGURE 16-19: Lock the phone and provide instructions for returning it.

▶ **Erase it:** This final "nuke from space" option (Figure 16-20) can be employed if you're sure the phone is lost or stolen for good and you're never going to get it back. If you go through with this, all of the content on the phone will be remotely wiped.

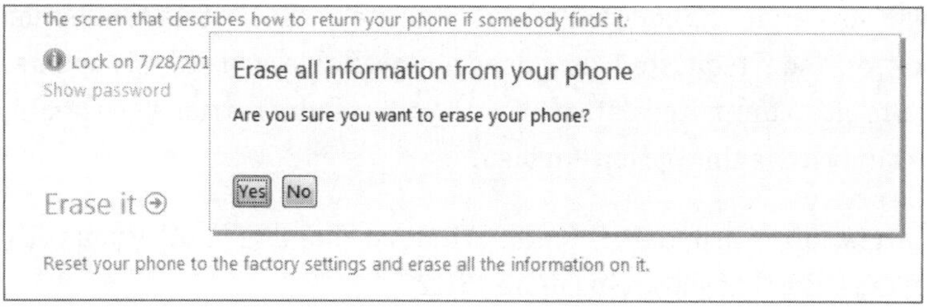

FIGURE 16.20: Erase the phone and at least you achieve peace of mind.

UPDATING WINDOWS PHONE

As noted previously, Microsoft will be providing frequent ongoing software updates for Windows Phone, and you may in fact be asked to install such an update the first time you boot up your new phone. As time goes by, you'll be prompted to install other updates, some of which can occur on the phone, over the air, while other, larger updates will require you to sync the phone to your PC via a USB sync cable.

It's very important that you allow Windows Phone to look for and install any updates. These updates will typically take two forms, both of which are very valuable. First, there will be bug fixes and, if necessary, security updates. These types of updates are typically very small and will often be delivered directly to the device.

Second, because Windows Phone is a brand new platform with an evolving feature set, Microsoft will also be providing bigger software updates that add new features and functionality. These updates, almost certainly, will require the USB connection.

> **NOTE** If you're curious, software updates that are 200MB or smaller will be delivered over the air, while those that are larger will require your PC. PC-based updates are delivered via the Zune PC software.

To ensure that your phone is correctly configured to receive software updates, navigate to All Programs, Settings, and then Phone Update. You'll see a screen like that shown in Figure 16-21.

In addition to a notification when new updates are available, you'll find two main options here, both of which should be enabled by default:

▶ **Notify me when new updates are found.** Windows Phone will notify you when a new software update is available. If you can install this update over the air, it will also provide you with the option to do so.

▶ **Use my cellular data connection to check for updates.** When this option is enabled, Windows Phone will use your phone's cellular data connection to look for, and if requested, download any available over-the-air updates. If you're on an unlimited data plan with your cellular carrier, you should almost certainly leave this option enabled.

When a new software update is found, Windows Phone will notify you with a full-screen message like that shown in Figure 16-22.

FIGURE 16-21: Phone Update Settings.

FIGURE 16-22: A new software update is available.

Most software updates are a one-way affair: Once you install them, there's no way to uninstall them. This is likely very different to what you're used to in PC versions of Windows. But on a smart phone, it makes a bit more sense, since these devices are more appliance-like, and most people won't ever need, or want, to micromanage the low-level software that's found on the device. More important, as new capabilities and updates are added to Windows Phone, Microsoft will rely on the presence of those capabilities and updates going forward.

SUMMARY

While the PC and web integration pieces in Windows Phone are somewhat disappointing, I expect these capabilities to improve over time. Indeed, if there is one mantra I've heard again and again from the Windows Phone team, it is their resolution to aggressively and constantly update their new platform so that it remains a uniquely powerful and innovative alternative to the iPhone and Android hegemony. The key to this, of course, is Microsoft's ability to provide updates to Windows Phone users directly, both over the air and through the Zune PC software, bypassing the cellular network carriers.

Looking ahead, you can expect Windows Phone to be supported by an ever-growing apps and game market, but also to be tweaked and improved by software updates both large and small. These capabilities aren't unique to Windows Phone. But they ensure that the platform won't stand still and that, over time, many of the early criticisms of what is otherwise a solid and fantastic mobile solution will simply fade away.

One thing I can say is that my excitement over Windows Phone has only deepened over time. And the more I learn about this platform, the more impressed I become, and the less interested I am in the competition. Because of the ever-improving nature of Windows Phone, I'll be monitoring and documenting the changes long after this book is published. So please, follow along at windowsphonesecrets.com, where you can join the discussion and enter this brave new mobile era together with me and other Windows Phone users. I look forward to seeing you online, and hearing about your experiences with Windows Phone.

Index